GEORGE FEDDISH
Nov 10 1981

The Art of Engraving

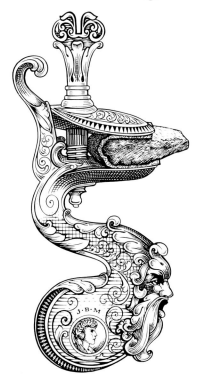

The flintlock hammer on the preceding page
is an elaborate and elegant embellishment
of a rather plain John Cookson (signed)
lockplate in the Victoria and Albert
Museum, London, and shows the engraver's
prerogative of designing and cutting something that catches his imagination.

The Art of Engraving
A Book of Instructions

by James B. Meek

Book Design, Drawings and Photographs
BY THE AUTHOR

F. BROWNELL & SON, PUBLISHERS, Inc. — MONTEZUMA, IOWA

Tenth Printing, April, 1980

TABLE OF CONTENTS

INTRODUCTION

About James B. Meek ("Bruce" to his friends) . . .

Even after 20 years, plus, of knowing Bruce and Jeanette Meek on an every-other-Sunday-dinner basis, I still get butterflies in my stomach whenever I watch Bruce work, along with a deep sense of awe over the man's complete dedication to perfection - a perfection carried to the nth degree. Whether it is doing an oil painting or a pencil sketch, faceting a precious gem, finishing and checkering or carving a rifle stock, casting a gold miniature, re-building one of his many Parkers, or engraving a beautiful shooting piece, Bruce spares no effort, ignores no avenue of research to insure a complete faithfulness of presentation. Such devotion in the complete artist results in finished pieces that are a delight to the critical professional eye.

When Bruce and I first discussed the possibility of his doing **The Art Of Engraving**, and during the 7 years following until the book was completed, his aim has been twofold - to do a book no one would surpass and to create a monument to the engraving art. During these years of endeavor, money, time and effort were of no consequence to him in his drive to produce a classic. To satisfy himself, he ended up with each original illustration being a photograph of an actual engraving. Originally, the hundreds of engraving samples and illustrations were all done with pen & ink, but, to him, did not "look" like quite "right". As a consequence he re-did them all - this time as actual hand engravings cut through a white lacquer coating into black plexiglas. He felt this mountain of extra work was the only way he could be honest with himself and the reader.

There is no way Bruce will ever recoup his investment in out-of-pocket money and hours of time spent. And here is where the artist bit comes out that only another artist will understand. Said Bruce: "...But I am not doing it for the money, Bob - but because I want to create something that is needed, that will be used and which will be beautiful." This I believe Bruce has accomplished. He worked under very unique circumstances which were all in his favor of achieving his ends. During the first four of the seven years of writing and drawing, he worked on the book before and after working hours as head artist for an advertising-printing company. He then retired and devoted the last three years on a full-time basis. Not many artists/writers have such a golden opportunity - nor the drive after retirement, for that matter - to do such an unusual project. But, Bruce is truly an unusual fellow.

As Bruce progressed with the book, still another facet of his abilities became apparent and developed - that of "teacher" (which was really the intent of **The Art Of Engraving** in the first place). When he first started writing, he exhibited the characteristic that all fine craftsmen seem to have and too often exhibit in their "how-to" articles or books, which basically is: "Heck, if I can do it, anyone can" and proceed on that assumption without giving any of the details as to just "how"!

In discussing the above with the author, I pointed out that most of the readers were not going to be accomplished artists, but just average people who wanted to learn; that every move, every detail, should be pointed out, described in depth and illustrated - even to a point where the readers should be told when to wipe off the sweat from their brows. Frank Brownell, who was editor for the book, and I are not artists or engravers - quite to the contrary; yet, because of Bruce's ultimate mastery of the teaching ability, we both have a yen to grab a graver and a piece of practice steel and start "cutting" every time we read some of his writings. We both feel that if he can so inspire a couple of fumble-fingered individuals such as we are, **The Art Of Engraving** will inspire anyone who reads it!

Finally, it is the hope and design of all of us in any way involved with **The Art Of Engraving** that the reader will find instruction, knowledge and inspiration between its two covers - That the person who wants to engrave can proceed with confidence because what he needs to know is here for him - That the person who appreciates engraved pieces will have a new and keen understanding and appreciation of the work, style and motifs created for him by the engraver - And that the fruits of James B. Meek's lifetime of devotion to his love of expression through art can inspire others to equal or surpass the ideals and abilities of this fine craftsman, instructor and author.

Bob Brownell

Montezuma, Iowa
August, 1973

FOREWORD

From the beginning of time there have been those individuals who have had an inclination to express themselves in some manner. As leaders in the military, in politics and in the arts, these men have left their mark. Among the earliest recorded art forms, the decorated caves of the primitives show this urge to create. The wealth of the early Chinese, Japanese, Indian and Persian decorative art is an amazing record of man's ingenuity and his ability to create. All of these, in addition to the Greek, Roman, French, German and English styles of ornamentation, which have had more of an influence on our own culture, make an imposing storehouse from which to draw inspiration.

With all of this treasure of accomplishment, the beginner has difficulty in finding explicit, detailed instructions to guide him in this formidable endeavor of beginning to engrave. Presumably, any instructions that were given to apprentices were given by word of mouth. This hard-earned knowledge and these "trade secrets" were not to be cast recklessly into the open market since reputations were built on craftsmanship of quality and style. The master engraver was a creative artist devoted to his craft, and the describing, explaining and relating in print of even a simple procedure could put a demand on his time that would have been prohibitive. Whatever the reasons, this lack of written information on the details of engraving imposes quite a handicap on the progress of the beginner. With this book we will attempt to anticipate and answer many of the questions the novice will ask, and give him a comprehensive coverage on each phase of the subject. It is important to the beginner that he be given more than the bare essentials of the topic, lest he get lost in an endless series of trial and error efforts.

There will probably be some of you who are interested in the processes and procedures, but have no intention of actually working at engraving. To you, we hope that you will find the book both understandable and interesting.

With the furor over the possession of guns and the fact that they may be restricted, it behooves the younger engraver to seek out new avenues into which to channel his talents. Many of the present gun engravers are, or have been, engaged in the die-making craft or as jewelers and engravers. Even L. D. Nimsche, who was so prolific in an era when the gun was so common, also engraved watches, spoons, plates and dog collars. In fact his card stated "Engraving on firearms - Lettering on all metals". The old saying that "you cannot teach an old dog new tricks" makes some sense, but some of you young dogs with a fresh viewpoint may start a whole new trend or fashion. So keep an open mind and an active one. You might contact your sporting goods stores and provide them with samples of your engraved, personalized, ornamental nameplates for their customers' golf bags, fishermen's tackle boxes or brief cases. Such an area might include individualized, decorated cigarette lighters. A smoker who is proud of his rifles and shotguns would surely have a similar pride in an object that he uses and displays so often. It would take some advertising and promotional work, but if it once caught the fancy of the public, who could predict where it might lead!

There are a number of fine engravers whose work I should liked to have included but space did not permit. Mr. Prudhomme's book the **Gun Engraving Review** has covered this field very well, with many fine reproductions for the beginner to study. To Arnold Griebel, Alvin A. White, John E. Warren, E.C. Prudhomme, Lynton McKenzie and John R. Rohner I particularly extend thanks for the photographic material that they so willingly and generously contributed. I want also to thank Lt. Col. F.B. Conway (Ret.) for comments and photographs that I am sure you will find interesting. Thanks also to all of those good friends who have permitted me to photograph their firearms for use in this book.

Especially valued is the inspiration, the critical interest, the experience and occasional prodding of Bob Brownell, the publisher, who has been largely responsible for the creation of this effort.

Next, a note of appreciation for my wife, Jeanette, whose encouragement and forebearance in social and recreational matters has made possible the time to accomplish the job.

I know that you are anxious to begin, and to get started you must have a design for your engraving. So now let us develop that design from the very beginning for the novice who has no idea even what a design is. Along the way I will give explanations and examples that should help to clear up any hazy conceptions or wrong directions. The areas of uncertainty will be replaced with a few concrete ideas that are basic, and from these, your ideas can then be expanded into elaborate and complicated layouts.

It is my intent and hope that this book will be a source of aid to the beginning craftsmen of tomorrow. So, to you young beginners - of whatever age - I should like to dedicate this book, with "Best Wishes" for many happy hours with the gravers.

James B. Meek

Newton, Iowa
May, 1973

The Art of Engraving

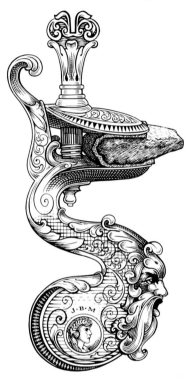

Chapter One
Design and Layout

any beginners want to take up engraving but are bewildered and perplexed at just how to get started. This is understandable because there is a scarcity of material on the subject, and the material that is available has been published in an assortment of different magazines and books over a long period of time. Most beginners are completely unaware of these articles or have no idea as to where to go to find them. So, to those of you who are taking up this fascinating art form for the first time, let us start at the very beginning.

It may come as a surprise that we will not begin by picking up the graver and starting immediately on the practice of actual engraving. To do a good job of engraving you must have a good idea of what you want to cut into the metal. So, let us go to work on the first requirement of a good engraving job, namely a good design. You should be able to put your design on paper, for by so doing you can alter and change the design until you are satisfied that it is what you want. This will give you some assurance that once the lines are cut into the metal, they will have been cut exactly where you wanted them. The clean, polished surface of a piece of metal is a distinct challenge, and having a well thought-out design will reduce the qualms about cutting into that beautiful surface.

Let us start by assuming that you have had no art training, and it is necessary to give you some simple facts that will help to organize your thinking about design. The two lines that are basic in all design are the straight line and the circle. Naturally, the curved lines will not all be segments of a circle, but they will be varying parts of the ellipse and the circle. The straight line is the least interesting because of its lack of variety. The perfect circle by curving uniformly in its entirety has this same lack of variety. This does not mean that the straight line and the circle do not have a function in design. These will be discussed as we get into the subject and as they relate to the whole design. Here are two simple examples which demonstrate the effectiveness of a few simple lines.

Figure 1a shows the effect of straight horizontal lines that one commonly sees in an early summer landscape; the long flat horizon line plus the flat bottoms of all of those white cumulus clouds drifting lazily across the deep

FIGURE 1a

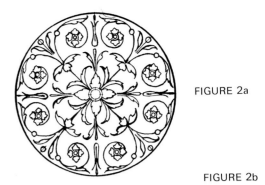

FIGURE 2a

FIGURE 2b

blue sky. All of these straight lines along with the straight vertical line of the tree contribute to the calm, peaceful character of the scene. To transform this calm, peaceful picture into one of tempestuous violence, a change in the character of the lines is all that is needed. A sudden, strong rush of wind, ushering in a storm, blows leaves and dust ahead of it which obscure that long clean horizon line. Black churning clouds are discharging a slashing attack of hail that further adds to the discord of the violent scene, while the force of the wind is seen in the yielding lines of the tree. See figure 1b. To return

FIGURE 1b

to a calm scene, had the straight lines been vertical instead of horizontal the same feeling of quietude would have resulted. For example, the feeling one gets while standing quietly in a forest of lofty redwoods or towering pines. Many of the great cathedrals with their tremendous vertical lines terminating in lofty arches convey this same feeling of quiet exaltation.

In figure 2a is a circle within which the straight line is used to divide the circle into eight sections. Notice that they are not hard, continuous lines but that the design has been drawn so the feeling of a straight line carries through. This combination of curves along with the straight lines makes for an interesting design. In figure 2b the straight line as it might be used for a border is shown. The scrolls

relieve the simple severity of a single straight line.

To get back to the original question of starting a design then, let's go back to the circle. As a distinct advance over the circle as a decorative device, the Greeks came up with the egg and dart motif. The circle, when it is drawn in perspective, appears as an ellipse which introduces some variety into the line that was a circle. The two ends of the ellipse, however, are still the same, so they added some variety by making the two ends different as in the shape of an egg. This adds a maximum of interest while the two sides (being similar) supply the touch of unity for the whole design. Figure 3 shows this use of the egg and dart in some decorative designs. The egg and dart has been the basis for many fine designs used by both the Greeks and the Romans.

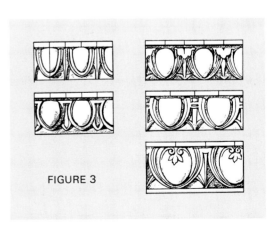

FIGURE 3

The popularity of the scroll with its infinite variety has always been a favorite with decorators and engravers. At figure 4 are shown two examples: the one is a demonstration plate by A. A. White showing different scrolls and the other is a typical example by the late Arnold Griebel. To get back to our scrolls again, a curved line that is of uniform thickness does not have the same quality as one that has some variation (from thick to thin). Figure 5 shows several scrolls, the right side of which shows scrolls with lines of varied thicknesses. The left side shows them cut to a more uniform width. The scrolls on the right side are def-

initely more interesting and lively because of the variation. The straight lines will of course be as straight and as uniform as you can make them. This will not be as contradictory as you might think for the curved lines of the scrolls are enhanced by the relief of some good straight lines. The straight line in nature tends to be associated with strength. The straight, clean lines of the well-muscled athlete as contrasted with the soft curves of the fat man.

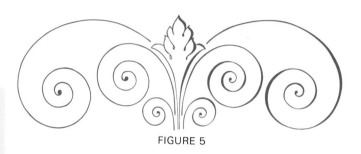

FIGURE 5

To those of you who want to become seriously involved with engraving, there is only one way and that is to engrave - engrave as much as you possibly can. I am convinced that almost anyone with an aptitude and a serious desire can learn to handle the tools, the chasers hammer and graver. The hand-propelled graver is another problem. This problem has now been solved by a new miniature pneumatic hammer which allows the use of both hands without that feeling of insecurity that all beginners experience when starting to engrave by hand. There will be more about this tool later in the book.

Before we start seriously with the pencil and layout, there is one point that I should like to impress upon you. It is difficult to explain and it may be even harder to understand. The eye by its very nature tends to focus on one point. The artist trains his eye to perceive (for example in painting a portrait) the complete subject. That is, he looks at the whole picture

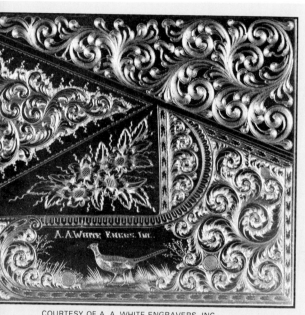

COURTESY OF A. A. WHITE ENGRAVERS, INC.

FIGURE 4

BY PERMISSION OF ARNOLD GRIEBEL

and in this manner he can get a true comparison of the color of the background, as compared to the color of the face. If he looks at the background only, the eye rapidly adjusts to what it sees in that area only. The color of one part effects the color of the surrounding areas. You will not be called upon to accomplish this, however the same effort will be a big help in laying out your design. By keeping your total area in mind you will be able to apportion your scrolls more effectively. Plan ahead so that the

FIGURE 7

FIGURE 6

layout fits the area that it is intended for, see figure 6. Until you have become an accomplished artist, it would be wise to adopt such a system of planning your drawings. At figure 7 two drawings are shown to give you an idea of how to proceed. In both drawings only the big proportions and the character of the subject are drawn. These are drawn in ink so as to reproduce sharply, but in your drawings they will be made lightly and in pencil. At this stage the drawing is easily corrected. Once all of the parts are as nearly correct as you can make them (as to proportion and character) then is the time to search out the details.

In the beginning portrait classes you would find the new students starting with the nose, the eyes or whatever part their eyes focused on first. After finishing that part they would find that it was not in the correct position, that it was too large or too small, and they would have to go through all the effort of redrawing it. Soon they would get the idea that it was faster and better to plan the overall drawing before starting to finish any of the details. See figure 7 again. Position the eyes, nose and mouth in

their correct proportions and determine, after careful observation, the variations of the parts of this particular model. You will find that practically everyone has one side of his face a little higher or lower than the other and that the two sides are not exactly alike. So plan your initial layout critically and the parts will fall into place like the parts of a jigsaw puzzle.

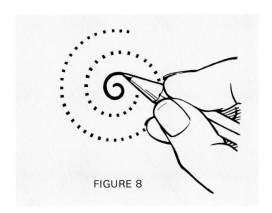

FIGURE 8

When you start to practice your scrolls remember the idea of the widened vision and try to develop its use because of the increased control that it brings to your work. The beginner has a natural leaning toward following the pencil point with his eye and it will be some time before he can transfer his attention to the whole scroll. If you watch only the pencil point you will probably end up as shown in figure 6, with too much scroll in too small a space.

Start to practice your basic scrolls using a medium soft pencil and a good white paper. As you practice, use a light touch with the pencil. Developing such a touch will help you later when you come to drawing animals and figures. Do not start making scrolls haphazardly even at first. See figure 8, and from the very first try to visualize the area into which the scroll is to fit. It is very important that you do NOT begin by picking up a pencil and dashing off scroll after scroll. Such effort will not develop the mastery or control that you will need.

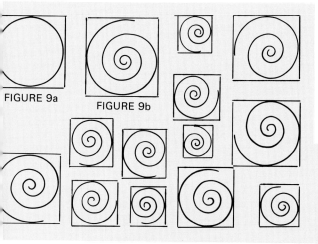

FIGURE 9a   FIGURE 9b

FIGURE 9

Draw each scroll rather slowly, concentrating on your control and making it as evenly progressive as you possibly can. This thoughtful, serious effort is bound to show results. Draw a square (which need not be perfect) and if it will help, you can even indicate a circle inside the square to help guide you in your first efforts, see figure 9a. The objective is to force yourself to make the scroll fit a definite area. Make your squares of assorted sizes, see squares 9b and beyond. Make them differently by reversing the direction of the scrolls since you will eventually be making them in all directions. Start a scroll

from one side, then start the next one at the bottom and reverse it. Each time that you do one, attempt to enlarge your area of vision so that you are aware of the whole area of the square.

You need not confine these practices to a square; try rectangles horizontally and vertically, see figure 10. With practice you will find them smoothing out. Be alert and do not let them become lumpy or uneven. You can practice these in odd moments of doodling (on scraps of paper, magazines, newspapers or old envelopes) if you have a pencil with you at all times. See how many ways you can place a scroll in that square or oblong. To repeat, start in one corner one time, a different corner the next time or in the middle of any one of the four sides. Do not allow yourself the habit of making all of the scrolls in one direction. You will probably make them more naturally in one direction than the other. The direction that

FIGURE 10

seems more difficult will require more practice. You can also vary the number of spirals in your scrolls to get some variety.

These scrolls are somewhat comparable to the notes of the scale, for after practicing

6

the scale to boredom, you are anxious to try a tune. So we shall explore the possibilities of extending this scroll and increasing the interest of the design. Put two squares beside each other, see figure 10 again. To add a little variation make one square smaller than the other. Within the two squares you can lightly indicate circles. Connect the two circles and complete the scrolls. Practice these in your doodling and you will have acquired a little larger stock of design capabilities. As with the single scrolls, practice variations of this arrangement. After making the first one, change the small square to the other side and connect them up differently. Make as many changes in this association as you can devise. Eventually these basic forms will become effortless to you. They become as much yours as is the alphabet, which you use without any conscious effort.

Until now, we have confined ourselves to the scroll and extended it to one additional scroll. Before we start a layout on a finished design, let us see how we can expand our design

FIGURE 11

and its interest by combining several scrolls. The running scroll is one of the first that seems to develop naturally. These can be fully formed as though the scroll was made in one of your squares, or it might be extended (as though it was made in a rectangle) which will give it a different effect, see figure 11. It may be that a given area will dictate what will most effectively decorate that space. For example, a long narrow area may call for a simple repetitious

FIGURE 12

motif, or you might decide on a modified, elongated scroll, see figure 12. You should build up a good file of reproductions of engraving from which you can find guidance for almost any situation that might confront you. In designing your first plates, keep them simple enough that you can execute them. As your talents and abilities develop you will experience the thrill of executing the more complicated cuts as though you were the first to ever do them.

As you go through your files and note how different engravers develop the scroll, you will find one that will execute one full scroll with a continuous cut. From this one he will take off and complete another full scroll, see figure 13a. A little more complicated but certainly a more flowing scroll is shown at figure 13b. By interrupting your cuts, a continuous flow of the metal connects one scroll to the next with no cuts separating them. The floorplate by John E. Warren is an example of the cutting as shown in figure 13a while the derringer by E. C. Prudhomme exemplifies the continuous scroll as shown in figure 13b. Both methods are commonly used. The scrolls at 13c are drawn from a reproduction of one of Kornbrath's engravings. The arrows point to two scrolls that show the use of each method.

FIGURE 13a

FIGURE 13b

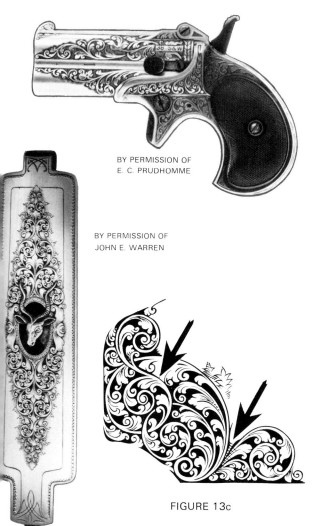

BY PERMISSION OF
E. C. PRUDHOMME

BY PERMISSION OF
JOHN E. WARREN

FIGURE 13c

he introduced a great amount of variety. Figure 14 is a drawing from a reproduction of one of his engravings. It does not do justice to the engraving, of course, since it is only a drawing and cannot show the sparkle and the mastery of the cutting.

You should have had a lot of practice by now with the pencil, making scrolls and carrying them on. Now you can increase the interest

FIGURE 14

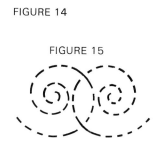

FIGURE 15

and complexity of your design by interweaving some of the scrolls to create the illusion of the lines passing over and underneath each other. To bring about this illusion you will have to interrupt your cuts and pick them up again. In the beginning, plan them carefully, as an unwanted cut can be difficult to cover up. Draw the intended scrolls lightly. Now pin down the intended lines that are going over the others by making them heavier. Stop the lines that are going underneath short of the lines that are passing over. Make a definite break so that you cannot mistake the fact that the one cut must stop, see figure 15. Carry a pencil and practice these scrolls in your spare moments, and you will be surprised at how much you will have accomplished. By doing your exercises with a pencil you can drill yourself and develop your procedure mentally. Here again do not forget to practice your training of the visual concept. This will be very important to you when you come to the cutting of the scroll.

From the middle of the 19th century until around 1900, an engraver by the name of L. D. Nimsche was one of the foremost engravers of his time. If you have an opportunity to study a book published in 1965 by John J. Malloy, entitled **L. D. Nimsche, Firearms Engraver** by R. L. Wilson, you should do so. From it you can study the work of a man who accomplished a tremendous amount of work (they estimate as many as 5,000 guns). He was equally at ease doing animals, portraits, or figures and he was a fine lettering man with his gravers. His scrolls were carried to a high degree of perfection. In addition to their flowing lines,

As you make the cut around the scroll, you must know where you are at all times and you must know where you are going to conclude the cut before you get there. If you can make a good accurate outline and follow it precisely, this will serve you well until you have developed the ability to "keep ahead of your cut" visually. The experienced engraver will indicate his scroll lightly as a guide to the area that it is going to occupy. This layout is a guide to the area only and will not be a line that is slavishly followed. As his cut progresses, it does so under his full command. The finished cut is so much smoother and cleaner than a hand drawn line that there is no comparison.

As you become more acquainted with engraving, you will see examples of engraving where the cuts are not all perfectly smooth and bright. In a later chapter we will explain and show photographs of the causes of the

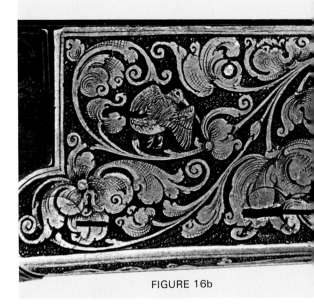

FIGURE 16b

enlarged view of a portion of the design to allow a little better study of the way that the cutting was done. Note that the cutting is not a real smooth, bright cut and that there are slight nicks here and there, but the conformation of the scrolls and the masterful design are all so well done that these slight imperfections do not detract from the overall impression of excellence. The woodcock at figure 16c is en-

FIGURE 16a

smoothness or the roughness of the cuts. The fact that the cuts are not perfectly smooth and bright does not necessarily mean that it is bad engraving, as is shown in figure 16a; this shows a well planned design and is one the beginner can study and profit from. Figure 16b is an

FIGURE 16c

larged still more to show you a fine example of how to cut a bird to get that modeled effect that shows so well in the overall reproduction. This also shows you that if you can make your subject into a good pen and ink drawing, it can be cut into the metal to get a very similar effect. From the boldness of the cutting, you can tell that this engraver knew what he wanted to say.

To review our steps this far: you should have a basic scroll quite well in hand. Secondly, you will be able to carry it into a second scroll in any position with no problem. Thirdly, your ability to continue these scrolls to cover an area will be well practiced by now. Finally you are increasing the variety and interest in these scrolls by interweaving and making them more intricate. Only after you feel that you have a good control of these patterns should you start to explore the field of finishing detail. Here again some of the good reproductions will be of great help to you. There is a very good book out, authored by E. C. Prudhomme, entitled **Gun Engraving Review** that would be a fine source of material for your study.

the finished surface presenting more of a texture than a bold design. Another example of this style of engraving is the floor plate by Kornbrath shown on the inside of page 6 of **The Gun Engraving Review.** The design at 17b has more of the background removed in relation to the scrolls and the details stand out quite well displayed and visible for some distance. In the same book just mentioned, on page 16, the second gun from the top of the page shows a fine design by the late Arnold Griebel that is typical of his excellent layouts. How you eventually feel about design will determine which of these two types of design you will want to work. A design to be displayed conspicuously must be well planned and executed as it is right out in the open for everyone to see. A design that goes to an overall pattern will not display its flaws so blatantly. They may be there but they are less easily detected. While you are examining the reproductions of various artists, use your pencil to fix some of these forms in your mind. Even go so far as to use some matte acetate or thin tracing paper and follow in detail some of their designs. You will be surprised at how easily the details will develop after you have the main lines laid out.

Most of our designs are based on things the artist has been acquainted with. The elements of decoration are many. You might develop geometrical designs, or designs based on flowers, leaves, vines or natural objects. Many are based on animal or human forms or sometimes a combination of the two, such as the centaur at figure 18a. On occasion, you will find the

FIGURE 17a   FIGURE 17b

Two examples of scroll work are shown in figure 17. Both are conventional in treatment, yet each is different in design to give you a basis for comparison. In 17a, the scrolls are kept very full with a minimum of background removed. From a little distance this makes for a tapestry effect with the design muted and

FIGURE 18a

FIGURE 18b

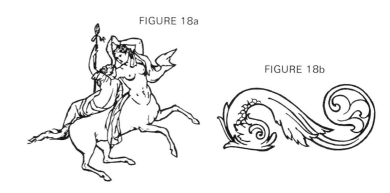

10

artist combining natural, foliage and human forms, or as is shown at 18b you might see a dolphin treated in a stylized manner combined with a decorative scroll. Instead of a human form on the body of a horse, you can find a crouching lion with a human head as shown in the sphinx at figure 18c. You could even find a sphinx with a lion's body and a ram's head while lions with wings in numerous variations (see figure 18d) are to be found.

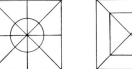

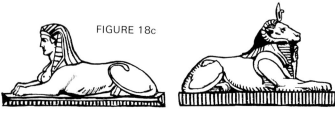

FIGURE 18c

FIGURE 18d

FIGURE 19

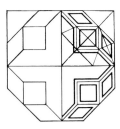
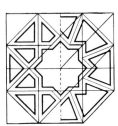
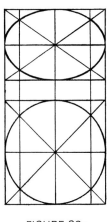

FIGURE 20a

The use of geometrical elements in designing goes back for centuries. The Greeks made use of them in the ornamentation of their pottery. Figure 19 shows several examples of ways of breaking up and using the square in design with three examples of repeat motifs. These may give you some ideas to work from in developing some of your own designs since the possible variations are unlimited. In addition to the square you have the rectangle, the triangle, the hexagon, the octagon and the polygon as well as the circle with its subdivisions and the ellipses with their various perspectives and subdivisions. At figure 20a is shown one way of drawing an ellipse. It is self-explanatory as

After the geometrical forms, the natural forms seem next in line. The Akanthos leaf is one of the most used as the basis for decorative purposes. The Akanthos is a plant (with a number of varieties) that grows in Southern Europe. Two of the natural leaves are shown at figure 21. The remainder of the illustrations in figure 21 are from decorative applications of the leaf. Its possibilities as a basis for ornamental use

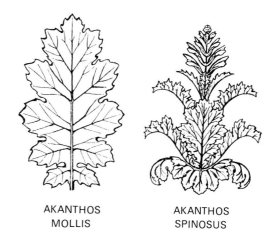

AKANTHOS MOLLIS   AKANTHOS SPINOSUS

FIGURE 21

the diagonal, vertical and horizontal lines intersect at the points in the circle that also establish the same points of the oval that is being drawn in the rectangle. By making the rectangle into which the ellipse is being drawn either wider or narrower, the ellipse can be made into a long slim oval or a wide fat one. For those of you who want to go into the subject more thoroughly, you can get the books **Handbook of Ornament** by F. S. Meyer or the **Styles of Ornament** by Alexander Speltz.

have been fully exercised. You will find variations of it used on our own paper money, for the obverse side (front side) of the dollar bill has a nice panel in the upper left hand corner

12

FIGURE 21-con't.

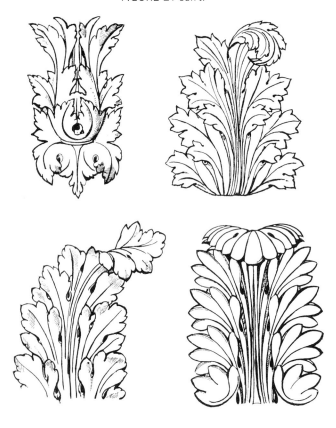

LAUREL

OLIVE

FIGURE 22

that can be used as an example in your engraving. In fact, the panel in each corner is suitable for such adaptation. Here again is an excellent example of the use of variety in design as each panel is different. On the reverse side of the dollar bill the Akanthos leaf is again used in one of its variations. The five dollar bill uses the same motif in much of its decoration. With a good magnifying glass you can examine in detail the modeling of the forms to use as a guide to the modeling of your own designs.

In figure 22 are the laurel and the olive leaves which have been used as symbols of distinction and peace for centuries. On your dollar bill again, on the obverse side, you find olive leaves worked in around the panel. The olive branch also appears at each end of the bill and here again note the differences that appear in each branch. As a symbol of distinction, the Greeks crowned the victors in the

Pythian games with a wreath of laurel. A "Laureate" was one crowned or decked with laurel as a mark of honor. Hence, one especially honored for poetic excellence was the "poet laureate".

Other leaves have long been favorites. The leaf of the mighty oak as a symbol of strength is still popular. The German engravers used it extensively in many combinations. You will find many examples of the engraved oak leaf as you build your portfolio of reproductions, see figure 23. As you examine many of these engraved oak leaves you will notice that they

FIGURE 23
BITTER OAK

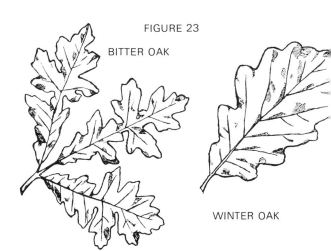

WINTER OAK

FIGURE 23-cont.

13

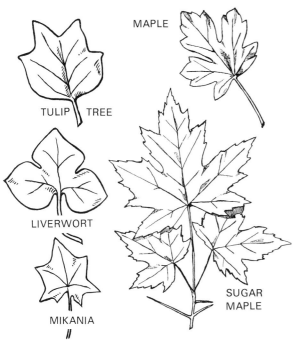

MAPLE

TULIP TREE

LIVERWORT

MIKANIA

SUGAR
MAPLE

ARTIFICIAL FOLIAGE

are not necessarily natural and actual representations of the oak leaf, but have been stylized by the engraver to conform to his own idea or method of engraving. Leaves such as the maple, the grape and clematis have been adapted to carvings, both in wood and in stone. If you come across a leaf that appeals to your fancy, take your pencil and make some drawings of it. If it still looks good to you, use it in your own engraving, trying to retain the character of the leaf. You need not copy each serration or indentation, but try to catch its characteristic shape.

The vine with its foliage, both natural and artificial, has long been the means of covering an area decoratively. The vine can be trained in a given direction and the leaves arranged in a decorative fashion. For the beginner, the vine (see the natural grape vine in figure 24) offers a means of covering an area with a design that does not require the experience and discipline of the scroll. The design can be an overall pattern and each cut can be made somewhat irregular by the very nature of the subject. Do not let the easy way entice you away from the more original, basic scroll, for once your fundamental scrolls are mastered, you are in a position to do anything that your fancy dictates.

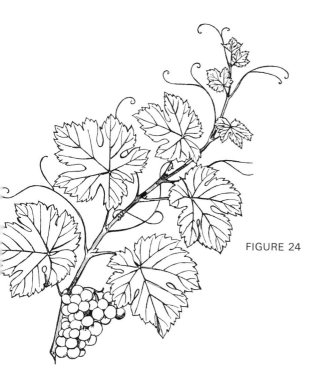

FIGURE 24

RHODODENDRON

WILD ROSE

CHRYSAN-
THEMUM

BLUEBELL

FIGURE 24a

FIGURE 24b

14

FESTOONS

FIGURE 25b

Next, let us consider the flowers. There is such a profusion of ideas for the designer in this area that we will confine our examples to those more commonly used. The wild rose and the chrysanthemum developing from a natural center are logical models for the rosette that you can use to cover hinge pins and large screws. All countries have included flowers in their firearms decoration. The wild rose, bluebell, chrysanthemum (see figure 24) and many others can be used in designing a floral arrangement. Not only are the individual flowers used, but they are also arranged in leaf and flower festoons and garlands. In figures 24a and 24b are shown two examples of flowers as cut by an engraver. Italy seems to have gone a little more to the use of flowers than some of the other countries and they have done it very effectively as can be seen in figure 25a. At figure 25b is shown an enlarged section of the receiver so that you can study it in more detail. You will note the treatment of the background that is quite often used to set the background back and to place more emphasis on the scrolls and main parts of the design. In this case many parallel lines are cut vertically across the background, but they may be cut in any direction

that seems appropriate. These lines are sometimes cut with liners. For the novice we have given a breakdown of the main lines in figure 25c. In all the confusion of detail, the uninitiated may overlook this underlying plan. Fruit as well as flowers was often used, and at times a combination of all three was employed - fruit, flowers and leaves - confined to a logical form with a ribbon.

FIGURE 25c

From all this exposure to natural motifs a stylized foliage has evolved. The resulting forms seem to be a logical outgrowth of nature being sifted through the human mind. Scrolls and

FIGURE 25a

COAT OF ARMS
ITALY

segments of arcs and ellipses seem to almost automatically collect these interesting and endless variations. Do not allow this huge field of past design to disconcert you. Stay with your scrolls and as you acquire proficiency in their use, your ability to assimilate and adapt other ideas will grow. All the time your awareness of the possibilities in design is becoming greater. Your storehouse of ideas would not be complete, however, without discussing briefly the use that has been made of animals, birds and the human figure, and some of the fantastic combinations that have resulted from these unions.

other decorative purposes. The English used the lion in their heraldry where it became their most popular animal figure. The combinations of an animal's body with a bird's wings and head led to the creation of the monsters. The Griffin has the head and wings of an eagle on a lion's body. The Chimera, a she monster, usually

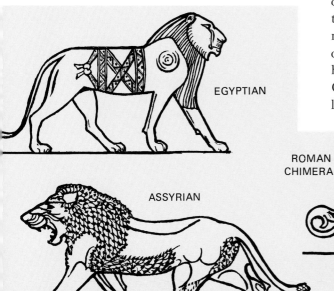

EGYPTIAN

ASSYRIAN

ROMAN
CHIMERA

GRIFFIN

The lion, the king of beasts because of his strength, courage and lordly bearing, has been used in many cultures as a decorative motif. The Egyptians and Assyrians made him a part of their design in their highly stylized manner, see figure 26. The Italians and Germans both used the lion in their coat-of-arms and for

WINGED LIONESS
FRENCH

ALL DRAWINGS
ON THIS PAGE
FIGURE 26

FRENCH

had a goat's body, lion's head and a dragon's or serpent's tail, see figure 26. The imagination and ingenuity of man has led to an endless variety of combinations that can be a spur to stimulate your own inventiveness and originality if you pursue the subject in more detail.

Ruger is a stylized example and one that is instantly recognized on a revolver. The dolphin was used on many old-time flintlocks. In its stylized treatment it makes a very graceful decoration and one that blends well with scroll work, figure 27. Shells are also naturals for adapting to your engraving, and several adaptations are shown at figure 27. The Shedd Aquarium in Chicago is an excellent example of applied design, for from the big bronze doors to the light fixtures, everything has been decorated (mostly in bronze) with marine life motifs in beautiful detail.

As you get into designing, you will encounter the grotesque masks and figures. These were produced in a free and capricious manner from a combination of human, animal and plant forms, sometimes quite ugly but always bizarre and fanciful. They have been used in architecture, armor and furniture to mention just a few of the many places they have appeared. The grotesque figure was drawn with a human head, a portion of the body, the arms replaced by decorative wings or scrolls and the body ter-

ALL DRAWINGS
ON THIS PAGE
FIGURE 27

The eagle, the dolphin and shells have all been popular as subjects for designs. The eagle has been especially prominent in the engravers' repertoire. You will find him portrayed in highly realistic portrayals or in decorative treatments, see figure 27. The trademark of the

minating with animal legs or foliage of fish tails, often a decorative treatment rather than a natural one. At figure 28 are shown several grotesque masks and three grotesque figures.

FIGURE 29

THE GROTESQUES

FIGURE 28

The Medusa head (in the circle) was one of the mythological subjects that was used on shields, armor, doors and above gates. The half figure is similar to the grotesque, except that the upper body is treated in a natural manner. In many cases the body is encircled by a decorative belt below the breasts or around the stomach from which the design is carried downward and outward. In other examples, the natural contours of the lower abdomen form a transition from the body to the decorative motifs of the design, see figure 29. The half figure has been a popular ornamental device for centuries. It has been used not only in low and high relief but in the full round as well.

THE RIBBON

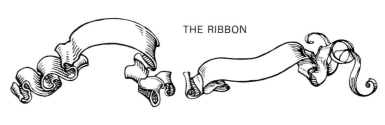

After this diversion into natural design forms, let us go back to the geometrical approach and include a further study of the "band" with some of its variations, see figure 30. The book **Handbook of Ornament** by Meyer has many more illustrations and information for the interested student. The fret band is a running border that was of Greek design used on

UNDULATE

VERTEBRATE

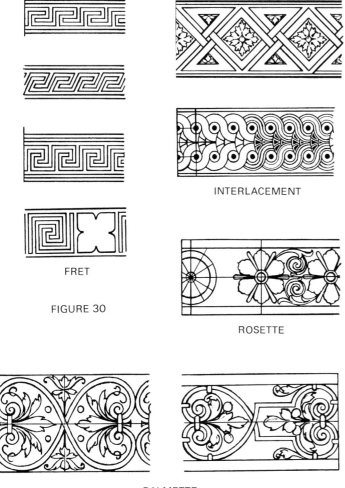

FRET

FIGURE 30

INTERLACEMENT

ROSETTE

PALMETTE

may be made up of square, round or oval links of any combination. You might want to start with a square link and alternate with oval links. Proceeding to the more intricate, you come to the interlacement bands. Many of these designs were intended for use with colors as in borders in tile floors. Among these bands you may find borders that you can adapt to your own jobs. From the rosette and palmette bands you can find ideas for many small running designs. The vertebrate band and the undulate band will also enlarge your choice of design. You will see among all of these designs, not only complete ornamental ideas, but many that you may want to take only a portion of and combine with something of your own design.

Included are some link borders and cresting borders, see figure 31. The link borders were running borders of foliage held together (or linked together) with scrolls. Cresting bor-

the cloth that they designed as well as on their pottery. It is of simple construction and can be varied to quite a degree. The chain band was often used and as the name implies is based on the links of the chain. No illustration is shown since it is easily imagined. The chain

LINK BORDERS

FIGURE 31

ders were used as ornamental crests on the top of the roof or ridge. The akroter acts as an ornamental terminal to the peak or gable of a

tombstones (or steles) were similar to the akroter and the antefix and they too are readily adapted to the engraver's use.

Decorative finials were used to terminate gables, balustrades, flagstaffs and parts of furniture, see figure 32. Many finials were of wrought iron and were also used on chandeliers and brackets. Two capitals, a pendant knob and a decorative shaft, are shown from which you can find decorative motifs.

FIGURE 31 cont.

CRESTING BORDERS

 KROTER
RESTS

STELE
CREST

MNHΣIΣTPATH

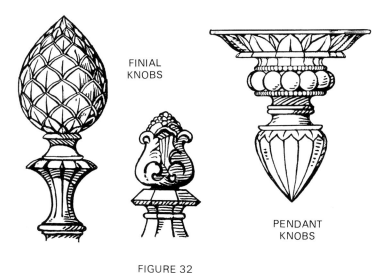

FINIAL
KNOBS

PENDANT
KNOBS

FIGURE 32

CAPITALS

DECORATED
SHAFT

roof. This element is very adaptable to the use of the gun engraver and you have seen it quite often as a decorative part of an engraving. The akroter was made of terracotta, carved in stone or sometimes cast in metal. When smaller ornaments of a similar nature were used on lower roofs they were referred to as antefixes. On a corner perhaps only half of the design would be used and for the engraver it is an ideal decoration to fill a corner. The crests on the Greek

In the illustrations of past designs that have been shown you will find much material that may be used as is, or which will enable you to develop your own drawings. The illustrations are slightly undersize and have been redrawn from cuts that appeared in the **Handbook of Ornament** by F.S. Meyer. The book is an unabridged and unaltered re-publication of the English translation of the last revised edition. It has 300 full-page plates with 3002 illustrations. This book is available from Dover Publications. The material from the book that is included here is only a small portion of that which is contained in the book. There is another book very similar in content, **Styles of Ornament** by Alexander Speltz. It has 400 full page plates and 3765 illustrations. This book is also available from Dover Publications.

After this short resume of past decorative design let us get back to your own scrolls and carry them on to their completed stage. We shall offer some suggestions and you will have your file to refer to also. Here again each individual will develop his own characteristic touches. You can start your scroll with a small spiral that is contained within the boundaries of the design, see figure 33a. An alternate choice would be to allow the border to run into and become the scroll, in the manner shown at figure 33b. Before you start developing each

pearance when the cutting is finished? The fullness that you give to the components and the amount of background you allow is going to determine the final appearance. Once you decide on the effect that you want, try to maintain about the same relationship in each of the scrolls. The individual parts in a scroll would vary even though you tried to make each exactly like the other. This variety is good and you should strive for a difference while retaining a similarity of character. See the six elements in figure 33c that are essentially similar in character but each slightly different.

FIGURE 33c

Heretofore your scrolls have been small or medium sized, the object being to cover your area with a network of related and interwoven scrolls. Now you will want to try your capabilities on larger scrolls that will form the main design on large areas, see figure 33d. This is a beginning on a Winchester single shot action with a central area left for a game scene. In designing these larger scrolls, your efforts will still be directed to the forming of smooth, well-formed scrolls. A large scroll that is ill-conceived is much worse than none at all. No attempt will be made at this stage to finish the details. The

FIGURE 33a   FIGURE 33b

scroll, you should decide what you intend the final appearance to be. That is, are you going to have a pronounced pattern, an overall textured effect or something intermediate in ap-

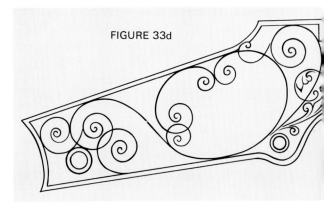

FIGURE 33d

FIGURE 34

BY PERMISSION OF ARNOLD GRIEBEL

scrolls will stand on their own merit if they are good enough. Working with a pencil enables you to correct and change the lumps and flat places which you will want to do when you lay out your scrolls on the metal, preliminary to scribing and cutting. After you have gained experience and confidence with the graver the cuts will become smooth and professional looking. While you are practicing with the pencil you will be working with a variety of arcs and curved lines and even at this practice do not work in an aimless, hit-or-miss fashion. Though it may be rough, indicate an area representing some portion of a firearm. This has been mentioned a number of times before because it is important that you force yourself to accommodate your design to a given, specific area. Working in this specific area, you may find that your scroll is running into a space that is going to force a radical change in the course of the arc, see figure 33e. In this case, go back a little and rearrange your scroll

large, they do not give the impression of overpowering or dominating the action. Again, while they are large, they are delicate and very graceful. Some of Griebel's large scrolls form borders for panels containing hunting scenes.

While you are studying his examples, give some attention to another style that he frequently used, see figure 33f. In Mr. Prudhomme's

FIGURE 33f

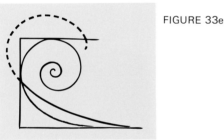

FIGURE 33e

so that it enters this restricting space with a smoother curve. Do not be content with just getting that scroll into the tight area, but insist that it be a well formed curve all the way. NOW is the time to change those scrolls if they are not easy and free flowing.

You will find many examples of large scrolls and these will usually be relieved by supplementary scrolls or decorative designs. Arnold Griebel has some exceptionally nice examples of these larger scrolls as applied to the large shotgun receivers, see figure 34. While

book **Gun Engraving Review** on pages 16 and 17 are some fine reproductions of this style that Griebel used so beautifully. The drawing at 33f does not do justice to his actual cutting, and if you have access to the book these designs would be well worth your studying. Note particularly the character of the lines that make up the scrolls. It is not a simple uniform line, but a line that is full of surprises, proceeding from a slender beginning and widening into an ornamental enlargement. It drops back smaller again, then forges ahead growing progressively larger until it develops into a different decorative idea. Finally after a number of variations it will terminate in a plain scroll, a free form or even a flower in the case of a screw or pin. In past issues of the **Gun Digest** are many examples of Mr. Griebel's art, done on Winchester 94's and single shot rifles, two examples of which are shown at figures 35 and 36.

22

FIGURE 35

The least expensive job is the simple line cuts. These can be from simple motifs to more extended coverage. These cuts are complete in themselves once they are made. Usually the cuts will vary in width of line, which adds interest to the quality and character of the cut but requires no additional time or attention. These can be completed in a minimum of time

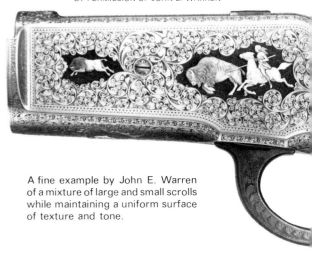

A fine example by John E. Warren of a mixture of large and small scrolls while maintaining a uniform surface of texture and tone.

This publication and its past issues contains the works of many other fine engravers worthy of your study. At figure 35 is a good example of a job that is cut quite simply but very effectively. The scroll work is simple line cuts that could be cut with very little time required, while the game scene shows his masterful handling of action and setting.

Before leaving the subject of design, there are a few general remarks that I should like to make. There is always the problem of to what extent an engraver should go to give the customer what he wants. A customer may have only a certain amount of money to invest in his engraving job. For the professional engraver, his less expensive job will be of as equally high quality as the best job that he produces. The difference is not in the quality but in the amount of time that he must put into the different classes of work. So let us examine some of the categories that he will have at his command.

and are consequently less expensive. You will note that there is no reference made to being cheap. Being done by a competent engraver, they will be of the same quality as the job that is carried on to a higher degree of detail and finish.

From the simple line job, the next step farther is to cut the design into an area with a little more detail. After the detail is cut, the background is given a different texture which can be done with various punches or different patterns cut by hand. This is very effective (many times it appears as though the background was set back) and since no time is lost in removing the background, it cuts down on the time invested in the job (and time is money).

The next step is often referred to as "semi-relief". This is quite a large field and covers

FIGURE 36

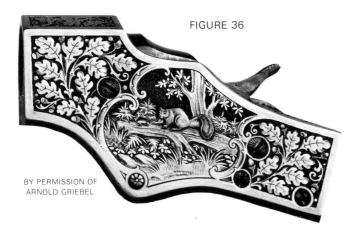

perhaps the larger part of the engraving being done. In this, the design is cut with the express purpose of removing the background to a depth of .005" to .010", exposing the design as a raised surface. Too much metal removed is unsightly and presents a cleaning problem. After removing the background it is sometimes stippled with a punch to present a uniform texture. Reproduced in figure 37 is a portion of a Charles Daly shotgun that shows the background removed with a graver. After removing the background, nothing further was done to it and the tool marks were left as a contrasting texture.

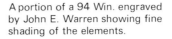
A portion of a 94 Win. engraved by John E. Warren showing fine shading of the elements.

Detail of a Diana Grade Browning showing the use of the liner for shading.

FIGURE 37

The detail in semi-relief engraving is usually cut by hand, that is, the shading of the elements. For this an onglette, square or lozenge graver is used with the shading lines being cut one at a time. Occasionally liners are used These cut multiple lines in the same cut, and are made in different widths with varying numbers of lines to the inch. They are used in gun engraving to accomplish some effects that are difficult to achieve with hand tools.

The ultimate is the "high relief" engraving in which the forms are modeled to reveal their full shape. Occasionally you will see an engraved object that has a portion done in high relief and the remainder done in semi-relief. In modeling the high relief, an assortment of die sinkers chisels and rifflers or files are used in addition to differently shaped scrapers, burnishers and punches to shape the intricate forms. You will not be attempting a high relief job soon, but you can see that such a job calls for a much greater investment in time.

For the beginner who is getting started, the material given here is only the doorway to a field that is wide open and almost without limit. There are many, many books from which you can build up your decorative sense. There are two such books by T. A. Strange that are huge reservoirs of decorative ideas. One is **French Interiors, Furniture, Decoration, Woodwork and Allied Arts**; the other is a similar book on **English Furniture, Decoration, Woodwork and Allied Arts**. Books of this nature will enrich your background and help to develop your innovative talents.

With the material presented here, I believe you can draw a workable design that you can transfer to your plate. So, now let us discuss several methods of getting the design onto the object you wish to engrave. The professional engraver with years of experience behind him may indicate his layout of a given area lightly

with a hard Arkansas point. He will indicate only the main lines of his layout and let the design grow from these. For the beginner, we will presume that he wants to do the best job that his limited experience will permit. In order to accomplish this he must be sure of what he is going to do, so he should plan each cut and stick to his plan. Eventually you will be able to make your supplementary cuts without any pre-planning.

A carefully prepared pencil layout is good insurance for the beginner.

To keep it simple we shall state that there are two ways to produce your design on the metal. By preparing the metal (cleaning and polishing) you can draw the design directly onto the surface that is to be engraved. The other method is to make your design on paper and then transfer it to the metal. Either course has its advantages. Drawing directly on the metal will save time but offers less leeway in changing the design. Developing the design on paper will allow many changes and even drastic alterations. If the drawing is made on a good grade of tracing paper, you can make changes by laying a new piece of translucent paper over the design and tracing off the portion that you wish to retain, then continue with any changes that you want to make. In making your design on paper, you will need an exact outline of the area you are planning to engrave—such as a floorplate. Later on we will show you how this

outline can be easily transferred from the plate.

In getting the design onto the metal, perhaps the oldest and most used item is the pan of Chinese White water color with which the engraver coats the metal before drawing his design. The water color artist has a choice of water color in tubes, which are often referred to as "moist water colors", or colors that are ground with water and binder and then poured into small pans where they dry out. These are called "pan colors" and the Chinese White is what is most often used by the engraver. When the artist uses this color he takes a brush, dips it into water and applies the wet brush to the pan of color. The water dissolves the binder, loosening the pigment which the brush picks up and applies to the drawing, or in our case to the metal. When the engraver coats the metal

When you are practicing, save the designs that you feel are your best. You may be able to use them for they will probably be better than one you might whip up on the spur of the moment.

with the Chinese White, he will moisten the tip of a finger with saliva and apply it to the pan of color, picking up some of the white which he spreads onto the metal where he intends to do the designing. The composition of the saliva is such that it acts as a wetting agent and aids in getting the pigment to spread. Winsor and Newton is an old-time English company that has a fine reputation for the manufacture of artist's colors, and if you can get their Chinese White pan color you will have the best.

The degree of polish that the metal has been given will effect the adhesion of the pigment. A finish that has been given a mirror-like polish will present the most difficulty in getting this Chinese White to adhere. Here again preferences as to finish will vary, but I like a finish that is free of any (even minute) scratches, stopping just short of the mirror finish. The mirror finish reflects everything around it and will not display the engraving to its fullest advantage. A fine satin finish such as can be gotten with a well worn piece of 400 grit wet-or-dry automotive paper makes an ideal background for engraving. On such a satin finish the Chinese White adheres quite well.

Any piece of metal upon which you are going to put a design for engraving should be cleaned thoroughly with a good solvent to remove any wax, grease or oil that may remain after the polishing was done. I have found lacquer thinner to be very effective. Only a small amount (such as a two or four ounce well-stoppered bottle) need be kept around and

used with the proper precautions as to smoking and ventilation. On a highly polished piece of metal, I sometimes give it a light coat of Blair Spray Fix (workable matte fixative) which can be purchased at art supply stores. As the name implies, it is a spray material that is used on pencil drawings as well as other mediums to prevent smudging and to preserve them. They make several different types of sprays, however I like the workable matte fixative sold under the number 100FL. After coating the metal with

All of the layouts shown are actual pencil drawings that were used on various jobs.

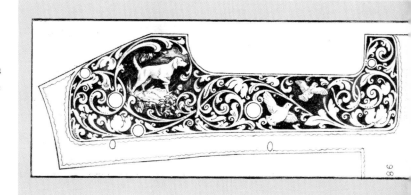

With new clients (especially those who are unfamiliar with your work), it is best to prepare a comprehensive layout. It is concrete evidence of what can be expected. When a sketch is agreed upon, the cost will be included in your price.

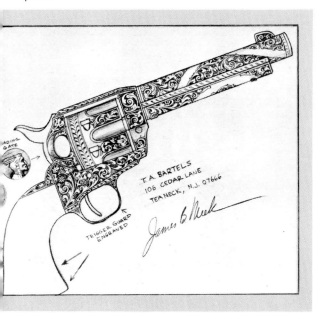

the fixative and it has dried, I then use our Chinese White to coat the area. After this has dried I usually give it another light spraying of the fixative. Except in rare instances this will permit the drawing to be done.

Another product that I have used is a paint-on lacquer made for machinists who use it to make their layouts on metal for machining, called Dykem Steel Blue. As the name suggests, this puts a fairly dark coating on the metal that stops glare and upon which a scribed line shows up well. This is available at machinery supply companies. Do not do layouts on this

directly, but put a coat of the Chinese White pigment on it to lighten it enough that a pencil line can be seen quite well. This Chinese White can also be given a light coat of the spray-fix which helps to protect the coating.

After some experience you can determine how well the ground is adhering when you draw your design. Many times I do my own cutting right through this ground if it proves to be adhering well. Otherwise, I go over the design with a steel scriber and scratch the design onto the metal so that it cannot be obliterated while it is being cut. After scribing, the coating can be removed where you are cutting a small design which you want to be super accurate; such as cutting a line of lettering.

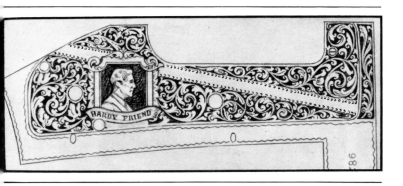

For the beginner I want to give a few facts about pencils that may help in making a choice for the job that you want to do. As you know, they come in different degrees of hardness or softness. This is controlled by the amount of clay that is added to the graphite. The harder the pencil the more clay and less graphite is used. Conversely, the softer pencils contain more graphite and less clay. As a starting point the letters "HB" are used and when the pencils are marked F, H, 2H, 3H et-cetera, the pencils are becoming progressively harder

with the higher numbers. Some pencils are made as hard as 9H which acts almost like a scriber on our tender metal coating. When they are marked B, 2B, 3B and 4B they are becoming increasingly softer, usually up to 6B. Where I want a real soft black pencil, I use one that is made in Germany, under the "Stabilo — #8008" trade name. It has the unique property of writing on glossy photos, glass and even steel.

Pencils play an important part in developing your ideas, and selecting the right pencil will make the job easier. Many preliminary ideas were developed in pencil sketches for the above catalog cover painting. The original was painted 24" x 30".

Another pencil that I have found most useful is a mechanical one sold under the name "Pentel", and available through many stationery stores. Its outstanding feature is that the lead is only 1/2 millimeter in diameter which practically

eliminates sharpening and it is very good when designing fine detail. Do not be disturbed if you encounter pencils marked other than those described above. You might see one marked "2 soft" or "all purpose 2". The system described above is used on artists' pencils so that the artist can choose the degree of hardness or softness that he wants for a particular job.

There is another product that I have found makes an excellent layout ground. It is a Borden product, Krylon Spray Primer, number 1315, which is described as "an excellent primer for bare, clean metal, highly recommended for auto undercoating, sheet metal, etc.", and was purchased at an auto supply store. The area to be coated should be masked off and only enough paint applied to cover; not a heavy coat built up. It dries in about 15 minutes and I have found it to withstand designing upon very well. When the work is done the remaining primer can be removed with lacquer thinner. You will note that this is a priming material, so that it is less rich than the finish coats.

Some of the finishing lacquers that I have tried formed such tough films that the scriber tended to loosen the coating on highly polished pieces.

Assuming that you do have a very highly polished surface, any of these bases for layouts will require that you handle them carefully. Where a manufacturer is applying a finish to a piece of metal that will be required to withstand abrasion, heat, cold and special conditions, he will destroy that high polish, using a metal-prep or an undercoat that will attack and bond tightly to the surface. You, of course,

Pen and pencil drawings are easily converted into line engravings.

will have to retain that high polish, so all that you can do is to see that the surface is perfectly clean before your coating is applied and then handle it carefully while you are working over it.

Under certain conditions you will find that you cannot work over your Chinese White layout without damaging the drawing. In order to be sure that the main lines of the design are not lost, most engravers will go over their design with a metal scriber, scratching the design onto the metal. Such scribers are made by Starrett, Lufkin and other tool makers, and have handles with replaceable points. These are commonly available at your hardware store or can be purchased from your engraver supplier. The engraver supplier usually carries a

28

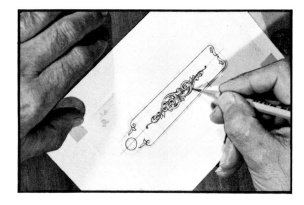

scriber that is a solid piece of steel (twisted in the center section for better grip) and sharpened at both ends. If you need a scriber right now, an ice pick makes a suitable substitute. Pull it from the handle and if it is needed, stone it to a sharp point. You can build up that part which you grip with tape so that it is large enough to hold onto comfortably.

So far we have been working directly on steel with our design. Now, let us draw our original design on paper and see how it will be transferred to steel. This will be only a short resume since in Chapter Seven I have gone into the subject thoroughly with description and photographs. Let us say that you are going to engrave a floorplate. After establishing your design on tracing paper we can proceed to the transfer. The drawing is done on tracing paper because it can be viewed from both sides. In this case we need to make a scribing of the design on either clear or frosted acetate and

this will be made with the drawing turned over and traced from the bottom with a sharp needle held in a pin vise. By scribing the lines of the design in the acetate, a burr is cast up where the point of the scriber is drawn through the acetate. After scribing, these burrs are charged with either powdered ivory black or with lamp black. In order to transfer these charged lines, the plate is coated with a thin coat of Damar varnish, a fast-drying artist's varnish. Before coating the floorplate with the varnish, our piece of acetate with the scribed design is taped to the floorplate so that it can be hinged down precisely in the correct position. Now you can see why the tracing was done on the bottom of the acetate (with the drawing turned over and traced from the back). Had the tracing been done with the drawing right side up it would have been reversed when it was turned over and transferred. With the tracing taped in place and hinged back, the varnish is applied and allowed to become tacky (in fact almost dry). When it has reached the right degree of tackiness, the acetate is hinged down and held firmly in place while a burnisher is used to press the charged lines onto the varnish. The tacky varnish picks up the black pigment and transfers the lines of your design.

For the beginner who may have some questions and problems with materials, supplies and equipment, I will try to answer these in the next chapter.

Chapter Two
Materials

any of the materials that you will be using are available around almost any home, like paper, pencils, erasers and scissors. Where I have found that specific materials are sufficiently superior, I have mentioned them by name in the operations that they are connected with.

Naturally you are especially interested in the tools with which you will be doing your actual engraving. So let's start with the tools that are going to do the cutting, the gravers. These come in a number of shapes and sizes, and the illustrations at figure 1 will show you the shapes and the numbers of the sizes in which the tools are available. These are shown somewhat smaller than actual size, for the large die sinkers chisels are approximately 7-1/2" long.

In time you will probably develop a preference to the tools you like best. The most commonly used tools are the onglette, the square (or lozenge) and the flat or chisel gravers. In addition to these, many engravers use the die sinkers chisels, also illustrated in figure 1. When the gravers come to you and before you try them, examine the points carefully. Generally you will find that in grinding the sides of the onglette gravers, the grinding wheel has cut a little deeper at the point, giving it a rounded appearance. When we come to the instructions on sharpening and clearances we will explain the reason why this is unsatisfactory and that the tool should be ground back until the sides are parallel, with this forward rake eliminated.

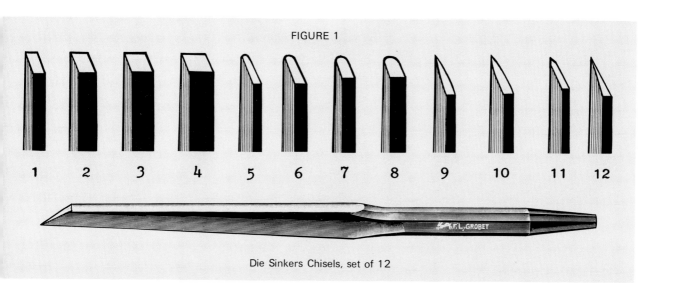

FIGURE 1

1   2   3   4   5   6   7   8   9   10   11   12

Die Sinkers Chisels, set of 12

You will need good handles for some of the gravers as you will eventually want to attempt engraving by hand. These are available with short and long shanks, so you may want to try several of each kind as they are comparatively inexpensive. You will probably find that some of your used gravers which have been sharpened to only about half their original length are easier to control than the new ones that project so far out of the handle.

sert a metal plug, turned to fit the hole tightly. This metal plug takes all of the hammer blows. Using the gravers gives you a wider choice of sizes as the die sinkers chisels come only in sizes 9 & 10 in the onglette. The gravers are only about half the price of the die sinkers chisels, although the price factor is not too important for either the chisels or the gravers will give you many, many hours of service.

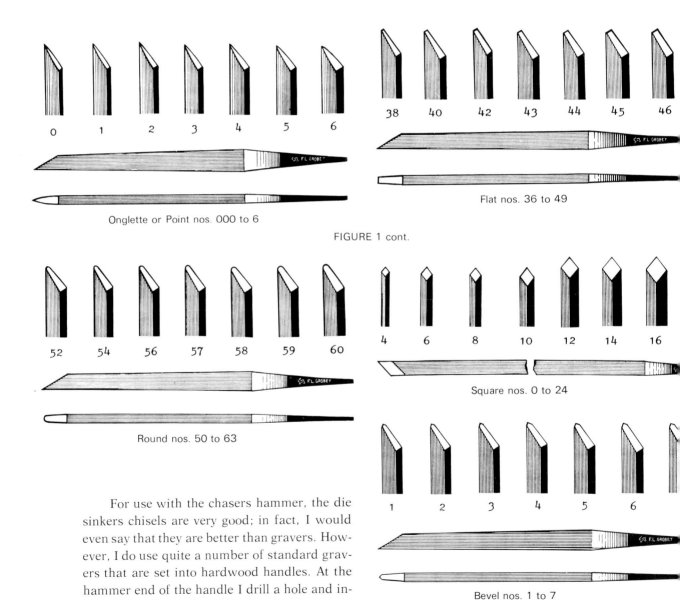

Onglette or Point nos. 000 to 6

Flat nos. 36 to 49

FIGURE 1 cont.

Round nos. 50 to 63

Square nos. 0 to 24

Bevel nos. 1 to 7

For use with the chasers hammer, the die sinkers chisels are very good; in fact, I would even say that they are better than gravers. However, I do use quite a number of standard gravers that are set into hardwood handles. At the hammer end of the handle I drill a hole and in-

You may find that you are having some difficulty with the hand graver when it comes to shading and giving form to the parts. The 00 and 0 are the smallest of the onglette gravers and they can produce the fine lines that you will want for your shading. If the gravers are fitted with handles as previously mentioned you can do the shading with the chasers hammer. It will be easier for you in the beginning

since the graver is more easily controlled. You should, however, continue your practice with the hand graver until you can handle it with complete confidence.

Once more I want to talk to the novice with no knowledge of sharpening metal cutting tools. The action of all cutting tools is one of wedging. For example, a cold chisel will really take a beating and force itself right through a bar of cold rolled steel. The ordinary knife blade

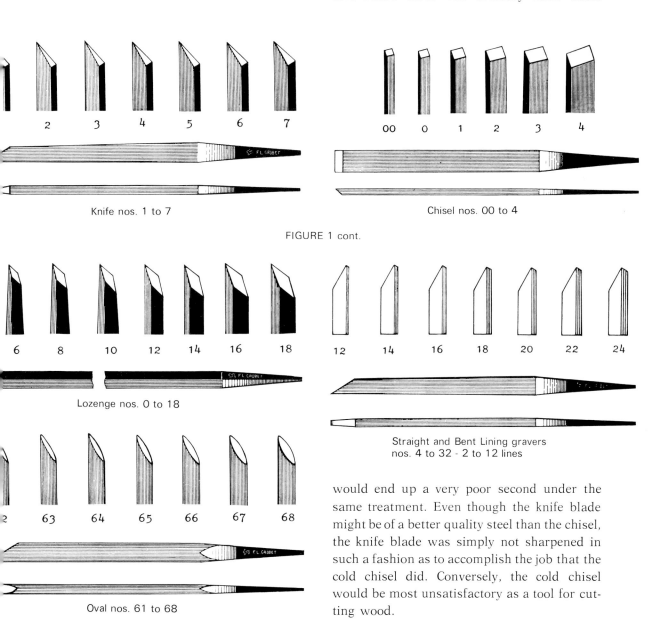

Knife nos. 1 to 7

Chisel nos. 00 to 4

FIGURE 1 cont.

Lozenge nos. 0 to 18

Oval nos. 61 to 68

Straight and Bent Lining gravers
nos. 4 to 32 - 2 to 12 lines

would end up a very poor second under the same treatment. Even though the knife blade might be of a better quality steel than the chisel, the knife blade was simply not sharpened in such a fashion as to accomplish the job that the cold chisel did. Conversely, the cold chisel would be most unsatisfactory as a tool for cutting wood.

Those of you who can remember the pleasure of watching an old-time cabinetmaker fitting the edges of two boards with his long plane can remember those long curls of fragrant pine. The final chip started at one end of the board and came from its full length, ending up as one long, perfect blond curl. When a knife makes a thin cut with the grain of the wood, the tendency is for the chip to curl in a similar manner. If the knife started at the end of a thin board and was forced into it, the cutting edge would start the cut, and as the thicker portion of the knife blade entered the wood it would act as a wedge and separate the wood curl from the rest of the board. So, when you

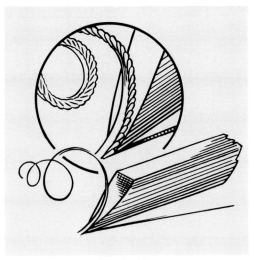

FIGURE 2b

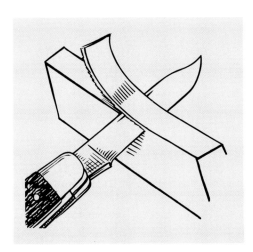

FIGURE 2a

parallel to and just back of the cutting edge into which the chip is guided and broken off into small sections. This eliminates the long curls sometimes seen coming off a lathe.

The only difference between your graver and the tool bit on the lathe is the time during which the action takes place. A lathe is built to be very rigid, with the work and the tool being supported as solidly as possible. The work is then turned rapidly against the tool, and compared to the engraver, a great amount of metal is removed in a short time. This action

take a knife and whittle on a piece of white pine, the chip comes off in a curl that is a result of the wood fibers breaking off in wedges, see figure 2a.

In metal cutting this same action occurs, see figure 2b. The curled chip that comes from the lathe bit or the curled chip that is cast up ahead of your graver is a result of this same wedging force. On many machine tools a chip-breaker is included when the tool is sharpened. This is a small groove ground into the bit,

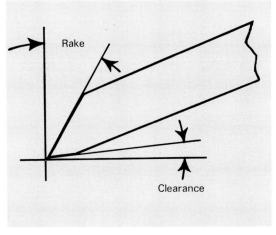

FIGURE 3

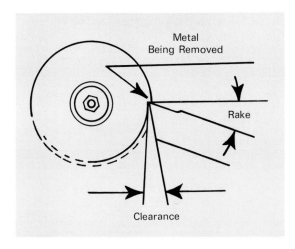

Metal
Being Removed

Rake

Clearance

FIGURE 4

in the machine develops a great amount of pressure and a tremendous amount of heat as this wedging action separates the metal. In the production room, coolants are flooded upon the turning work to dissipate the heat as it is generated so that a good rate of removal can be maintained.

In the case of the production lathe above, the tool bit is usually of a special steel, with very careful attention given to the angles used to sharpen the bit. With so much pressure and heat, the angles at which the tool is ground must be such as to give the cutting edge as much support as possible with as small an amount of clearance as will permit the tool to enter the work. And, as the tool moves toward the headstock, there must be clearance on the forward edge of the bit to allow the carriage to advance. (There is another clearance angle needed in lathe work that is omitted here for the sake of clarity.) The two angles that you will be concerned with are the rake angle which will be the face of your graver and the bottom of the tool which will be the clearance angle, see figure 3.

The engraver is not faced with the heat problems of the production room. He does, however, have most of the other problems in sharpening his tools. I shall attempt, by word

and picture, to explain the angles used in sharpening gravers and the reasons involved. We are going to take an onglette and sharpen it for general cutting in steel. The illustration shown at figure 4 shows the angles that we will be most concerned with. The rake angle is that angle formed by the face of the tool and a perpendicular at the point where the tool enters the work. When the hammer end of the tool is raised so that it can be made to enter the work, the angle formed by the bottom edge of the tool and the surface of the work will be referred to as the clearance angle.

To refer back to the cold chisel, we can describe it as a tool that will cut a 1/4" rod in two easily. Actually it does not CUT the rod, but it does displace the metal in such a manner as to accomplish the same result. In actually cutting metal, some of the metal is removed as in lathe work or cutting a rod with a hack-saw. Since in engraving you want to cut a groove and remove some metal, your tool will cut more efficiently if it is ground to have the necessary clearance and rake.

The onglette graver as it comes to you is approximately straight along the bottom edge and the face is usually ground at an angle of about 45 degrees. As was mentioned before, examine the edges at the face of the tool to see if they have been rounded in grinding. If they are rounded they should be ground back all the

FIGURE 5

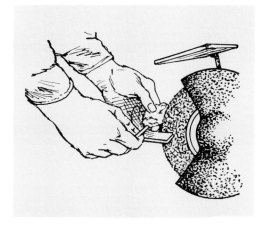

34

way until the sides are perfectly straight to the face of the tool.

In grinding these tools great care should be exercised in order to maintain the original temper. Do not overheat the tool in a hasty attempt to get it ground. Have your water supply handy and use it often. The tool should be in the water as much as it is on the wheel, and do not leave it on the wheel long enough to build up heat. In my grinding I use a paper towel, soaked in water, and wadded up around the point of the tool. As you press the tool against the wheel, also squeeze the wad of paper and force more water onto the point where contact is being made. You cannot see the tool, but with frequent inspections you can grind about where you intend to. This takes off the bulk of the metal that is to be removed, and after the excess metal has been taken off you can finish it to the exact shape that you want. Do this final finishing in the conventional manner, keeping it cool by dipping. See figure 5.

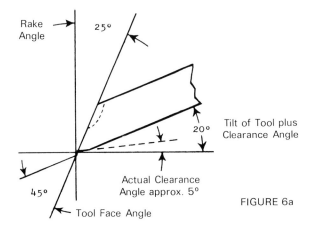

FIGURE 6a

In the illustration showing the angles at figure 6a, note the dotted line at the face of the tool. This portion is usually removed at the rough grinding. By removing this small amount it is easier to maintain the sharp point by stoning without the necessity of taking off the thick portion of the tool with the slow stoning.

Now let us sharpen our first tool. Grind the face of the tool to an angle of 45 degrees with the bottom edge of the tool, making sure that this angular face is square with the length of the tool, see figure 6a. This angle does not need to be precisely 45 degrees, for as you acquire experience this angle will vary with the material that you are engraving. The softer the materials, the less strength is required in the point so that it can be sharpened with an angle that is more acute. The harder, tougher materials can use a rake angle as small as 10 degrees. The more acute the angle becomes, the more you will sacrifice in strength, so a 45 degree angle will be a good one with which to start.

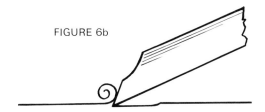

FIGURE 6b

Having ground the first angle, the procedure from here on becomes a little more difficult to explain. Since you have the face of the onglette ground to the 45 degree angle, let us examine it carefully. Look at figure 6b showing the tool as it would appear when it was tipped to enter the work. This is only slightly exaggerated so that you can see what a weak, unsupported point is presented to the metal that is being removed. Taking the tool in its present shape, you would, of necessity, have to work with the hammer end of the tool quite close to the work. If you raised it very much, the tendency of the tool would be to cut deeper and deeper. In order to reduce this weakness to a minimum as well as to allow more working room, an additional 15 degrees will be stoned off the bottom at the point as shown in figure 6c, which will make the actual cutting angle of the tool 60 degrees instead of the 45 degrees to which it was originally ground. This angle will be better stoned than ground since you are not going to remove very much metal. You do not need to stone it back more than 3/32" from the face of the tool (again see figure 6c which is not actual size). The shaded area is the part that will be stoned off. Here again this can be slightly more or less without effecting the strength or cutting quality appreciably. You will end up with an included angle of 60 degrees and a tool that looks like the tool in figure 6d. By referring back to the figure at 6a, you will note that this 15 degrees plus the additional 5 degrees that is the actual clearance will not only improve the cutting quality but will improve the strength of the point as well.

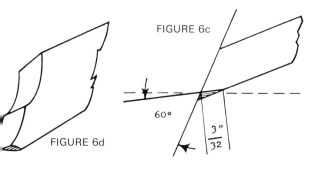

FIGURE 6c

FIGURE 6d

60°

3"/32

Now we come to the critical part. Take the onglette that you have sharpened to the 45 degree angle squarely and as you read these instructions follow along with the tool and a stone or any flat surface that you can think of as a stone. Simply reading the instructions may sound confusing, but if you can actually see what is happening I think they will be easily understood. Let us start by laying the tool flat on its side on the surface of the stone. The face of the tool is at a 90 degree angle to the stone, see figure 7a. Now if you raise the hammer end of the tool straight upward until the tool makes approximately a 20 degree angle

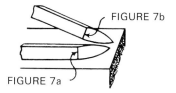

FIGURE 7b

FIGURE 7a

with the stone, you find that the face angle of the tool is no longer square with the surface of the stone, see figure 7b. Holding the tool by the top and bottom edges you can rotate the tool as shown in figure 7c. By rotating the top

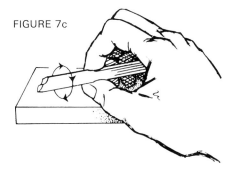

FIGURE 7c

edge toward yourself you can again bring that face angle back until it is at a right angle to the stone. Figure 7c shows the tool rotated past the 90 degree angle for stoning. If the tool were stoned at the 90 degree angle there would be no clearance for the cutting edge of the tool. This would give the edge its maximum strength but it would lack the cutting quality that we are after. By rotating the tool to the correct angle and checking the height of the back end of the tool you can bring the tool into a position so that the center line of the tool is parallel to the surface of the stone, see figure 7d. With the

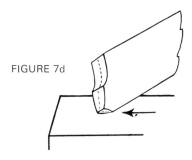

FIGURE 7d

36

tool in the correct position proceed to stone this one side until you are down to the center-line. When looking down the bottom of the tool, this part that you have just stoned should be a straight continuation of the bottom edge of the onglette. In stoning this angle, it can be stoned perfectly flat or by using a wiping action and rotating the wrist, you can maintain the contour of the onglette. The opposite side is stoned maintaining the same angles except that they are reversed. When finished the tool should look like figure 7e. There is one other angle to be considered if you are going to stone these

round gravers the face is tipped a small amount and rotated to stone a small clearance all the way around the cutting edge.

There is one final tip for you in this shar-pening act. With the tool completely sharpened we take it and give one light pass over a fine ruby bench stone (a fine hard Arkansas stone would be as good). Hold the tool so that the face is at right angles to the surface of the stone in this final pass. We want to emphasize that this is only a light, polishing touch and very little metal is removed. It will, however, impart a burnished effect to the cut, leaving the cut bright. We also break the very bottom of the point with a light rolling touch because the very tip is quite vulnerable as a sharp point. Once the point is chipped or broken the cutting quality is gone. This is especially evi-dent if you are cutting by hand. When the tip goes is usually when a slip occurs. The amount of metal removed is not apparent to the naked eye in this final touch.

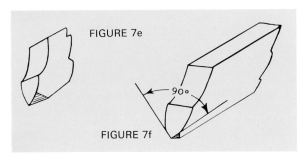

FIGURE 7e

FIGURE 7f

angles flat. I suggest that you stone them to a 90 degree angle as shown at figure 7f. This will give you a good strong point. Here again for the harder materials you can increase this angle somewhat for a still stronger point; for average materials or finer lines this angle can be more acute as this point is well supported. It is quite important that you double check to see that the centerline of the bottom of the tool is perfectly straight. If the face is not square with the tool and the centerline is off, the tool will want to drift off to one side in use.

The square and lozenge gravers are shar-pened in the same manner, using the same angles. The face angles of the flat and round gravers are ground the same. The clearance angles on the round and flat gravers are the same except that we do not extend the stoning back beyond about 1/32". On the flat graver this clearance is, of course, stoned flat. On the

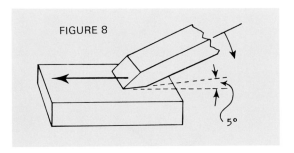

FIGURE 8

John Rohner, the engraver, whose work you have seen reproduced on the cover of **The American Rifleman** and in the **Gun Digest,** uses a somewhat different approach to the sharpening of the tool that he prefers. He uses a flat tool, the front edge of which is sharpened to an included angle of approximately 35 de-grees. After this angle is ground, the tool is stoned against this front edge, see figure 8.

Place the edge of the tool on that part of the stone that is nearest you. Place the angle flat on the surface of the stone. Now raise the back of the tool up about 5 degrees. With a firm pressure move the tool forward across the stone and as you move forward drop the back of the tool down. Try to coordinate the two movements so that as you reach the end of the stroke, the tool is back down to the flat from which you started.

Now for the power behind the chisels and gravers. Aside from hand power, chasers hammers are the most generally used hammers for driving the gravers and chisels. The chasers hammer heads are available in different sizes, which also means different weights. If you plan to buy only one hammer, I would recommend that it be the 1-1/4" face which is the largest one. On some of the heavier cuts this extra weight will be an advantage, and on the lighter

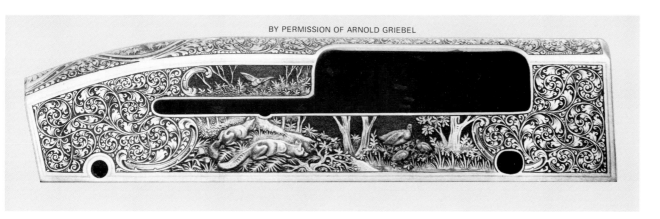

BY PERMISSION OF ARNOLD GRIEBEL

Here and on other pages are shown some excellent examples of engraving for the beginner to study. The novice can learn much from Arnold Griebel's work, shown above.

This somewhat rounded, chisel-like edge gives you a burnishing cut that is very bright and shiny. This makes a strong point and as is obvious you are getting two cutting points with the one sharpening. In use the tool is tipped up at an angle. The tool must also be held at slight angle to the travel of the tool. With some practice cuts you can determine the angles for holding the tool while cutting. This is a good tool to use when you want to make a line graduating from fine to wide and back to fine. This about covers our methods of tool sharpening and any special grinds will be covered where they are called for.

cuts you will use shorter, gentler strokes of the hammer. With these chasers hammer heads you will use the regular chasers handles which are slender and springy. Naturally, you can use any hammer that is available, but the ones that have been designed for the purpose and in use so long have their advantages. If you should use a regular hammer, let it be comparatively light and scrape the shaft of the handle down until it has a little flexibility.

With the tools all sharpened and ready to go, you will start thinking about the work and how you are going to hold it. Many engravers work in a standing position and this has been recommended for it allows a freedom of movement in changing positions. So in all probability the most feasible plan in the beginning would be to try an ordinary swivel vise which many of you may already have. This can be left free to swivel and it will hold your work and serve the purpose quite well. Your floorplates can be attached to a block of wood and the block clamped in the vise. When you are clamping an automatic or pump action shotgun receiver in the vise, be alert to any chance of springing the action out of shape as the bench vise has a lot of power. This is also true for any action with thin parts. I have never tried any of the "all position" vises but I do know of one engraver who does use such a vise. They might be worth investigating, and would surely be less expensive than an engraver's vise.

grow it and turn it in on a more advanced outfit. Each time that he trades he must take a loss. So he has not only lost his money but has lost all the advantages that he could have had with the better equipment. So it is with the engraver; if he is reasonably sure that it will be a rewarding hobby or avocation, then he would likely be wise to invest in a good engraver's vise. There is always the possibility that in the event he should change his mind, he could recover a substantial portion of his investment in the second hand market.

For those wishing to make their own vise, I am showing a set of photographs of the vise that I made. This vise is more complicated than is necessary because it was designed to make use of the two good bearings that I had available. My finished vise measures 5-7/16" at its

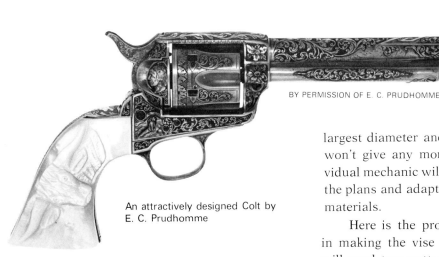

BY PERMISSION OF E. C. PRUDHOMME

An attractively designed Colt by E. C. Prudhomme

largest diameter and weighs 22-1/4 pounds. I won't give any more dimensions as the individual mechanic will no doubt want to simplify the plans and adapt them to his own ideas and materials.

Here is the procedure that was followed in making the vise that is shown. First, you will need two patterns for the foundry to use in casting the parts. The patterns are made from clear white pine. It will be necessary to glue several thicknesses together in order to come up with sufficient thickness to turn the large diameter of the ball. In gluing the boards together use a good casein glue or something equally waterproof. Not being an accomplished pattern maker, my patterns were simply made, see figure 9a. You might consult the foundry or if you are acquainted with a pattern maker, get him to help you. The patterns diagrammed

The engraver's vise is the ultimate and is, of course, the most expensive. It is like buying a camera. The amateur will buy a cheaper camera as long as it will take a satisfactory picture. The serious amateur who firmly believes that he is going to continue to be serious about photography is wise to buy the best equipment that he can afford at the outset. If he buys the cheaper equipment he will soon out-

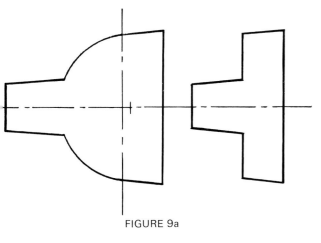

FIGURE 9a

The finished ball shown at Figure 12 is 5-7/16″ in diameter at the largest circumference and weighs 22-1/4 pounds.

The top section of the vise was machined first, see figure 10. This part was set up in the chuck with the flat side of the top of the casting against the chuck. After centering the piece, turn the stub on the bottom to accept the bearings. You can see by the photo that the main bearing is a large taper bearing. The large diameter gives a broad base that is a distinct advantage. Here again, a large thrust bearing would serve equally well and be considerably cheaper since it need not be a precision bearing. There are also available various needle bearings for both radial and thrust loads that could be used to good advantage.

did work, but by using cores or splitting the patterns you could possibly save some machining. I paid for my ignorance by boring the entire hole in the base and milling the whole slot for the vise jaws. These parts could be made from solid, round bar stock if no foundry services were available. In making your patterns, be certain that they each have the required taper as indicated in the drawings so that the patterns can be withdrawn from the molds. After finishing, they should be given several coats of shellac.

Some of the other parts that were used in constructing the vise.

FIGURE 10

Keep in mind the fact that the top should be large enough in diameter to support the jaws when they are opened to their widest capacity - and some of the shotgun receivers are of good size. In addition, extra room will be needed since you will use pieces of leather or offset printing press blanket for padding and protection from marring by the vise jaws. To the many of you more richly endowed with mechanical perception, the photographs will show the working principle which can be modified to suit your own ideas. After the lug is turned, remove the piece from the chuck and reverse it, holding the piece by the lug. The outside is turned to size and the top faced off.

The ball part of the vise is now chucked into the lathe with the flat part of the casting against the chuck. After centering, the lug can be center drilled and supported by the tailstock if yours is a small, light lathe. With the casting centered and supported, the lug with its taper from the pattern is turned straight. The main portion of the ball can be rough turned round, as close to the chuck and to the lug as is practical at this time.

After turning the lug, remove the piece and using the lug, chuck it with the flat face out. If your chuck is universal it should run true. If not, center it and face off the top. Rough turn the remaining portion of the ball that was not turned because of the jaws that held it. Now bore the opening to fit the bearings of the top section, see figure 11. Finish-turn the outside of the ball as far down as is possible.

FIGURE 12

off just outside the radius of the casting. You will have to reverse the lathe jaws and using the hole just bored, chuck the casting and center it. Now all that remains is to finish-turn the rest of the ball and blend it with the outside circumference.

The screw will need a right hand thread on one side of the center and a left hand thread on the opposite side. It will work either way, of course, but it did seem more natural to have the screw turn clockwise, or away from the operator, when closing the jaws. For the right handed man, the left hand screw thread should be the end that has the wrench on it. You will also note the screw slot on the end of the screw. This is to facilitate the starting of the jaws onto the ends of the screw. The Dixon engraver's vise uses a T-handled screw driver for actuating the jaws, but it was felt that the hex-headed screw would have superior wearing qualities so the one end of the screw was milled to fit a cap screw. A large handle was turned, knurled, bored and threaded. Into this a cap screw was inserted, turned up tightly and riveted. The vise shown in figure 12 has been in use for over 25 years now and it looks as though it might wear out a couple of engravers, instead of vice versa.

FIGURE 11

If the two parts fit correctly, you can now take the casting out of the chuck. Saw the lug

Observing the jaws, you will note that one jaw has two 1/4" holes (these were reamed) and a ninety degree slot milled in the face of one jaw. The other jaw has the two 1/4" reamed holes with a third hole drilled and reamed in the center between them. This is a 3/8" diameter hole. If the piece to be held has parallel sides, it can be held by the four pins similar to the two shown in the photo. The swivel jaw shown gets ninety percent of the work, however. It is even used in holding straight

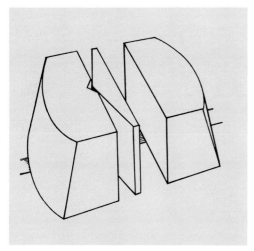

FIGURE 9b

pieces. It is not too apparent in the photo, but there is a groove filed in the edge of the swivel jaw that prevents floorplates from popping out of the vise while being worked on. Also, the notches on the tops of the pins are slanted back slightly. These pins, the swivel jaw and the screw were all made of tool steel and sent to a heat treating firm where they were hardened. After all these years of use they show no wear.

There is one other important accessory that was omitted in the photographs which is too valuable to pass over, see figure 9b. This is a supplementary jaw that is used in conjunction with the vertical slot in the face of the one jaw. It is simply a piece of 3/8" thick cold rolled

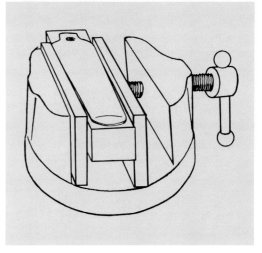

FIGURE 9c

steel and it is machined from the center to the outer ends. The ends are 1/8" thick. This permits the holding of parts that are tapered or irregular in shape. Incidentally, the vertical slot in the face of the jaw is used for holding large screws while engraving the heads.

There are more simple holding devices that can be used. If you are of a mechanical nature but do not want to go as far as making a ball, a simple holding device as shown at figure 9c could be cast and made up. The orientals used similar holding arrangements with the work held in by wooden wedges for working on ivory, gold, silver and jade. There are also simple engravers' balls without the turning top vise. These are inexpensive and would do a good job when using the chasers hammer. They are not easily turned when using the hand graver. Two such vises are shown at figures 9d and 9e.

FIGURES 9d and 9e

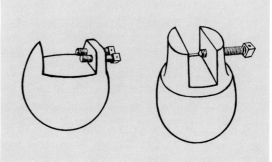

The ball at 9d is a die sinkers ball and it was available in weights from fifteen to forty-five pounds. As far as I know these are still available from William Dixon, Incorporated. Leather ring pads are also available for these balls.

Sometimes when I am using the hand gravers I like the ball to turn quite freely, so I have turned a wooden ring out of rosewood to replace the leather ring. The engraver's ball shown in the photo has been given a good smooth finish and when it is used in the wooden ring it turns very easily. Figure 13 shows a cross section of the ring that I made. You will

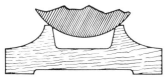

FIGURE 13

notice that it is relieved under the ball and that the bearing surface upon which the ball moves is reduced to the very minimum. With the natural oils in the wood it moves with very little resistance. If a little more friction is needed, the ball is simply lifted out and a piece of cloth is laid over the ring. In case still more friction is wanted, some of the powdered rosin that is used on barrel bushings is sprinkled onto the cloth at the point of contact with the ring. The ball shown is the conventional one with the turning vise. With the foregoing information I hope that you can overcome your holding problems.

Let us now turn to another phase of our tool requirements. In your engraving or inlaying, you will find yourself needing and using punches of various shapes and sizes. These can be purchased, but you will find that it is more convenient to make them yourself from either oil or water-hardening drill rod. Since the shapes are simple and holding tolerances are no problem, the regular water-hardening drill rod will probably be more often recommended. Most punches needed can be made from 1/8″ or 5/32″ drill rod. Brownells have Carpenter tool steel available in the Green Label Tough Timber (water-hardening), as well as the Stentor steel (oil-hardening) in any size that you may want. Their catalog has the instructions for the heat treating of these steels as well. **The Machinery Handbook** has quite a complete explanation of the heat treatment of steels. This book contains almost 1900 pages of information on all kinds of machining and tools, as well as tables of all kinds relating to mechanical functions, and is an excellent addition to your working library. To get back to our punches, however, the 5/32″ size is preferred as it seems a little easier to hold if much punch work is to be done at one time. Here again it is nice to have the handles knurled for easier holding, but in the interest of saving time I compromise and wrap the holding portion with masking tape. This gives a good, no-slip surface and takes very little time or material to achieve.

The rod is cut into 2-1/2″ lengths. Unless your fingers are unusually large, this is ample length for comfortable holding. The blanks are

BY PERMISSION OF ARNOLD GRIEBEL

cut (usually 8 or 10, in the interest of saving time) and made in a group. Since the background punch is so often used, let's use it as an example in making our punch. With the background cut away in a pattern, this punch is used to give a uniform texture to the area. The punch is slightly concave on the end, giving a small raised dot each time it is struck, eliminating the graver marks and giving a nice over-all texture to the background.

The punches are machined on a lathe. They can be shaped in a drill press with a file; however, in a pinch they can be filed by hand. After the blanks are cut to length, a blank is chucked in the lathe. With the compound set at 15 degrees off center, the point is turned down until approximately a flat of 1/32" diameter is left at the point, see figure 14a.

the back, hammering the forms up from the rear, then refining and finishing the detail on the front.) This punch that you must make is a

Gold line inlaying at its fine-line best. This is shown at about actual size.

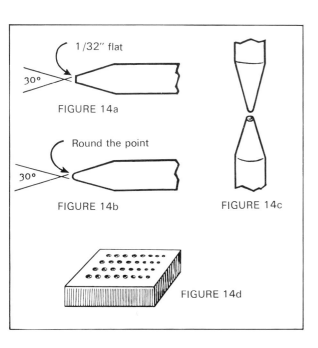

1/32" flat

30°

FIGURE 14a

Round the point

30°

FIGURE 14b

FIGURE 14c

FIGURE 14d

simple one with about a 1/32" radius on the point, see figure 14b. After it is shaped and hardened, put a high polish on the rounded point. To use it, take one of the punch blanks that you have made and holding it securely in a vise, place the dapping punch in the center and tap it lightly. If the impression is centered, replace the punch and deepen the punch mark until it almost reaches the outside edge of the punch, see figure 14c. With the punches being made on the lathe, it is a simple matter to chuck the punch blank into a collet in the headstock and put the dapping punch into a tailstock chuck. Bring the tailstock with its punch close to the punch blank and lock the tailstock in place. Turn the lathe on at a moderate speed and with some center lubricant on the punch blank, force the dapping punch into the punch blank. It doesn't take much force as the dapping punch is only forced in until the dimple almost reaches the outer edge of the punch face.

At this point we will have to stop and make a dapping punch before we can finish our background punch. Dapping punches are made in a number of graduated sizes, and are used in repousse work to form circular convex forms. (Repousse is the working of thin metals from

44

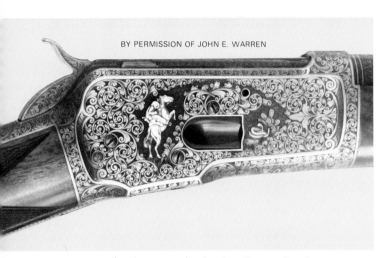

BY PERMISSION OF JOHN E. WARREN

Another example showing the results of careful planning and workmanship. The beginner should study these engravings not only once, but many times.

depressions are made into which the punch can be laid so it will not roll off at a critical moment. Before laying the punch in place, however, coat both ends with a paste of bone black and sperm oil or Smith's carbon putty, which is a welder's product available at welders' supply stores. This is done to protect the metal as much as possible from oxidation. Place a spot of Tempilaq in the center (this is a temperature indicator about which I will give you more information later). With the torch set to show a slight feather (at least not oxidizing) the heat is applied slowly to raise the temperature to about 1450 degrees or a dull cherry red. Use a pair of small tongs to transfer the heated punch to the quenching bath (oil or water, depending on the steel you used).

The method that I use for making my punches employs a beading die. I prepare my punches as we have just done but from there on I do not use the dapping punch. Beading dies similar to the one shown in figure 14d are available from William Dixon, Gesswein or Southwest Smelting and Refining Company. These are special dies that have been made with a number of different size impressions. At the bottom of each die mark is a round, raised dot that is a portion of a sphere. These blocks are made of hardened die steel, and in use the shaped punch is placed in the size desired and struck with a hammer. This forces the punch down over the raised dot, forming a part of a sphere in the end of the punch very simply and quickly. After punching, the tools are hardened.

The punches are now ready for heat treating. Following is an explanation of the method that I use. Since I do not have an electric furnace, I use an acetylene torch for my heat source. Set up a small furnace out of fire bricks on your bench, see figure 14e. Lay two small pieces of fire brick about 1/2" apart near the back. Since fire brick is real soft, two small

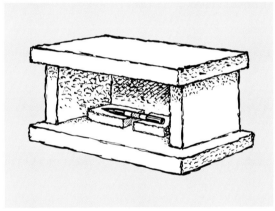

FIGURE 14e

I want to interject at this point a few words about "color" in heat treating. Here is a quote from **The Machinery Handbook:** "the U.S. Bureau of Standards states that SKILLED (the capitalization is ours) observers may vary as much as 100 degrees in their estimation of relatively low temperatures by color; beyond 2200 degrees F it is practically impossible to make estimations with any certainty". The same book lists the following in Fahrenheit:

752 degrees - red heat visible
     in the dark
885 '' - red heat visible
     in the twilight
975 '' - red heat visible
     in the daylight
1077 '' - red heat visible
     in the sunlight
1292 '' - dark red
1472 '' - dull cherry red
1652 '' - cherry red

It can be seen from the above that the light which is available where the heat treating is to take place has an important bearing on the colors that will be seen. Another factor to be considered is the individual's ability to perceive color, for many people are color blind or partially so. Thus it boils down to a fact that heat treating by color can be quite inaccurate.

There is a product on the market that is made for just such a situation, tradenamed Tempilaq, and is distributed by Brownells, Inc. It is a liquid carrying a pigment-like substance that is applied to the steel to be heated. It drys to a dull finish, and when it reaches the correct temperature, the Tempilaq melts sharply. All color changes are disregarded as the piece heats up. Tempilaq temperature indicators are available in 27 different steps from 350 degrees F. to 1550 degrees F., and a 2 ounce bottle will serve for many, many heat treatments.

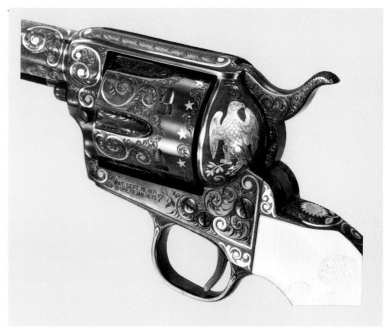

Recoil shield detail showing gold inlay and engraving by A. A. White on a Colt single action revolver. One of a pair custom-made for collector R. O. Sutherland. Courtesy of A. A. White Engravers, Inc.

You will be making many punches in addition to the background punches just described. As you get on with the modeling of the animals, flowers and scenery, you will find yourself needing a variety of shapes and matting textures to get the forms or surfaces that you want. Here again, in attaining any form or texture that you are working for, do not be confined to conventional means. Use all of the ingenuity and imagination that you possess. You may develop something entirely original and completely your own. The end result, that which the customer sees, is the all-important goal. Make it look as professional as possible regardless of the "sweat and tears" that you have to put into it.

Another material that you will have occasional use for is the wax used by engravers to transfer the pattern of an already engraved surface to a new surface for cutting. If you were to engrave one segment of a revolver cylinder and wished to duplicate it, you could

A portion of the receiver of a Charles Daly shotgun.

46

transfer the design with the engraver's wax. In the process of transferring the design you will need some light-weight card or heavy paper. You may have seen instructions where material such as a business card has been recommended as an appropriate weight stock. If you have a printer near you, he could doubtless supply you with some suitable business card-weight material. Several sheets will transfer all the designs that you will want to transfer for a long time to come. I have been using some scraps from a print shop that were picked up for the asking. It is a white, antique finish, sixty-five pound Hammermill cover stock, and works perfectly.

To transfer the design, rub some of the transfer wax into the design. With several trials you will be able to judge about how much of the wax to use. Do not use too much or you will find the wax spreading and blurring the design when you transfer it. The wax is colorless and comes as a translucent paste. Although I understand that it can be obtained in colors, so far I have not found it. I did take some of my

The above is enlarged over nine times to give you a good idea of how the effect at the left was achieved. The small photo is actual size.

wax and melted it on a plate and while it was liquid mixed in some powdered ivory black. This seemed to improve the visibility only a small amount. The transfer wax gives the polished metal a frosted appearance.

With the wax rubbed into the design, the card lubricated and moistened in water, you are ready to make the matt. With your burnisher in one hand, place the card on the design and start to press the card into the engraving with the burnisher. The card must not be allowed to shift its position while you are doing the burnishing. Burnish a small area at a time until you have covered the whole design. When the card is moistened it should not be sopping wet; dip it into the water and right out. After it has been out for an instant wipe it off with a cloth. The card must be soft and flexible so that it can be forced down into all the fine detail.

When you lift the card off and examine it, you will find a reverse of your engraving. All

The photo at the left illustrates why an engraver must know the anatomy of animals.

Note at the arrow how the upper rear leg bone is going to knock the wind out of the critter every time the leg comes forward.

Normally, this bone is set at such an angle as to pass on the outside of the paunch as it comes forward. Also the drawing of the hock is not clear.

Below is shown a tracing of the same animal with a more natural action.

Any kind of craft work, such as the catalog cover above, sign painting or stock work can be a stepping stone to an engraving career.

of the low places are now the raised portions of your matt and have picked up the wax from the low areas of your engraving. The matt is now placed wax down in contact with the new surface to be engraved and again it must be held firmly in one position. Rub the matt into contact with the new surface with your burnisher. You used quite a firm pressure in making the matt, but in transferring the design considerably less force is needed to transfer the wax. If your design came out successfully and is well transferred, you will need to go over it with your metal scribe to make it withstand handling. The transfer wax will not stand up to any handling by itself.

Another area we should discuss is the precious metals used in inlays. Inlays can and have been made from base metals such as copper, German silver or brass, as well as the precious metals platinum, palladium, ruthenium, gold and silver. These can be purchased in sheet form or as wire. In inlay work, much of the figure work is done with the flat plate unless the subject is unusually complicated or intricate, in which case 24k gold wire is used.

The flat material as well as the wire is usually sold by weight but is designated and measured by the standard B&S (American) gage numbers. You will probably never use anything thinner than 36 gage which is .005" thick, or thicker than 18 gage which is .040" thick. When you get your catalogs from the various suppliers you will find complete charts of sizes, weights and measures. You may develop a different preference, but I will give you the sizes that I have found suit my requirements, including three sizes of 24k gold wire which were bought because of the convenience. You could get by just as well with only one size by using a draw plate. My largest wire is 1 millimeter or approximately 18 gage which is about .040" in diameter. I use this where I want the rich full color of the pure gold and in fully modeled inlays. On occasion I use my draw plate and reduce the diameter where I do not need quite such a thick wire. I also use a 22 gage 24k gold wire that is about .025" in diameter and

Extra floor plates are available and make fine practice plates. They are smooth and have a slight contour that gives some preparation for the more complicated surfaces that will be encountered in gun engraving.

48

makes quite a good sized gold line inlay. My smallest wire is 26 gage which is about .016'' in diameter. This still makes a good-sized gold line, and where I want a nice fine gold line I reduce this to the smallest draw hole in my plate which gives me a wire of .011'' diameter. This smallest wire is used for inlaying gold lines where the design requires a delicate line that is not going to overpower the area in which it is used. Special tongs are made for drawing the wire through the draw plate.

The flat stock that I use is purchased in 18k gold, 20 gage which is .032'' thick. This is perhaps a little thicker than is actually needed, but it gives ample material where a rich, fully

where it is beaten out from the back side with the round end of a small ball peen hammer or with punches. Be careful however, for the tendency is to go too far. It does not take very much driving to punch the gold out .015'' or .020''. Various punches are used to model the main forms and it can be worked from both sides. After the big forms are completed, it is cemented to a block of wood with some engraver's or chaser's cement. The gravers are now used to refine and add the fine detail. The reference here is to a firearms inlay, when speaking of the depth of draw on the lead block. In the field of repousse work on silver, gold or brass the possibilities are much greater, and

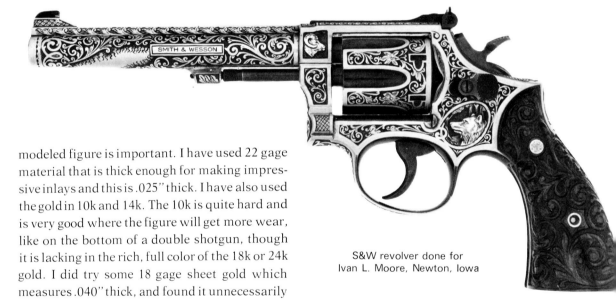

modeled figure is important. I have used 22 gage material that is thick enough for making impressive inlays and this is .025'' thick. I have also used the gold in 10k and 14k. The 10k is quite hard and is very good where the figure will get more wear, like on the bottom of a double shotgun, though it is lacking in the rich, full color of the 18k or 24k gold. I did try some 18 gage sheet gold which measures .040'' thick, and found it unnecessarily thick, for the extra .010'' was not being used at all.

There was a very good article on engraving and inlaying a trigger guard and floorplate by Roy Vail in the February, 1950, **The American Rifleman,** showing this method of preparing the gold and attaching it to the plate. By using his procedure, a repousse process mentioned earlier, a thinner piece of gold can be used and still attain the fully modeled appearance of a very thick piece of gold. The figure is cut out and laid on a piece of lead

S&W revolver done for
Ivan L. Moore, Newton, Iowa

many fine works show the item has been punched out until the work appears to be almost in the round.

The matter of cost of the various thicknesses is relatively minor. The prices given here are from an old catalog and are the prices per square inch in the different gages. Today you will not find published prices given in catalogs, but you will be charged the price of the metal on the day of the sale. The prices shown here are only to give the novice some idea of the relative prices at this time. 22 gage (.025" thick), in 10k is $2.90, 14k is $4.25, 18k is $6.30 and Palladium-Ruthenium is $5.12. In 20 gage (.032" thick), in 10k is $3.61, 14k is $5.35, 18k is $7.90 and Palladium-Ruthenium is $6.46. Sterling silver in 22 gage is 24 cents per square inch with 20 gage at 30 cents per square inch. The 24k gold wire cost approximately $2.50 per foot in 26 gage, $3.30 per foot in 22 gage and $4.40 per foot in 20 gage.

The plate can be bought in about any size desired up to 6" x 24". When sheet gold is purchased, I have it cut into 2" squares which make a handy size to manipulate in sawing out the figures. The loss in laying out the figures is minimal as they can be juggled around to fill the space to best advantage. As a conservative estimate, the 2" square piece of metal will yield at least eight inlays, and you might get as many as twelve or fourteen. So if you were to use the 10k gold in the 20 gage at $3.61 per square inch, you would have 4 square inches for a total cost of $14.44. If you got ten inlays from the piece your cost per inlay would be quite inexpensive. This is not allowing anything for overhead which you would have to account for if you were in business, but it will give you an idea of the relative cost of the material as compared to the cost of the time that you will expend on installing it.

Silver is used on firearms inlays, but its tendency to oxidize makes it a second choice at best. Platinum or palladium is often used where a silver-colored inlay is wanted as it retains its silver color without the oxidizing problem. Goldsmith Division of National Lead, Hoover & Strong or Southwest Smelting and Refining Company are all dealers in the precious metals mentioned. There are doubtless other refineries or dealers that might be closer to your location.

There is one other item that you can use to good advantage; an oval template. Mine is a "Rapidesign, number 77 Ellipse Master". It is a very flexible, fairly thin plastic template with sixty ovals cut into it ranging in size from 1/4" to 1-3/8" long. They are accurately and cleanly cut, covering four projections from quite round ovals to fairly narrow ones. The two axes are marked so that they can be lined up accurately if need be. By shifting the template slightly, the inside and the outside lines of an oval panel can be laid out exactly. They are available from Dick Blick and will save much time in laying out oval panels. There are many more ovals besides the one described, but this one will do ninety-five percent of your work. If you do not have an art supplier near you, the above company has a very complete line with a catalog available.

After this review of materials, any special tools, equipment or supplies that will be required will be dealt with at the time they are called for to go on with the work.

Chapter Three
Anatomy

ome idea of the structure of the various animals and birds is necessary if errors in drawing are to be avoided. Not only will the actual drawing be made more easily since you know what to look for and where to find it, but your drawings will be made faster and with the authority that is bound to show in the finished work. This is especially evident to the viewer who is well acquainted with the subject that was drawn.

I wish to state at the outset that I do not consider myself to be "a naturalist". This will be only a basic explanation of the structure of some of the animals and birds more commonly used as subjects in the engraving field. I hope that this information may help prevent some of the more blatant errors from showing up, and urge the novice to get some good books on this subject. There is a wealth of information by many competent men in this field, and I have included a list of a number of the better ones.

The skeletal structures of man, beast and fowl are nothing more than a system of levers. In their most simple form the arms and legs can be thought of as straight sticks. See figure 1a. When one of the sticks is actuated in one direction a muscle must contract to move it. In order to move that stick back to its original position there must be a muscle on the opposite side to accomplish this. So you have just learned one of the fundamental facts: muscles come in pairs. In the following description of

muscles, they are named and along with the name is given the origin and insertion of that muscle. Also, is important to know that the muscle that is contracted is actually acting on the lever below the joint. For example, with the biceps contracted the lower arm is flexed. With the muscles in the forearm actuated the action takes place in the hand. So when Atlas on the beach wants to exhibit his muscles, he sends a message to both the biceps and the triceps to energize themselves and the resulting conflict fills out both the front and back of the arm with quivering power, see figure 1b. I believe that

FIGURE 1b

this form of exercise is now called isometrics. Since all of the muscles come in pairs, it is this conflict between one muscle and its opposite that results in the beneficial exercise.

FIGURE 1a

The anatomy offered in this chapter will be an attempt to give the beginner only the main facts about the construction of the human figure, animal or bird that is the subject. The books listed below contain detailed information on these animals, and they give all the details of the bones and muscles if the knowledge is seriously sought, making them valuable additions to your library.

Books available on the human figure include **The Human Figure** by J. Vanderpoel; Bridgman's **Constructive Anatomy** and **An Atlas of Anatomy for Artists** by F. Schider. Although **The Human Figure In Motion** by Muybridge is not a book on anatomy, it does show hundreds of action shots of both the male and female human figure in motion.

For the books on the anatomy of animals there are **An Atlas of Animal Anatomy for Artists** by Ellenberger, Baum and Dittrich; **Animal Drawing, Anatomy and Action for Artists** by C.R. Knight; and **Animals in Motion** by Muybridge which contains hundreds of shots of animals in motion. W.J. Wilwerding's **Animal Drawing and Painting** is published by Dover Publications, Inc. Another book giving an amateur good examples of free, artistic renderings with effective methods of handling sketches and expressing action is Fredric Sweney's **Techniques of Drawing and Painting Wildlife**, published by Reinhold Book Corporation. This is an excellent book on the art of sketching and drawing animals. All of the above are listed in the back of the book along with the publishers.

Perhaps ninety percent of the figures you will engrave will be either animal or bird. However, there will be occasions where you must use the human figure, so we shall begin with the essentials of the human anatomy. Whether it be man or animal there are three principal masses to keep in mind: the head, the chest and the pelvic areas. In order to draw them, you should have a clear mental picture of what is taking place in these three principal

masses. Observe carefully the tip and tilt of the head, study the position of the rib cage and determine exactly what position the pelvis is assuming. For example, when a deer has been alerted his hind legs are brought in under the body and the pelvis is tipped in toward the rib cage to give him more purchase when he takes that first leap in flight. The structure of the deer and that of man are not too greatly different but what the understanding of one will be a great help in the drawing of the other. See figure 2.

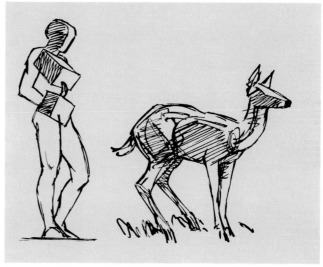

FIGURE 2

To begin our study of the human figure let us start with the framework and the larger muscles that go to make up the outline of the figure. The muscles will be diagrammed and named so that they can be located as we talk about them. The bones are shown in figure 3 and only the larger ones will be named. Starting at the top is the skull with the spinal column connecting the skull, the rib cage and the pelvis. The ribs in the front are attached to the sternum, commonly referred to as the breast bone. At the top of the sternum the clavicle or collar

52

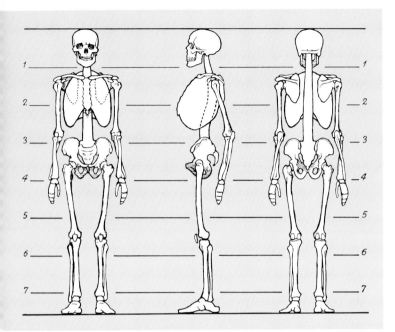

FIGURE 3

bone is connected to it and it makes a very firm but movable attachment for the whole shoulder and arm assembly. The scapula or shoulder blade is attached to the outer end of the clavicle. The scapula has two boney prominences that form the socket for the upper arm bone, called the humerus. The forearm is made up of two bones. The ulna is hinged to the humerus and is the bone that is prominent at the back of the elbow joint and it can be felt as it continues down to the little finger side of the wrist. The radius is the other forearm bone and it is connected at the upper and outer side of the elbow joint and when the hand is palm down it crosses over the ulna and is evident on the inside of the wrist. The hand consists of the carpus or wrist bones, to which are connected the metacarpals that form the palm of the hand and to them the phalanges or finger bones. The carpus or wrist bones are attached to the radius and the ulna with the larger portion of the wrist connected to the radius which

gives the hand such a great latitude of movement.

The longest bone in the body is the upper leg bone or femur. Here again, as in the forearm, the lower leg is comprised of two bones. The main bone, the one that carries most of the weight, is the tibia and is usually called the shin bone. The smaller bone that is evident at the outside of the knee and is again conspicuous as the outside ankle bone is named the fibula.

The foot is made up of a number of bones as is the wrist. The bones of the foot are made for carrying a great deal of weight so they are larger and assembled in a different manner than those of the wrist. In function, however, they are similar to the wrist in that they are required to assume a great variety of positions. The heel is the most prominent, to which the tendons of the gastrocnemius muscle is attached. This tendon is commonly called the Achilles tendon. There is a group of bones upon which the tibia rests that carry the weight of the body and these form the arch of the foot. Beyond the arch, of course, are the bones of the toes.

Figure 3 shows the front, the side view and the back view of the skeleton. The head is customarily used as a unit of measurement. It is also generally accepted that the average figure is drawn so the height is seven and one half times the height of the head. The proportion and placement of the parts of the skeleton are reasonably accurate. No attempt has been made to go into intricate anatomical perfection since you will not be making medical drawings. For example, the rib cage is drawn as a mass, ignoring the individual ribs. Also the hands and feet are simplified masses. You will also notice that the arm is not hanging in a relaxed, natural position in the side view but has been held a little to the rear to show a full side view of the pelvis. I shall use a similar simplified view and explanation of the muscles when we come to giving the muscles of the various parts of the body, shown in figures 4 and 5.

1 Trapezius
2 Pectoralis Major
3 Deltoid
4 Lastissimus Dorsi
5 Serratus Magnus
6 External Oblique

7 Rectus Abdominus
8 Gluteus Medius
9 Sterno-Cleido- Mastoid
10 Gluteus Maximus
11 Teres Major and
    Teres Minor

1 Rectus Femoris
2 Vastus Externus
3 Vastus Internus
4 Gluteus Medius
5 Gluteus Maximus
6 Tensor Fascia Lata
7 Sartorius
8 Gracilis

9 Patella
10 Gastrocnemius
11 Soleus
12 Tibialis Anticus
13 Peroneus Longus
14 Semitendinosus
15 Biceps Femoris

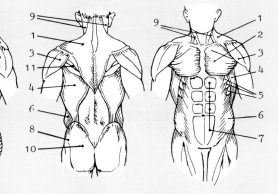

FIGURE 4

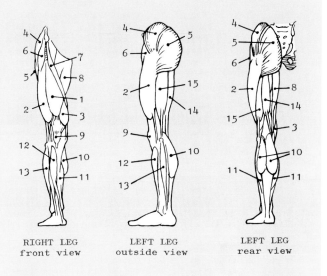

RIGHT LEG
front view

LEFT LEG
outside view

LEFT LEG
rear view

FIGURE 5

Now, let us take the body, one part at a time, and explore some of the main facts about each of them. Let us start with the head. When a child draws a head it is usually represented by a circle. Two of the instructors at the Chicago Art Institute used to employ the oval in constructing a head, see figure 6. With both the circle and the oval there is no point along these curves that you can pin down as a definite change of form. If you can think of the head as having a front and a back, two sides, a top and a bottom it will give you an image that has a feeling of substance, of volume or mass. Any lines that you draw are placed so as to convey this feeling of solidity. As you become more adept at drawing, the character of the lines used to express this feeling will become more varied and expressive. In figure 7 you can see how the head might be thought of as a simple mass in locating the action of the head. The details can be added with some assurance that the action will be correct when the head is completed. When you lay out the head as in figure 7 you will not only be thinking of it as a mass

but you will be thinking of the character of the block. Is it long in relationship to its width? What is the comparison of its width to its depth? It is not only the eyes, ears and nose that are going to tell the story of the particular head, for you can easily recognize a friend several blocks away when these details are completely invisible. You know him by the shape of the head, the way that the head sets on the shoulders and by the way he walks.

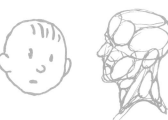

FIGURE 6

FIGURE 7

When drawing the head, whether it be man, animal or bird, be sure of the big proportions and see that they are as true as you can possibly make them before going on to finish any details. You must always be aware of the mass. When the pencil makes a mark it is not only a line, but it is also a boundary for one of the parts of the mass that makes up the subject.

In drawing the masses of the head (or any figure), the light under which they are viewed is very important. A single light source is excellent, such as the sun in nature or a single light bulb. You will find that such a light will separate your subject into three distinct tone values. The area upon which the light is falling directly will be the lightest part of your drawing. The part that is on the opposite side away from the light source and receives no light becomes the darkest part of the drawing. And those planes that are transitional from light to dark where the light is passing across the planes are referred to as half-tones since they are neither lighter or darker. Single light sources are excellent for showing the structure of the masses in any animal form. When you have a foggy, diffused light or a number of lights, these forms tend to merge and it takes a discerning eye to detect the subtle shapes.

Lighted from above, these masses of the head show up as definite shapes and are basically quite similar from man to man (also true of animals of the same species) and it is a close

attention to the correct portrayal of these shapes which shows that you are aware of the forms that are there. For example, take a coin from your pocket and hold it under a single light source with the light shining across the surface of the coin. On the Jefferson nickel the forms are very well defined; the underside of the jaw, the zygomatic arch, the eye socket and the temple are all clear and definite. The Kennedy half dollar contains perfect lessons for the beginner to study and use as a guide, see figure 8. The engraver cuts these shapes or masses to varying depths into the metal as opposed to the artist who uses a variety of tints and shades to record the same shapes.

From the side view the skull constitutes the principal mass while the jaw and the face are a subordinate mass. From the front, the skull is still predominant as can be seen at figure 9. Once the big proportions are estab-

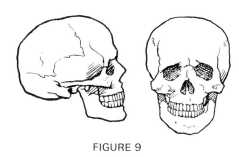

FIGURE 9

lished, it is time to go into details such as the eyes, ears, nose and mouth. **The Human Figure** by Vanderpoel shows the basic shapes of these various forms quite thoroughly. Let us begin by examining the construction of the eye. The boney prominences of the orbital cavity that protect the eyeball play a great role in expressing the character of the model. Is the brow prominent with deep set eyes? Are the eyes protruding? Is the bridge of the nose high, flat, narrow or thick? All of these points are the setting for the eye and they are an inseparable part of the construction of the eye.

FIGURE 8

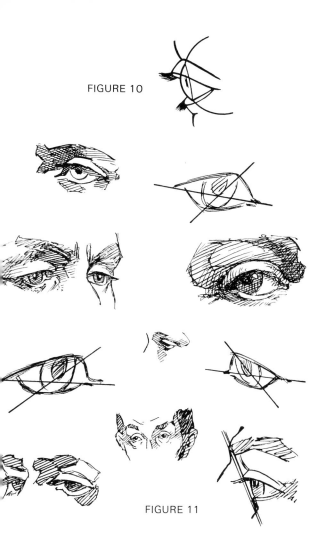

FIGURE 10

FIGURE 11

The nose comes in an unlimited number of shapes and sizes. The top of the nose, the two sides and the under portion at the tip of the nose will give you the shape of the nose and the lines you put down will show your understanding of the shapes of these parts. The boney part of the nose (which is part of the skull) makes up only about one half its total length. The ethmoid bone is a perpendicular bone that divides the nasal opening vertically in the skull. Cartilage extends on down to the tip and separates the nose into the two nostrils. Noses may be large, very large, small or anything in between. They can be convex, concave, straight or crooked. The tip of the nose may be turned up, turned down or straight. The wings of the nostrils may be high or low, narrow or flared. All of these variations can be defined by the shapes of the shadows and half-tones in your drawings. Figure 12 shows a few of the shapes in the construction of the nose.

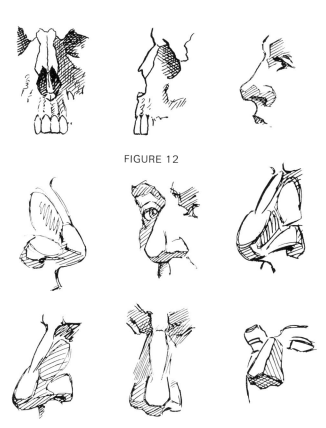

FIGURE 12

In drawing the eye remember that the outside of the eyeball is round but that the lens of the eye extends a little beyond the sphere of the eyeball. The eyelids reflect this feeling of roundness, see figure 10. It is the upper lid that is most mobile so most of the action is reflected in the upper lid. Also remember that the upper lid moves with the eyeball as the lens moves up or down in a vertical movement. Normally the upper eyelid covers part of the cornea or the lens. Only in certain forms of insanity and when persons are in a state of extreme fright or terror does the lens portion show completely. The upper lid is thicker than the lower lid and along with this thickness the eyelashes shade the lens and usually cast a shadow upon the eyeball. Figure 11 shows some of the characteristic shapes that are a result of the forms that make up the construction of the eye.

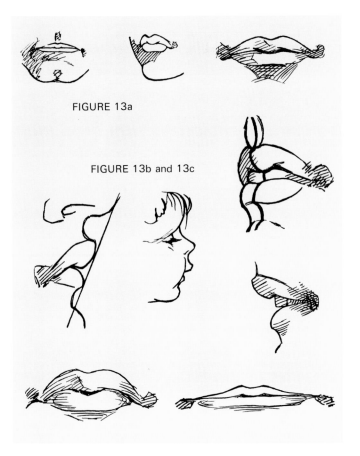

FIGURE 13a

FIGURE 13b and 13c

jaw and the teeth are more nearly flat across the front, this mouth will have lips that are straighter such as a thin-lipped, stern mouth, see figure 13a. The mouth may be thin-lipped or full, wide or narrow, curved or straight. Figures 13b and 13c show some of the details of the construction of the mouth.

Let us now look at the ear. Viewing the head from a position at one side, the ear would appear as you see it in figure 14a. While ears come in all sizes, generally you can construct the ear so that it falls between the brow and the base of the nose while the front of the ear lines up with the rear angle of the jaw. The top of the ear is tipped outward away from the skull and the lobe of the ear is in closer to the jaw as it follows the natural contour of the skull and jaw. See figure 14b. From the side view the ear can be divided into three equal spaces. Naturally these proportions will vary from one individual to the next but this is a point from which to start. At the top is the helix or rim of the ear. This continues on down and at about the lower third it begins to blend

The mouth, like the eye, is very flexible and has a great variety of expressions. The only attachment of the lips to the bone is at the base of the nose and about half way down to the bottom of the jaw bone which allows the lips a great deal of freedom of movement. While the lower jaw moves and the lip moves with it, the upper jaw is immobile. When the muscles move the lips as in a smile, the upper teeth are usually more exposed than the lower teeth. When there is a whole-hearted expression of merriment the lower teeth will also be more exposed.

The shape of the skull as it holds the teeth plays a large part in the form which the lips take. The fully curved lips are formed over teeth that are set in a jaw that shows a nice curve. When the teeth are set in a more angular

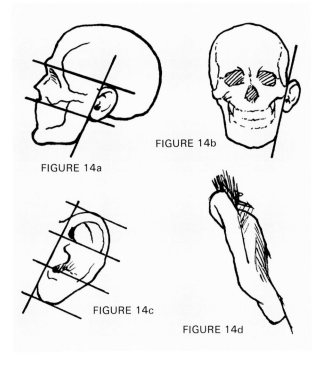

FIGURE 14a

FIGURE 14b

FIGURE 14c

FIGURE 14d

into the lobe of the ear. On the middle third at 14c is the tragus which is a protective covering for the opening into the ear. And the lower third is the lobe of the ear. The planes of the front of the ear blend into those of the face. From the rear, however, the contours of the skull and neck fall away. The cartilage of the ear is attached here at the cup of the ear, see figure 14d. This attachment carries on down to the lobe of the ear and the way that this connection occurs can vary considerably. From these points it moves outward to the rim of the ear. Naturally there are countless variations in these forms from ear to ear. There are large long ears, small oval ears, round ears and even some that are pointed. They may lay close to the head or extend outward from the head. The facts given here are basic and with a book on anatomy you can uncover many more interesting and informative details.

Some of the characteristics to look for in drawing the neck are that in the male the neck is shorter and heavier than in the female. It also assumes a more vertical position in the

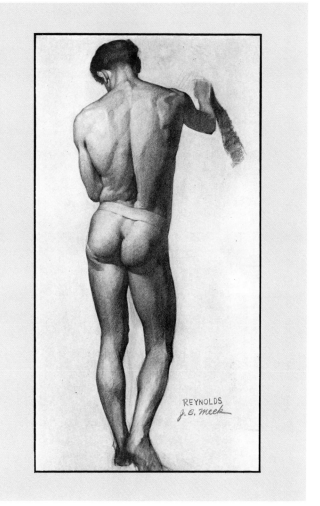

FIGURE 16

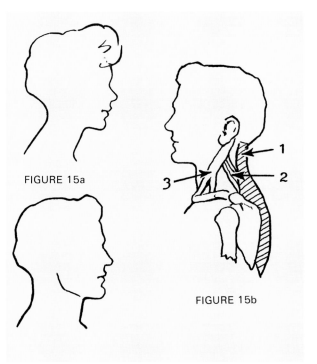

FIGURE 15a

FIGURE 15b

male. In women the neck slopes forward slightly more than in the male and is somewhat longer and more graceful than that of the male, see figure 15a. You will also note at 15b-1 that the trapezius attaches to the base of the skull in the rear and makes this attachment in a higher plane than the connection of the lower jaw to the neck at the front. This means that the connection of the head to the body appears to take place at an angle, also shown at 15a.

The three most prominent muscles of the neck are the trapezius at 15b-1, the sternocleidomastoid at 15b-3 and the levator of the scapula at 15b-2. The trapezius is the big tri-

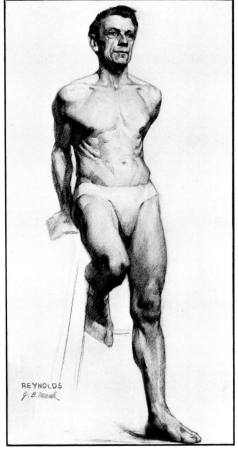

FIGURE 16 cont.

angular-shaped muscle that has its origin at the base of the skull, the seven cervical and the twelve thoracic vertebrae. The muscle is inserted at the outer third of the clavicle and the spine of the scapula, see 15b-1. The prominent muscles on each side of the neck are the sterno-cleidomastoid. Its origin is the upper part of the sternum and inner border of the clavicle and is inserted into the mastoid process back of the ear, see 15b-3. The third of the three muscles is the levator of the scapula. This muscle lies somewhat beneath the trapezius and runs down to the upper angle of the scapula or shoulder blade from the upper cervicle vertebrae. As the name implies, it lifts the angle of the shoulder blade. Here again I would like to emphasize the importance of some good books on the subject. If there are art classes available in your area for figure drawing by all means take advantage of them. Shown at figure 16 are two such studies and a sketch that were done while attending eight years of studies at the Chicago art schools.

Even while the body remains in one spot there can be a variety of actions expressed. The body can be bent forward, backward or sideways. The hips can remain stationary or they can be tipped from side to side with one hip higher or lower than the other. The pelvis can be tilted forward with the buttocks bulging to the rear (we are speaking of the top of the pelvis or the iliac crest as being tilted). If the

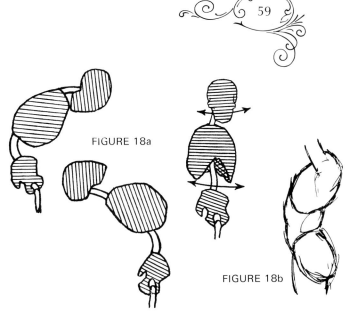

FIGURE 18a

FIGURE 18b

top of the pelvis is tilted to the rear in relation to the lower portion of the pelvis then the buttocks will be brought in under the trunk. The hips can remain stationary, with the chest and shoulders rotated about the axis of the spine. Or the chest may be held in one position while the hips are turned. With the upright torso, the silhouette of the front view and that of the back view will be the same but the actual drawings will be entirely different, see figure 17a. In the back view at 17b, showing the muscles of the shoulder and hip, the spine of the scapula and the iliac crest are landmarks to look for as they tell the location of the shoulder blade and the pelvis.

Most of the action of the spine takes place in the cervical vertebrae or the neck, and in the lumbar vertebrae or small of the back. In this flexing of the body back and forth the thoracic vertebrae (the vertebrae to which the ribs are attached) may be considered as practically stationary. There is only a small amount of movement in each of the vertebrae, but in total it adds up to quite a degree of movement. When the body is bent forward or backward

most of the action takes place in the areas just mentioned, see figure 18a. However, with the body rotating about the axis of the spine, most of this action takes place in the lumbar section. The trunk should be thought of as having three principal masses; the chest, the abdominal portion and the pelvis, see figure 18b. Before starting to put a line on paper, study the action and the interrelationship of the parts. Establish firmly in your mind the action that you wish to express, see again the figures at 18a.

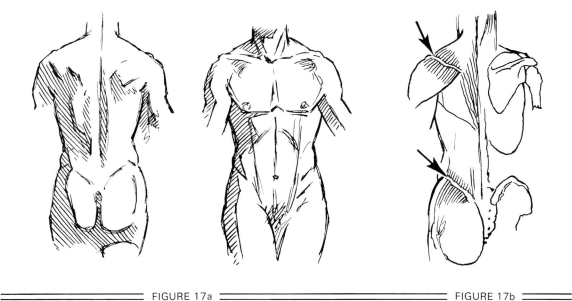

FIGURE 17a   FIGURE 17b

While the muscles on the rib cage alter the outline only slightly, the rib cage itself is the form that is most evident. This is not the case in considering the pelvis. The form of the pelvis is largely concealed by the big muscles that connect it to the legs and those that attach it to the spine and rib cage. This is one reason that the iliac crest, the symphysis pubis and the sacrum are so important in determining the position of the pelvis. Figure 19a shows the gluteus maximus or the big muscle of the buttock that has its origin at the upper rear portion of the iliac crest, the sacrum and coccyx and is attached to the upper end of the femur (the long upper leg bone). At the front of the

the large muscle on the front of the upper leg. It is the one that is used to straighten the lower leg when one is walking or kicking a football. These two muscles form the outline of the upper leg where it attaches to the pelvis. If a line were to be drawn from the fold below the buttock to a point where the erectus abdominus (belly muscle) appears to intersect the muscles on the front of the upper leg, this line would form the lower boundary of the pelvic mass, see figure 19 at a and b.

The arm, by the very nature of its construction and attachment to the body, is capable of a great range of movement. The only solid attachment is at the sternal end of the clavicle, and the ligament attaching it to the sternum, see figure 20d, permits quite a lot of movement at its outer end where the upper arm attaches. The outer end of the clavicle (collar bone) attaches to the acromium process (figure 20a) of the scapula which can be moved up and down as well as away from the spine or in toward the spine. The acromium process, and the coronoid process at 20b are the parts of the scapula (figure 20c) which form the socket into which the humerus (20e) or upper arm bone fits. The clavicle (20d) shows the position of attachment to the shoulder blade. Attached to the

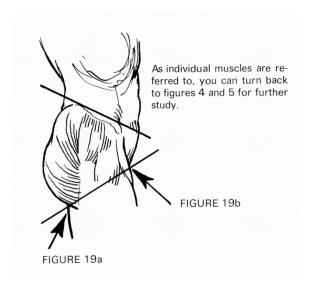

As individual muscles are referred to, you can turn back to figures 4 and 5 for further study.

FIGURE 19b

FIGURE 19a

pelvis, at the forward point of the crest of the ilium, the sartorius muscle has its origin and it is inserted at the upper, inner portion of the larger of the lower leg bones. This muscle is sometimes referred to as the tailor's muscle because it is the one that lifts and crosses the lower leg when he sits cross-legged on the bench to sew. Attached to the pelvis just below the sartorius is the rectus femoris which is

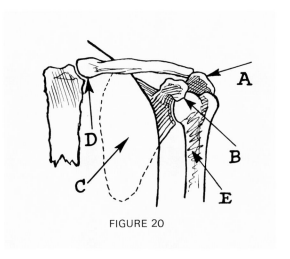

FIGURE 20

lower end of the humerus are the two bones of the forearm. The bone that is prominent at the back of the bent elbow is the ulna, see figure 21a, and it is again evident at the little finger side of the wrist. The end of the radius at the wrist has flared out until it is quite large and to it is connected the greater portion of the wrist, see figure 21c. This view is shown from the front with the palm turned in toward the body. The eight carpal or wrist bones, figure 21d, move almost as a unit with the metacarpals (which form the palm of the hand) since they are all closely connected with ligaments and muscles. The hand can be flexed or tensed to something under ninety degrees. It can also be moved from side to side but to a much lesser degree. The hand cannot be rotated at the wrist

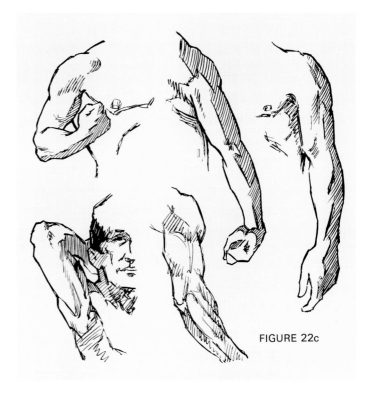

FIGURE 22c

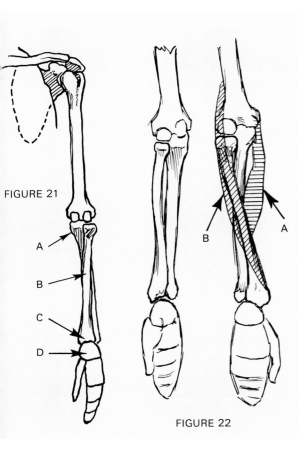

FIGURE 21

FIGURE 22

since this is a function of the forearm. The drawings in this short synopsis should not be taken as perfect anatomical drawings (these you should study in your books on anatomy), but are reasonably accurate as to proportion and function.

The lower arm is made up of two bones and these two bones give it great mobility. We have already spoken of the ulna which can be felt from the point of the elbow to the little finger side of the wrist. The other bone, the radius, runs from the outer side of the elbow to the thumb side of the hand. When the hand is palm down, the radius crosses over the ulna, see figure 22. The muscle at 22a is the pronator radii teres and is the muscle that accomplishes the action of turning the hand palm down. The supinator shown at 22b is the muscle that turns the hand up or toward the front. For some typical shapes of the arm see figure 22c.

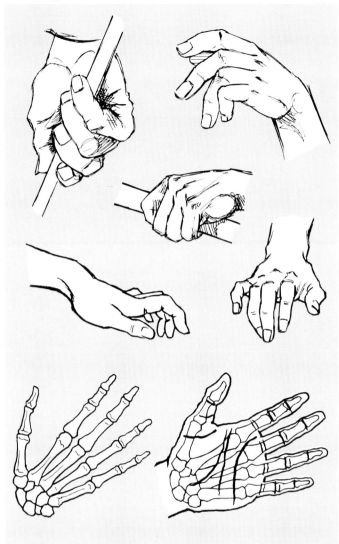

FIGURE 23

back of the hand, the joints of the fingers are of unequal length and they get shorter toward the ends of the fingers. On the palm side of the hands the pads of the fingers are approximately equal in length, see figure 23.

The leg, as in the arm, has its three main parts, the thigh, the lower leg and the foot. In contrast to the arm, the muscles in the leg are heavier and each of the parts taper more rapidly than corresponding parts of the arm. The femur, the longest and heaviest bone, is slightly curved when viewed from the side, and the whole leg from the hip to the ankle has the effect of a gentle reverse curve. This effect is emphasized by the bulge of the rectus femoris on the front of the upper leg and the swell of the gastrocnemius or calf muscle on the back of the lower leg, refer to figure 5.

As the upper leg bone descends from the pelvis to the knee, it normally angles inward when viewed from the front. From the knee to the ankle the two lower leg bones (the tibia and the fibula) assume a more nearly vertical descent. As the femur approaches the knee it suddenly broadens from side to side and length-

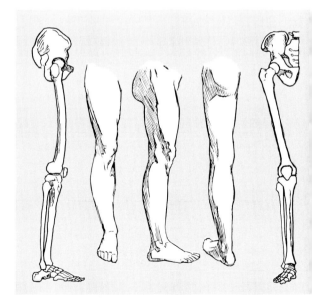

Hands have been a difficult part of anatomy to draw for many a commercial artist. Actually, the hand is not too much of a problem if you are fully aware of some of the facts concerning it, for which you can be on the lookout. The hand is thicker at the wrist and tapers toward the fingers. It is wider at the knuckles and tapers backwards toward the wrist. The palm of the hand extends out to half the length of the first joint of the fingers. Looking at the

ens from front to back, giving this joint a larger, stronger bearing surface since this joint carries practically all of the weight of the body. The top end of the tibia is similarly enlarged to match the femur. The front of the tibia is quite evident all the way to the ankle as the shin bone. The inner side of this bone, on the inside of the leg, terminates as the inner ankle bone. The second lower leg bone, the fibula, originates slightly below the knee joint and to the rear, on the outside of the leg. From there it descends, to become the outside ankle bone at its lower end. The outside ankle bone is always lower than the inside ankle bone.

The advantages of a good basic knowledge of the human anatomy will become increasingly evident as we get into the study of the structure of birds and animals.

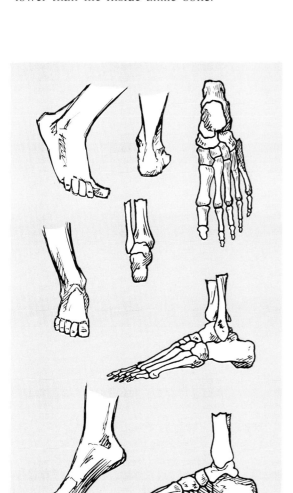

The leg joins the foot back of the center and has the effect of joining it at a slight angle. The foot is a marvelous mechanism when you stop to consider the thousands of pounds of shock that it absorbs each day. (There is an average of one hundred and fifty pounds of shock coming down on each foot at every step.) The arched construction permits this shock to be distributed gradually. The heel, the ball and the outside of the foot carry the weight. The type of action determines which section receives the initial shock. When walking, the heel receives the first impact. In running and jumping the ball of the foot absorbs the shock.

As mentioned earlier, this human anatomy discussion has been quite sketchy. The books listed will take you as far as you wish to go. There are almost unlimited opportunities today to study anatomy simply by applying conscious observation. With our television coverage of sporting events such as boxing and track, you have perfect models who have trained away their fat and have developed their muscles.

64

With the latest TV equipment now in use, you can watch excellent close-ups for detail and medium shots for action. So take your pencil and have a go at some quick sketches from your television set. If you get a sketch that looks fairly good, take a piece of tracing paper and your anatomy book and make a study of the muscles that are creating the action. Any such practice will make the drawing of your people or animals easier and more fun to do.

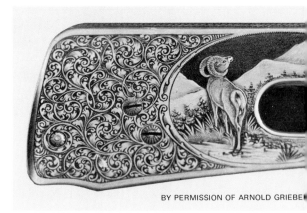

A portion of a receiver showing Arnold Griebel's treatment of an animal.

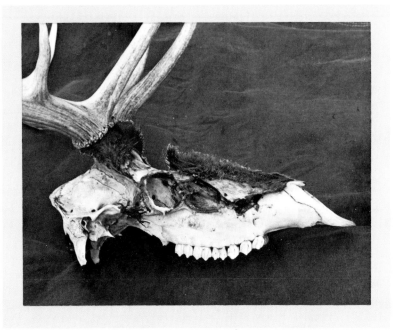

The skull of a deer, shown above, gives a very clear picture of the placement and attachment of the antlers to the skull.

On the animal side of the engraver's art, the deer with its grace of form and movement has long been a favorite subject. So let us study the make-up of the animal. Here again we will not go into the characteristics of the various species, for the books mentioned will give you all the details you might desire. Most of the drawings shown are from photographs taken

in the Rockies using a Leicaflex with 50mm, 90mm and 280mm telephoto lens and a Beaulieu Super 8 movie camera with an Angenieux 8-64 zoom lens. The 280mm telephoto is a fine lens for animal still shots since it gives a large image on the negative; and for catching animal action, the Beaulieu with its f/1.9 lens is an extraordinary instrument to get some difficult shots. The camera is not intended to replace sketching if you have the time. I have done considerable sketching, using seven power binoculars to bring the animals up close so that the details show up almost as though you were in a zoo. If you are near a good zoo or top museum, you can do your studying with a minimum of wasted time.

As with humans, the animals show a variety of shapes and sizes. One deer of the same species may be shorter, taller, heavier or lighter and their temperment may show up in the way they carry themselves. The deer family is worldwide in its distribution and there are so many varieties that we will study only the bone structure and muscalature of the deer.

As the anatomy instructor at the Chicago Art Institute used to say, "learn the anatomy thoroughly, and then forget it." His idea was that the anatomy should not become the end result so that every drawing was an anatomical rendering, but that the finished drawing should be able to stand up to a critical analysis as far as proper physical construction was concerned.

There are tissues, skin and fur that cover up these muscles so that many of the smaller ones are not apparent at all. The larger ones, of course, influence the form. The very nature of the coat of fur breaks reflections so that masses become soft and somewhat fused into one another. So, as an artist, you must see, select and emphasize those shapes and actions that will best portray the true character of that animal. Illustrated in figure 24 are two standing deer. One has the forelegs drawn in a straight up and down position. Remember that a vertical line is a static line, and the resulting drawing leaves something to be desired as a picture of a living animal. Anything that you can do to give that animal a life-like quality is going to be recognized and appreciated.

"A worker in precious metals, fine woods, ivory and pearl is a rather rare breed of firearms craftsman today-" quoted from the American Rifleman feature article on Alvin A. White, January 1967, p. 15. All items illustrated in this informal portrait of White were made in their entirety by him. Courtesy of A. A. White Engravers, Inc.

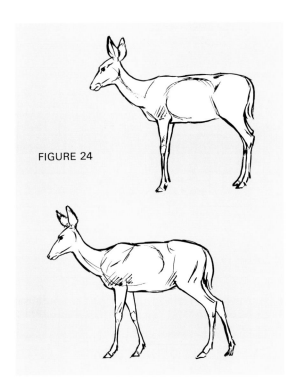

FIGURE 24

There is one other point that we should like to touch upon. In fine art there is one quality that is not too often noticed or mentioned. It is a quality that makes a picture desirable and easy to live with and is called "repose." Most of the great paintings that have survived and been loved through the centuries have this attribute. Perhaps the one we are most familiar with is the Mona Lisa. Let us consider it a moment. An animal in violent action is eye-catching and exciting. But, is it going to become stale and tiresome after seeing it day after day? Would a less violent action, one that is transitional, give the quality of life desired, yet not be so overpowering in its excess of energy? The engraver is naturally going to give the hunter something that he has experienced and can relive in his memory. The shocking flurry the pheasant makes as he takes off from almost underneath your feet. The excitement of the ducks planing in for a landing in the cold, damp morning air with their brakes all set. On the other hand, what sight is prettier than that of an old rooster pheasant slowly strutting his stuff, his head held high and the bright sun bringing out those glorious colors. Or there is the flock of mallards that lit on the pond and rested for several days with all kinds of interesting and relaxed poses, both in and out of the water. The figure that you cut into the metal or the gold inlay is going to be there for a long time. Give it some thought; consider its repose.

The deer as presented here will deal only with the basic facts. It is hoped that many of you will become sufficiently interested to seek more extensive and detailed information. In the skeleton of the deer shown, the vertebrae and rib cage are shown simply as the area that they occupy. Also the bones are named to correspond to the human skeleton. In the forelegs

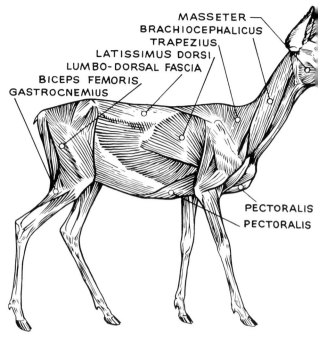

FIGURE 26

the carpal bones are those of the wrist in the human animal. The tarsal bones are those of the ankle. The knee is very similar to the human knee and in the diagram of the muscles, the position of these bones show up quite clearly, see figure 25. This is a good example of the benefit to be derived from the study of anatomy. If you know what to look for and where to expect to find it, your drawing immediately becomes more easily accomplished. The same is true of the skeleton. Since these bones are fixed as to length and restricted as to range of movement, they can only assume positions that are governed by the laws of mechanics and perspective. So the first thing to be aware of in your drawings is the position of the skeleton. All of this becomes evident at once if you know where to look for the shoulder blade, the humerus (upper arm), the elbow, the knee and the heel.

The musculature of the deer as shown here, see figure 26, is again held to the big muscles. They are strikingly similar to those of man. The latissimus dorsi (the big muscle that pulls the swimmer through the water), the

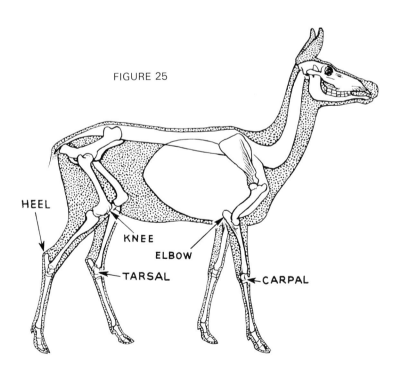

FIGURE 25

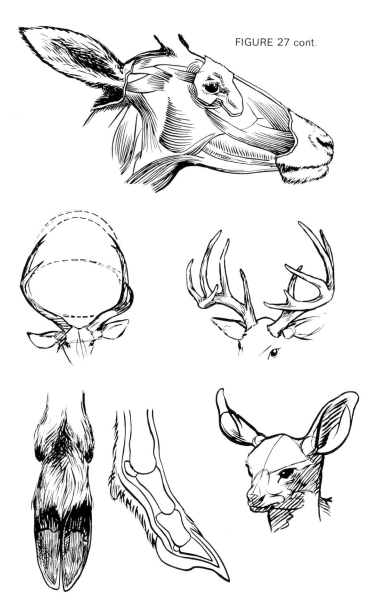

FIGURE 27 cont.

trapezius, biceps femoris and the gastrocnemius all have their counterpart in man. The muscles of the upper foreleg correspond to the flexor group of the lower arm in man which moves the hand up or down. In the deer these muscles move the lower foreleg forward or backward.

The detail of the foot shows the bones that would be the bones of the hand or foot in man. The cross section of the hoof shows that the center of the hoof is raised, the weight being carried on the outside edge of the hoof.

The skull is shown in side view as well as top view for a better understanding of the form. Note that the lower jaw only has teeth at the front end of the bone. The antlers take off at an angle, up and to the rear. Antlers are difficult to draw so try visualizing arcs that will connect up the opposite side. This may help in establishing the main lines of the beams

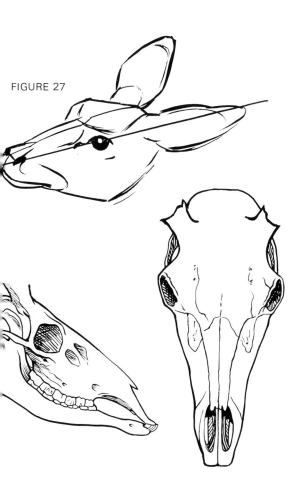

FIGURE 27

and the tines. They are practically never symmetrical, and it is these small differences that makes the sketching of antlers such a challenge. While on the subject of the head, note the eye position. A line from the nostril to the ear will locate the eye with but little variation. See these details in figure 27.

In man, the eye, the mouth and even the nose all contribute to an expressive countenance. In deer, however, the ear is its most active signal of its feelings and is very mobile, covering almost one hundred and eighty degrees. The ears can move together or they may be moved independently of each other. One sketch here shows a deer with his right ear directed forward while the left ear is rotated ninety degrees and is pointed to the left.

The two mounted heads shown above were photographed at the University of Colorado museum, at Boulder, Colorado. Printed by permission of John R. Rohner, Curator.

Drawing animals can be most aggravating to a beginner, so it is especially good if you have a zoo available to study at since you can usually find some of the animals in a pose you can use. Make many quick action sketches that do not go into detail, but catch the spirit of the pose. As your knowledge of construction and detail improves, you will be able to complete these action studies.

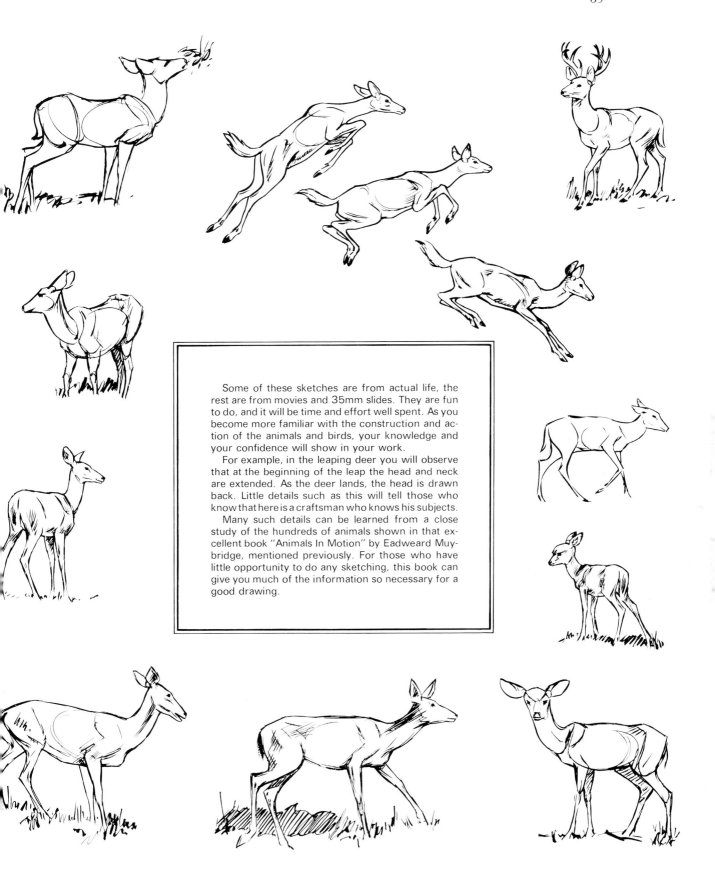

Some of these sketches are from actual life, the rest are from movies and 35mm slides. They are fun to do, and it will be time and effort well spent. As you become more familiar with the construction and action of the animals and birds, your knowledge and your confidence will show in your work.

For example, in the leaping deer you will observe that at the beginning of the leap the head and neck are extended. As the deer lands, the head is drawn back. Little details such as this will tell those who know that here is a craftsman who knows his subjects.

Many such details can be learned from a close study of the hundreds of animals shown in that excellent book "Animals In Motion" by Eadweard Muybridge, mentioned previously. For those who have little opportunity to do any sketching, this book can give you much of the information so necessary for a good drawing.

After familiarizing yourself with the deer, the studies of the rest of the deer family will be easy for one basic construction is almost identical and it is simply a matter of differences in proportion, size and identifying characteristics.

The antelope is very close to the deer in its form and actions although the general impression is of somewhat more rounded forms. The neck seems slightly shorter and heavier in comparison. The lower legs of the antelope are very slight. The body itself appears to be less angular than that of the deer. The horns are a little flattened on the sides. He carries his head in much the same manner as the deer when he walks. When on the alert, his head comes up, forming quite an acute angle with the line of the back, see figure 28. This is characteristic of the deer, the antelope and the elk.

The elk, while not the largest, is the most elegant and impressive of our large deer family. His huge rack and the ease and grace with which he can maneuver it through timber is purely a sight. In spite of his huge bulk, he is lightfooted and his natural elegance makes him a splendid subject for the engraver.

The two antelope heads are from the University of Colorado museum, at Boulder, Colorado. Printed by permission of John R. Rohner, Curator.

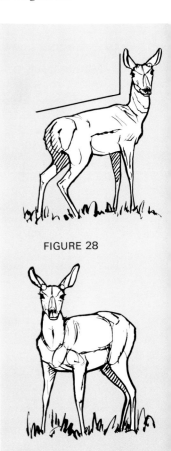

FIGURE 28

four and one half to five feet tall at the shoulders, they are an appropriate animal for the majestic country that they occupy. They range from the meadows in the high mountains in the summertime down to the valleys as winter closes off the high country. In spite of their size they are very active and sure footed as they move about among the cliffs and rocks. For short distances they can build up quite a burst of speed.

During May and early June the young are born and by late autumn they are on their own. By this time too, the last of the velvet has been rubbed from the antlers and the rutting season begins. The clear, bugling challenge of the bulls signals the beginning of many fierce battles as the big, powerful animals fight for the possession of the herd. It is during this time in an elk's life, when he has attained his full vigor, that the antlers will be at their best as trophies. As the bulls pass this peak, the horns become smaller by the year.

Sketches made in Wyoming where there are many fine herds. South Dakota also has many antelope, and is where some of my best action movies were shot.

The elk is an animal whose size is deceiving when he is seen in his natural surroundings. He is usually seen in country that is itself big and overpowering. The large, mature bulls will weigh up to nine hundred pounds, with the record bulls going to around one thousand pounds. Measuring eight to nine feet long and

The elk has a rugged constitution and is capable of quite a long life, providing he survives the rigors of everyday life. One authority quotes a life span of fourteen years and as much as twenty five years in captivity. Another authority tells of a bull, still in good condition when shot, that was found to have been tagged thirty five years earlier. All in all, the elk is a subject that is worthy of an engraver's skill.

Some sketches made in Colorado. These were made from quite a distance, using 7 power binoculars.

The largest of the deer family, the moose is probably the one with which people are the least familiar, since they do not adapt to captivity like the deer. Therefore, about the only place left to find them is as mounted specimens on display in museums. The mounted heads make an impressive trophy.

Their habitat in the United States is limited to some of the northern border states, principally Maine, northern Michigan and Minnesota, western Montana, Idaho and small portions of northwest Colorado and southeast Utah. Canada and Alaska are, however, the prime source of the world's largest hoof-bearing animal as game or trophy.

The moose, despite his huge bulk and unusual and ungainly appearance, can move

through the timber and undergrowth with a minimum of commotion. The large males will reach a height of five to six and one-half feet and weigh between eleven and twelve hundred pounds. One writer tells of some Alaskan moose that weighed up to eighteen hundred pounds and stood ninety-two inches at the shoulders.

Like the deer and the elk, the rutting season occurs in the fall, and the antlers are shed during late December to February. The young are born during May and June. During the summer months they live largely on aquatic vegetation and are very much at home in the lakes, beaver ponds and muskegs of Canada.

Mounted moose head from the University of Colorado museum. Courtesy of John R. Rohner, Curator.

Anatomically, the moose is much like the rest of the deer family. The legs are longer, with the shoulders more massive and hunched. However, the same skeletal and muscular landmarks found on the deer are present to help and guide you when drawing the moose.

The caribou is the only remaining subject in the deer family on the North American continent. It is a somewhat curious fact that engravings of caribou are relatively few. My files on engraving are quite extensive, and there are only a few that have used the caribou.

The barren ground caribou are found in large herds and mostly in the tundra areas of northern Canada and Alaska. They are never long in one place and are continually on the move, moving south in the winter time and north in the spring. Like the moose he has no aversion to water and in his migration (rather than detour around it) he will swim right across a lake.

The male caribou will stand up to four feet at the shoulder and weigh from two hundred and fifty to four hundred pounds. This is one animal on which antlers will be found on both the male and female. The feet of the caribou are large and more nearly round than the feet of the deer, elk or moose.

The woodland caribou range a little farther south in Canada and are found in the muskegs and pine forests. They move about only short distances compared to the barren ground caribou, (more like the elk) and will migrate up or down the mountains. They also are larger than the barren ground caribou with larger horns and may weigh as much as six hundred pounds.

All of the smaller sketches of the caribou are offhand with the idea of expressing an action or pose. No detail is drawn. This can be good experience and the practice will help prevent becoming involved in details before you have established the proportions and character of the pose.

The transition from the large four-legged animals to the smaller canine group (the family which includes the dogs, foxes, coyotes, wolves and jackals) is quite easy. Except for the antlers, feet and proportions, the muscular and skeletal make-up of the two groups is much alike, which is only natural because the functions of the bones and muscles in each case is so similar.

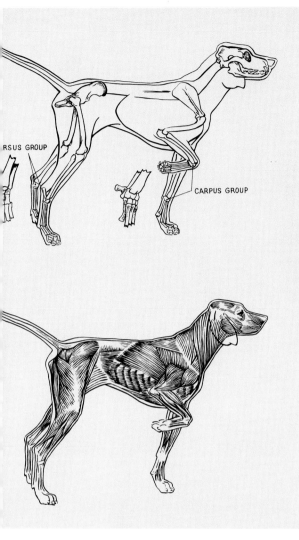

FIGURE 29

ward. Each dog is an individual and the way the tail is carried on point may vary from straight out to raised. There are many fine pictures of dogs in action in current books and magazines. If you have a good bird dog, or even a friend who has one, take a day off with a 35mm camera and make a number of shots of the dog in action. A telephoto lens is a great asset in this type of shooting since you can fill the negative with the dog, which is what you want to study, and this can be done from a reasonable distance. With a normal lens, the dog will be lost in the scenery unless you are very close to it when the picture is shot. If your dog finds plenty of birds, the variety of poses will be a revelation.

Occasionally you may encounter a customer who wants a bench-show type pose rather than a hunting stance. This is an alert but relaxed and classy pose. The head is held high with the front feet planted evenly under the chest. The back feet are placed farther to the

FIGURE 29 cont.

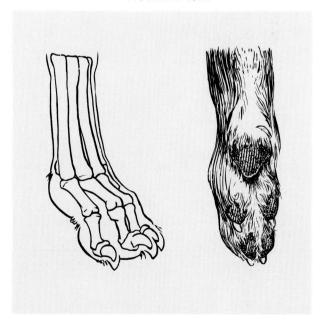

The canine group with its pointers, setters and retrievers has been one of the favorite subjects for the engraver since he first started to decorate firearms. The skeletal and muscle structure of the pointer is shown, see figure 29. Many paintings are seen of the pointer with one foot raised and folded inward. When the pointer picks up the scent of the bird, he may freeze with all four feet on the ground. He may set with his head held high or extended for-

rear and a little farther apart than a dog normally stands. This drops the hind quarters and makes a nice, long sloping line from the tail (which is straight out behind) up to the head. The whole effect is one of leaning forward as though about to take off.

The setters make splendid subjects for the engraver and you will no doubt have calls for depicting them. The English, Irish and Gordon setters are all beautiful dogs and their proud owners will like to see them reproduced on their favorite guns.

For the customer with an individual preference, it is a practical idea to have the customer supply a photo or reproduction of the dog that he likes. Or, you may furnish a drawing of the dog that you propose to engrave for his approval. By doing this you may avoid such comments - when the work is finished - as, "the tail is too long" (or short), "the tail is carried too high (or low)", "the ears are too big (or small)." It is another good idea to have a library of dogs and various animals because a good book of hunting dogs will show the best of these dogs at work, and many of the questionable points can be cleared up to a customer's satisfaction. It will be on your own file and library that your reputation will be founded, so it is to your own advantage to start and build up the best source of material that you can assemble. No matter how imaginative an artist you might be, there is no substitute for the facts. If it is not drawn correctly, it may fool a good proportion of the people who will see it, but there will always be those who will know that it is not a true, clear-cut statement of the facts as they are.

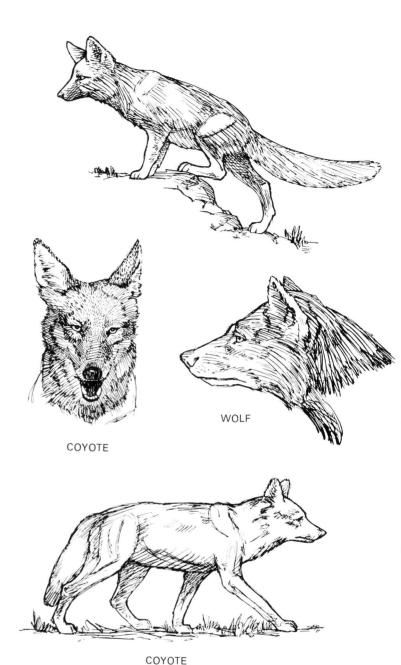

WOLF

COYOTE

COYOTE

Let us turn from the domesticated members of the dog family to the wild ones. These will make suitable subjects for varmint rifles, revolvers, pistols and even shotguns, and have been used many times in the past. Not too long ago, one of the number four Browning shotguns listed in their catalog an engraving of a fox bringing back a game bird to a couple of her pups.

The foxes, coyotes and wolves are all similarly constructed, the differences being a matter of proportion and characteristics. The foxes and wolves carry their tails high when running, while the coyote carries its tail low. The wolf is a large, powerful brute and it is easy to understand how a pack of them could bring down a moose or deer. For this reason, the wolf's head is heavier throughout with the ears smaller in proportion than those of the fox. The fox, preying on smaller animals and birds, is constructed along more dainty lines with its slender muzzle and slight build. The tail or brush of the fox is larger and more bushy when compared to that of the wolf or coyote. Taken as a group, there are many incidents in their daily lives that will make interesting subjects for the engraver.

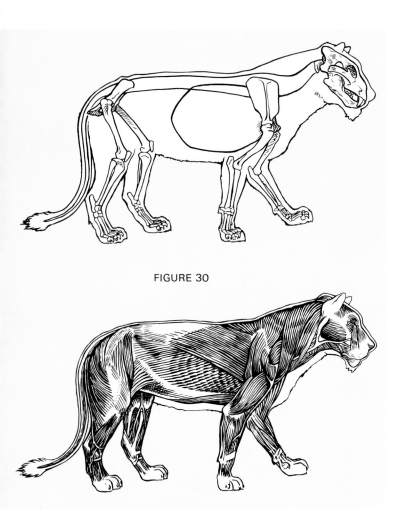

FIGURE 30

I have included several sketches of a house cat, see figure 31. If you have a choice, pick a cat that is large and muscular as they are nearly a miniature of the larger animal as to actions and character.

The feet with their comparatively large paws and retractable claws are the principal difference between the cats and dogs. With eighteen unsheathed claws and saber like teeth, the cats are well equipped for attack or defense.

When the teeth are exposed you will note that there is a gap between the upper canines and the upper incisors. This gap is the space occupied by the lower canines when the jaw is closed, so when engraving a snarling lion with its teeth exposed, be sure that the drawing is correct.

The lynx and the bobcat are members of

FIGURE 31

The cats make up another group that come in for their share of attention. At the head of the list, of course, is the king of beasts, the lion, see figure 30. Since very few of us will have an opportunity to study these animals first hand, it might be interesting to know that Allen St. John, who illustrated many of the early Tarzan books in the late twenties and thirties, based many of his drawings of lions on studies made from his cat. Mr. St. John was also an instructor at the Chicago Art Institute, and there might still be some of these Tarzan books around your public library. If so, his handling of pen and ink are splendid examples of how to handle this medium. For examples,

the same family. With his characteristic tufted ears, the lynx sports a tail that has black all around the tip. The bobcat has this same short tail with the black at the tip, but on top only. The general effect of these two cats is that they seem a little closer-coupled with longer legs than do lions and tigers. The large pads of the lynx serve almost as snow shoes when he is pursuing small game in the snow, for he is an animal of the Canadian forests and swamps with a few as far south as some of our northern border states to the east and far west. The bobcat is found from southern Canada to Mexico, in the mountainous western states as well as in southern and northeastern states. The bobcat is quite adaptable!

BOBCAT

LYNX

COUGAR

Bears hold a certain fascination for the hunter and the gun fancier because of their size and the many stories about them.

Because he is heavily furred and quite lumpish in form, the muscle structure is not much in evidence and may not be of as much value as an understanding of the construction of the skeletal make-up. Here again, having an understanding of the construction of the rest of the wild animals will have supplied you with a basis for comparison. The big differences once more are in proportion and detail.

The most notable divergence is the absence of the hock. This contributes to that

squat, close-to-the-ground effect so characteristic of the bear family. There are the black
bear, the grizzly, the polar and the brown or
Kodiak bear in order of size from the smallest
to the largest. The grizzly and the brown bears
have a pronounced hump at the shoulders, while
the black bear does not. Also, the grizzly and
the brown bears have a face that is concave or
"ski-nosed". The nose of the polar bear is more
pointed and not as large as that of the grizzly
and Kodiak. All of the bears are supplied with
five claws on each front foot. Sometimes the
inside one may be high on the inside of the foot.
The claws vary in relative size, with the grizzly
being the largest, the brown bears smaller and
those of the black bear the smallest of the three.
Most zoos will have some of the bear family on
display that can be studied by sketching or by
photography.

POLAR

BROWN

GRIZZLY

Sheep and mountain goats are often used
as subjects by the engraver since they are splendid trophies that are becoming increasingly
difficult to come by. The white sheep or Dahl
sheep is slightly smaller than the bighorn sheep,
but with his beautiful white winter coat and
gracefully tapered horns, he is a prize trophy.
He is found in the mountainous areas of north-
western Canada and Alaska. When the spring
thaw comes and he starts living close to the
earth again, the beautiful white coat becomes
soiled and discolored, giving a measure of protective coloration.

fall saw some of them in the Black Hills National Park. They can get into mountainous areas that are inaccessible to anything else but a mountain goat. You will need binoculars and telephoto lenses to get a close look at these animals unless you are lucky.

The only large Western animal that we have not mentioned is the buffalo or bison. He is a large, dark-brown beast that may weigh from 800 to 2,000 pounds with a large, shaggy head and shoulders. His horns are not shed each year as are the horns of the deer family, and will be found on both sexes. Most of the buffalo today are found in our National Parks. The Black Hills National Park in Southwest South Dakota has a large herd that roam free and many times are quite close to the highways

The bighorn sheep of our Western mountains have been quite thoroughly hunted and are most likely to be seen in our national parks or protected areas. He may grow to three and one-half feet tall and weigh up to two hundred and seventy five pounds. This grayish brown sheep has a whitish rump patch and his horns are large and heavy. When two of these older rams are engaged in one of their battles during the rutting season, their clashes can be heard from great distances. They back off until they are about thirty feet apart, then at top speed they ram into each other. After so much of this, too dazed to continue the contest.

The mountain goat has long white fur, a beard and spike horns that are his distinguishing features. I have seen and photographed these in Glacier National Park and only last

where good photos can be taken at almost all angles.

One problem often encountered is getting studies of the buffalo in which the feet are showing for they are usually seen grazing in deep grass. When you are fortunate enough to find one on bare ground, make a number of shots from all possible angles. The buffalo is an impressive animal and will make a striking inlay. The sketches shown were made in the Black Hills and from photographs.

The small animals such as the squirrel and the rabbit are often-used subjects of the engraver. These are quite common to most areas of the country and can be studied and photographed by anyone who is interested.

Finally, let us look at the bird family, both water birds and game birds, with the object of eliminating the more common errors by sticking to the essentials. For this study you might find some mounted birds available that could be studied at your convenience.

In this connection, the two mounted eagles shown here were photographed at the Museum of Natural History at the University of Colorado, Boulder, with the permission of the curator, Mr. John R. Rohner. At the time, he made the

FIGURE 32

following comment regarding the two eagles and I quote, "taxidermists are like engravers; there are good ones, then there are those who are not so good. The pop-eyed appearance of the golden eagle is due to the taxidermist neglecting to build up the skull above the eye, to replace the cartilage that nature put there originally. This build-up of the cartilage gives the eye of the bald eagle that fierce, deep-set look which is normally present also in the eye of the golden eagle", see figure 32. If you are using mounted specimens, be sure that they are good examples of the taxidermist's art lest they mislead you in certain tell-tale details. Good reference books are a must if you want to check specific details of anatomy.

The skeleton of the bird is generally much the same as that of man. The bones are lighter in structure because of the requirements placed on them. But their function is the same as any animal. In birds, however, the muscles are much less in evidence than those of fur bearing animals. The feathers are forms in themselves and effectively hide the musculature. In de-

picting birds one must rely on the big forms and the distinctive markings of the subject.

The waterfowl family covers a wide variety of birds, but we will concern ourselves here only with the ducks as representative of this entire group. (Geese are much the same as ducks, only on a grander scale.) Much of the variety that occurs between the different families shows up in their general conformation but especially in the length of the neck and the wing size.

The accompanying diagram of the duck is labeled with the common names used in referring to the comparable bones of the human skeleton, see figure 33. With a knowledge of these bones and the areas in which they function, you can avoid drawing the different members in positions that it is physically impossible for them to assume. The two outline drawings of the ducks with their bills open is an example of what not to do. These two tracings are from actual engraved guns of German origin, but I have seen the same drawings on some of our early double-barrelled shotguns. The duck's bills are opening like a pair of pliers as though the upper bill was hinged also. Actually the upper bill is a continuation of the duck's skull and as such is immovable. Also, the lower bill is hinged quite far back under the skull so that in opening, it appears more as shown in the duck on the wing.

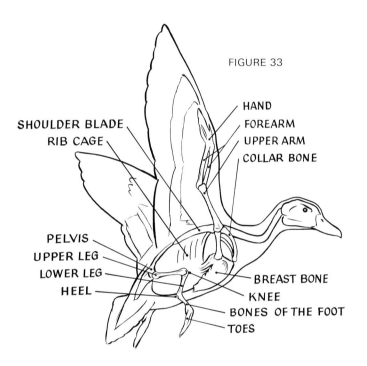

FIGURE 33

SHOULDER BLADE
RIB CAGE

HAND
FOREARM
UPPER ARM
COLLAR BONE

PELVIS
UPPER LEG
LOWER LEG
HEEL

BREAST BONE
KNEE
BONES OF THE FOOT
TOES

view and underside view of the wing. You will note that the underside of the wing also has its coverts which serve in windproofing the wing. The rough action sketches of the four ducks in flight are shown to illustrate another important factor in drawing the wing. The curve of the wings is quite pronounced and takes place both from the body to the tip of the wing and from the leading edge of the wing to the trailing edge.

The wing, as it is shown, is basically the same for most of the birds, so it will not be repeated when we come to the land birds. The primaries are the feathers that attach to the hand and finger section of the wing. The secondaries are those feathers attaching to the forearm portion of the wing. The tertials are the ones that are attached to the upper arm section of the wing. The scapulars are the feathers that cover the shoulder blade and form a connection between the wing and the bird. The wing coverts, as the name implies, cover the shafts and bases of the feathers where they attach to the wing. I have shown both a top

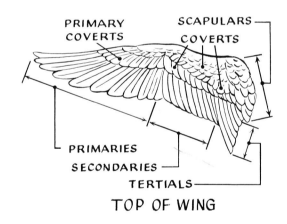

PRIMARY
COVERTS

SCAPULARS
COVERTS

PRIMARIES
SECONDARIES
TERTIALS

TOP OF WING

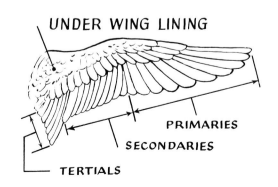

UNDER WING LINING

PRIMARIES
SECONDARIES

TERTIALS

When you are observing birds, either in flight or resting, try putting your impression of the action down on paper. The sketches of the geese and some of the ducks were made in a game refuge and show some of the actions that result from irritation, alert attention, resting and simply being on the move. This live drawing practice will be especially valuable to you if you are serious about becoming an engraver for it helps fix in your mind the characteristic actions of the subject. If you can capture the correct action, the details can be found in text books, manuals and photographs. Here again a movie camera is a valuable addition in the study of live action, because the films can be shot in slow motion, and the action slowed to the point that specific phases of it can be truly observed.

In all birds in flight, the tail feathers appear to originate from a common center, see figure 34. This, along with the length of the feathers and the breadth of the spread is what determines the identifying characteristics of the different birds. The accompanying drawings show the tails of ducks, geese, grouse and pheasant.

FIGURE 34

Now to game birds. A few of the more commonly used game birds are illustrated here; the pheasant, quail and the grouse. You will have no difficulty in assembling a good and extensive library on these birds if you are serious about your engraving. Along with these

drawings you will find the head of a golden eagle and a woodcock. In this drawing of a live golden eagle, the cartilage above the eye is clearly evident, giving the eye that deep-set,

fierce look missing in the stuffed one shown earlier. The woodcock and grouse are shown about nine times larger than actual size to give you quite a clear picture of how this particular engraver acheived the detailed and lifelike quality that shows up so well in the finished work. This was not done by extensive modeling, but rather by the bold, correctly placed individual cuts. Here is a perfect example of how a simple, direct statement in pen and ink can be converted into an engraving.

Also, I have included the two sides of one gun frame, slightly undersized, to give you an idea of the finished appearance of the two birds.

In concluding this chapter on anatomy, let me once again reiterate that my sole aim is to help the novice in avoiding some of the more common errors and to give him aid and support in his understanding of those figures that he will be required to draw and engrave. And, as one last bit of advice, do not neglect your own files and library; be known for what they contain, not what is missing.

Chapter Four
Lettering

t is indeed a rare individual who does not get a thrill out of seeing his name beautifully engraved in all of its sparkling beauty. This is especially true if the name is done in gold, silver or even polished brass, and attached to some valued possession. As an engraver, you will receive many requests to cut initials, names or inscriptions, and this can be potentially a tremendously large market for your talents.

Cutting of lettering is another phase of the engraver's job that will require study and a considerable amount of practice for the work to show the superior quality which you wish to imply you can do on your engraving jobs. The lettering must be, first of all, spelled correctly, well laid out, and cut with authority. That little catch about the correct spelling should not be taken lightly. It is quite easy to become engrossed in the layout and omit a letter, or become so interested in the design that the correct spelling is overlooked. After the layout is finished and the lettering job completed is the very worst time to find out that the spelling is incorrect. Check and double check the spelling!!

I know of two books dealing with lettering as related to the jewelry field that contain a great deal of information which would certainly be of benefit to anyone who plans to attack the problems of lettering seriously. Both of these books are available from the Southwest Smelting and Refining Company, Incorporated. The earlier book was written by Albert A. Winter, and entitled **A Practical Course In Jewelry Engraving**. The second book, a more recent one, was written by John J. Bowman and R. Allen Hardy, and is called **The Jewelry Engravers Manual.** Both of these books have much to offer and the novice will find many of the answers to his advanced questions. My concern in this chapter is to give the beginning engraver the information he needs as he turns to this special phase of the engraver's art.

Anyone who seriously intends to become good at lettering must accept the fact that it requires a careful study of the various letter formations. For this reason, do not waste your time and effort with a graver as you endeavor to learn the shapes of the letters. It is both a lavish and misspent use of your time and energy for you can accomplish so much more with pencil and paper without the frustrations attendant on the use of unfamiliar engraving tools. You must first be aware of what constitutes a well-formed letter. After you can draw the letters acceptably well, then you can begin engraving with some chance of success.

There are hundreds of alphabets that have been and are still being used, which greatly contributes to the confusion of the uninitiated. In an effort to reduce this confusion to an understandable level, we shall restrict this mass to four basic alphabets from which all the rest have been derived.

The first and most simple is commonly called the Gothic. This is an upright letter of uniform width throughout all its parts. It is a very legible letter, and is used extensively. The second and perhaps the most widely used of all the letter forms is the Roman letter. This was one of the early Roman art forms, and has come down to us in practically its original form using letters in which certain members are thick while others are thin. You often see Roman letters made by amateurs in which the wrong members are emphasized, and these always stand out like a sore thumb. Aside from learning which is correct, you can check yourself by remembering that the "down" strokes are heavy, and the "up" strokes are thin, as are the horizontal strokes, see figure 1. The

The inside of the cut approaches a straight line while the outside shows a nice curve.

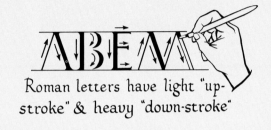

Roman letters have light "up-stroke" & heavy "down-stroke"

FIGURE 1

third group of letters has come down to us in many of the old manuscripts in Latin, German and English, and can be summed up under what we now refer to as Old English. This is quite a decorative text, and you see many certificates and diplomas with the names lettered in this Old English letter. The fourth big category is script, or a natural derivation of the hand written word which the engraver has developed into an elegant and graceful letter form. Once you have mastered these four basic alphabets, you will be equipped to do any kind of lettering job from simple names to elaborate trophies.

The Gothic and the Roman letters will be found as either vertical or slanted letters. When these letters are made on a slant they are referred to as Italic, for example, Roman Italic or Gothic Italic, and it is quite common to find these letters used either way. The Old English letter is always constructed with the main stems vertical. The script letter is practically always a slanted letter and only on occasions is it drawn as a vertical letter.

Since I have urged the study of the letter formations, we will first go into this part of the

ABC
Gothic

ABC
Roman

AaBb
Old English

𝓐𝓑
Script

extreme curves result in many broken points.

for more strength and character use straighter cuts.

four basic alphabets. Then we will discuss the subject of the tools and their use in cutting the letters.

Script letters, because of their beauty and popularity, will be taken up first. In searching for some of the reasons why script is the beautiful letter that it is, we can refer back to our explanations of design. The straight line is usually thought of in conjunction with strength, while the curved line is one of grace and beauty. The basic cuts in the script alphabet contain this combination to a very high degree. You will note in the illustration of the two basic shade cuts that the inside of the cut assumes an almost straight line, while laying the tool over and bringing it back out again makes a full, graceful curve on the opposite side of the cut. Look again at the illustrations of the upper and lower case A's in figure 1. The first two show an example of too much curve being given the cut which results in not only a weaker letter, but also a cut that is hard on graver points because of its extreme twisting action. The second set of A's show what a little restraint with curves can do. Not only will your tools last much longer, but you will get a stronger, more flowing letter.

Lynton McKenzie's treatment of a lettering job. This is a portion of an elaborately engraved and cased set that will be shown later.

Let us start in with some general remarks before beginning on the design of letters. Script letters are designed and cut at an angle similar to the angle one uses in writing. Some script alphabets are cut vertically, but this is an exception and is done as a special request or for a definite reason. You will find different degrees of angle being used and I have encountered 45, 54 and 60 degree angles being recommended by different engravers. This particular point can become a matter of personal preference as it is in handwriting. The important point to keep in mind is that whatever angle is chosen, it must be maintained consistently. Figure 2 shows the three angles mentioned and shows the use of guide lines. These guide lines should be used when you are laying out the lettering to insure that the letters will be of a uniform slant. The template shown is a pattern that I use, with the exception that it is shown shorter in order to conserve space. My template actually measures 2" wide by 6-1/2" long overall, and it is made of an opaque white plastic about 1/64" thick. I made some templates originally out of clear plastic, but could never locate them when they were laying on the bench, so I changed to the opaque white plastic instead. Do mark the angles and use the angle that you like, the one that seems to work best for you. The 45 degree angle is one that I seldom use.

FIGURE 2

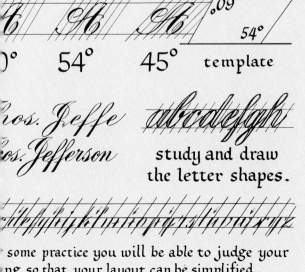

It is useful if you have a long space and a comparatively small number of letters to occupy that space; however, script is a letter that looks better if it is cut rather condensed. The two Thos. Jeffersons were drawn to demonstrate the difference graphically.

When you are going to study letter design, do not attack it with a mad rush. Instead, take a letter or two at a time, and after drawing them take the time to give them as critical and unbiased a comparison as you can possibly make. Only by ferreting out the mistakes that you are making, then correcting them, can you expect to make any progress. It will do you no good to continue to practice making poorly-formed letters. So the amount of practice is not the whole answer; but careful, thoughtful work will bring its reward. Study and draw the letter shapes until they are firmly fixed in your mind. When you do start the cutting, it would be well to lay out the work as carefully as you did while studying. Eventually, when you have acquired the ability to judge the spacing required by the shade cuts and the hairlines, you will be able to simplify your layouts as shown in the alphabet illustrated in figure 2.

As you accumulate a file of engraving and lettering examples, one of the first things that you will encounter in script is the great variety of styles used. One engraver may indulge in many decorative loops, while another will be content with a simple, straight-forward letter. In any case, the letters must have a relationship to each other if there is to be any unity within the finished lettering. To accomplish this unity I have illustrated the alphabet and used the oval as a basis for each of the letters. Keep this basic oval rather long in relationship to its width. The length of the oval shown is approximately two and one half times its width. As a tall stately woman is more graceful than a short fat one, so it is with the oval and the script letters, see figure 3.

There are numerous so-called keys to building up these letters, and the ultimate end of all of them is to design a letter that is easy-flowing and natural. The use of the small ovals for the minor portions of the letters acts as a guide toward attaining a uniform and even flow to the lines, and a likeness to similar portions of other letters. You will find that constructing these ovals lightly will be a definite help, and I recommend that you use them in your studies. By using the alphabet showing the direction of the various cuts (figure 5), and following the suggested use of the ovals, you should experience little difficulty in developing a good working knowledge of the script alphabet.

The basic hairline cuts (shown at a, b, and f), and the basic stem cuts (c,d,e,g and h), are illustrated in figure 4. Once these are fixed in your mind, the letters develop quite naturally. Most of these basic cuts are accomplished with a single cut. There are, however, a number of parts of letters which will require two cuts to get the shape of cut needed. In the illustrated script letters showing the direction of the cuts, the portions of the letters just referred to that call for a double cut are shown with a slash across that particular part of the letter. On the h, K,k, M,m, N,n, p, R,r, U, V,v, W,w, Y, the

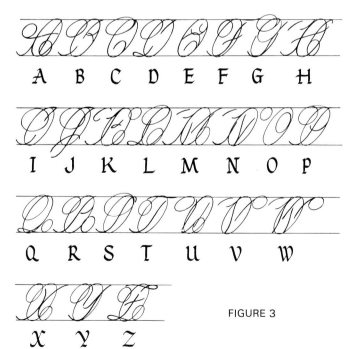

FIGURE 3

ampersand "&", and the figure 8, a part of the letter will necessitate a double cut. The reason for the double cut is that both ends of the stroke have a rounded shape. Look at figure 4g. The first cut of the n starts with a flat entry of the tool and terminates with a nice curved end as the tool is brought out of the cut. On the second cut of the n both ends of the cut show this rounded end, which means that the cuts must start somewhere in the middle. In the beginning, it will seem a little difficult to make the two cuts appear as one finished cut, but with practice it will become as natural as the single cut. Shown at figure 4l are the tops of the F, T and the bottom of the L which are also cut as two single cuts.

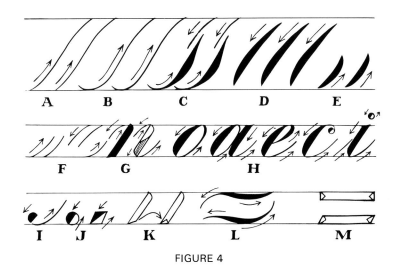

FIGURE 4

FIGURE 5

You may experience a little difficulty in getting your tool started squarely on the line when beginning such cuts as the first cut of the n. A very slight deviation from the square is acceptable, provided all such cuts are the same.

94

A practice used by some engravers is to make a slight cut that will make the bottom of these cuts end squarely on the line, as shown at figure 4k. These are small triangular cuts where the tool makes a squaring-up cut and is immediately brought out. These small cuts can also be used to square up the ends of bars or dashes, as shown at figure 4m.

There is one more operation that the jewelry engraver makes use of that the firearms engraver himself can employ. A metal that is too thin to withstand a script bright-cut is usually "closelined." The lines are a series of shallow cuts, and where the lines of the letter become wider, another cut is placed closely beside the first one. Each successive cut starts from the preceding one, and merges back into it. As many cuts are made as are needed to bring the desired width to that member. The engraver may not be too concerned about the thickness of the metal, but this closelined method works well where a large letter, such as a monogram, is to be used.

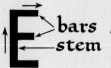

FIGURE 7

As was mentioned earlier, there are many variations of the script alphabet, so I have deliberately confined the study here to one that has a definite quality, but is not over-embellished or complicated. As you gain in proficiency and experience, the basic alphabet that you have studied may yield to your own characteristics and preferences. The books that you acquire, along with your expanding file of lettering art, will also influence your selection of what eventually develops as the style that suits you best.

The Gothic letter is a very useful engraved letter because of its legibility along with its ability to withstand hard usage and the deterioration of time. I am sure many of you have seen old silverware on which family's initials have practically disappeared from usage. The fine hairlines are naturally the first to be worn away. With the Gothic letter, which is cut with a round tool, the cuts are comparatively deep; and being of a uniform depth no one part wears away before the other.

Gothic letters can be cut with the round tool or with the flat tool. The designing of these

FIGURE 6

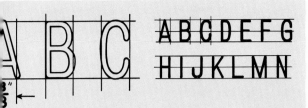

construction of Gothic by mechanical means

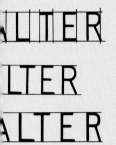

The first Walter is spaced mechanically. The second is spaced visually. The third is spaced visually so as to occupy the same space as the first Walter.

FIGURE 8

letters can be done mechanically, making each letter the same width, with three exceptions. The I being a single stem letter obviously does not require a full space. The M and the W because of their extra components need more room to avoid a crowded, illegible appearance. The Gothic alphabet is shown at figure 6, and the letters are constructed larger than you will normally ever make them. For the first few times at least, lay out your letters this size in order to familiarize yourself with the shape of each letter. After becoming acquainted with the alphabet, drop the size down to 3/16" or 1/4" and lay out some names. Draw the top, bottom and center line horizontally. Make the width of the letters approximately one half the height. After laying out several names, the first thing to become apparent is that some of the letters do not seem to have been spaced evenly. This is because certain letters, due to their construction, have more blank space than do others. These letters are called "open letters". For example, the letter A fills the bottom of its allotted space quite well, but there is a big blank area at the top of each side. The letter L

leaves a large blank area above the lower bar. The letters A,C,E,F,J,L,T,V,W,X and Y are all open letters and will require special attention in your lettering. In the conventional Roman alphabet, the letters D, G, O and Q are also open letters. Figure 7 gives some additional information on the Gothic letter as it would be designed and cut with the flat tool.

Illustrated in the name "Walter", at figure 8, is the effect of mechanical spacing. To correct this bad-looking spacing, you must space it visually. The second "Walter" is visually spaced as it was lettered, and results in a shorter name because of the closing-up of the extra spaces between the open letters. The third "Walter" shows spacing by eye so that the finished name occupies the same space as that of the first one. You will need to learn to fill a given space with evenly spaced letters since it is often required.

FIGURE 9

HENRY AINSWORTH – CLEVELAND

The example above demonstrates what the result will be if close attention is not given to the starting, and stopping of each cut, precisely on the guide lines. All of these cuts are within .010 of an inch of the guide lines. Even with this small deviation, the result is a ragged line of lettering. Below is shown the result of closer attention to this detail.

HENRY AINSWORTH – CLEVELAND

ROSES
GRACE
JUICE

When cut with the round tool, the Gothic letters C,G,O,Q,S and the lower parts of the J and U should extend slightly beyond the guide lines. See text.

PRESENTED TO

RICHARD SMITH

WINNER

OF THE

OAK HILL

COUNTRY CLUB

TOURNAMENT

PROPERTY OF

JAS. AUSTIN

MADISON, WISC.

These two plates are
designed with Gothic
letters ～ The top plate
cut with flat tools ～
The larger plate on
the left as cut with
the round gravers ～

FRANK S. JOHNSTONE

JANET RICHMOND

DRURY LANE   MICHIGAN

The two simple nameplates above are
laid out as described in the text ～～～
Each letter being allotted a space equal
to one half its height ～～～ The spacing
being done visually ～～ The top plate
in Roman, the second plate in
Roman Italic ～～ Address in Gothic ～

FIGURE 10 and 11

After you have become familiar with the letter formations you can try some layouts, using smaller letters. A letter that is cut 1/8″ in height makes quite a large letter when it is applied to a small area. These smaller letters will demand especial attention to the detail of uniform height. One letter that is slightly short of being full height with a letter next to it that is slightly over can result in a line of lettering that has a ragged, amateurish appearance. The smaller the letter, the more accurate it will need to be. When cut with the round tool, the Gothic letters C,G,O,Q,S and the bottoms of the letters J and U should extend slightly beyond the guide lines in order for them to appear equal in height to the other letters. Several examples of this are shown in figure 9.

Gothic letters, whether cut with the round tool or the flat tool, are usually used for inscriptions that are purely informative. It is not a decorative letter in itself, as are the Old English, Roman or script. It can be used effectively by the beginner for small plaques or name plates, especially if he is careful with the layout and gets a little variety by the use of varying sizes and/or the introduction of some lines in italic, see figure 10. The use of italic letters, whether Gothic or Roman, will effect a change

CDEFGHIJKLM
PQRSTUVWXYZ
2 3 4 5 6 7 8 8 9 0 &

may be thought of as an engravers Roman
it is based on equal spacing for each of the
s except the "I", "M" and the "W".

FIGURE 12

Note", "The United States of America", "Five Dollars" and even the small "Washington, D.C.". The eye travels over these letters smoothly. The serifs on any line of lettering serves to give that line an entity of its own, and makes for smoother reading. As further evidence, observe the "Five"'s on the reverse side of the bill, in the lower corners. These are practically Gothic letters fattened up, with serifs added. See figures 12 and 13.

in appearance and add a little interest, as is shown in the "Janet Richmond" plate at figure 11.

The Roman letter is perhaps the most used of the various letter classes. The main reason for this seems to lie in its construction, which by the use of thick and thin strokes, immediately projects a more interesting impression. The serifs add considerably to its clean image and legibility. (For the benefit of the novice, the serif is a short line at the top and bottom of a stroke, and terminates that stroke. It serves a very real purpose. The plain Gothic letter, without any caps or serifs, has all of the stems ending on the guide lines. Examine a one or five dollar Federal Reserve note to graphically demonstrate these points. First, examine the two lines of Gothic letters without any serifs, "This note is legal tender for all debts, public and private". If you do not read it at a glance but let the eye travel over the individual letters, it will go something like this: It starts out straight and smooth over the T, hits one bump of the H and then the second, hits another bump of the I, then up and over the S, across a space and two more bumps of the N, and so on down the line. As a contrast, observe carefully any of the lines of the Roman letters, "Federal Reserve

In the early 1700s, Caslon designed a type style that bears his name and has come down to us virtually unchanged. The fine Roman alphabet below is one of the Caslon family.

ABCDEFGHIJ
KLMNOPQR
STUVWXYZ
&abcdefghijklm
nopqrstuvwxyz
fifffflffiffl1234567
890$

FIGURE 13

The 19th century Roman alphabet shown here gives you a more decorative treatment of the serifs. The serif at figure 14a shows it as it was originally designed. The serif at 14b is a suggested modification that might be considered when using these letters in an initial or in monograms.

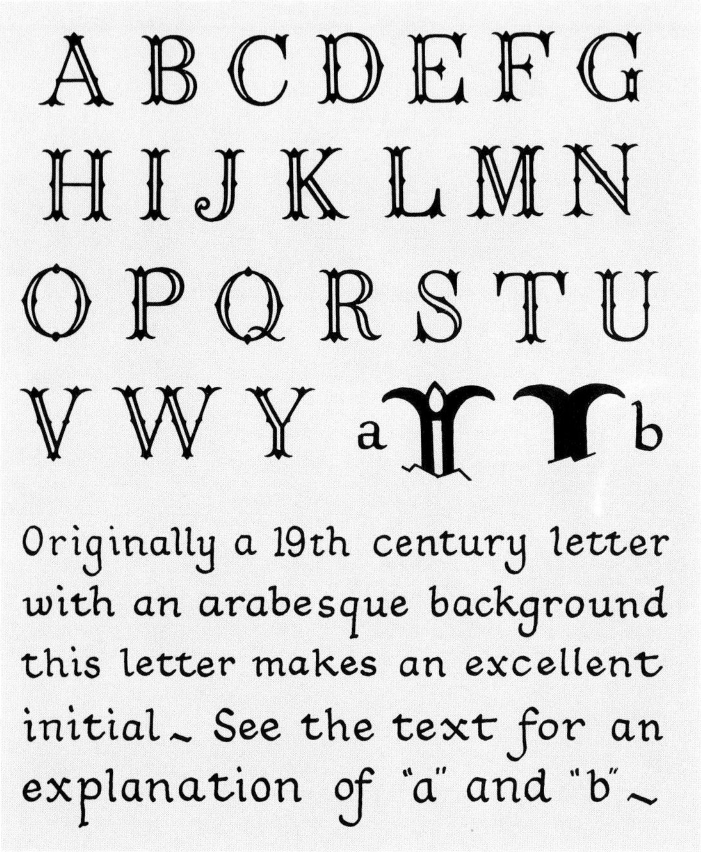

ABCDEFG
HIJKLMN
OPQRSTU
VWY a𝕴𝕴b

Originally a 19th century letter with an arabesque background this letter makes an excellent initial. See the text for an explanation of "a" and "b".

FIGURE 14

FIGURE 15

In studying the Old English alphabet you may be confused by the differences that will be found in the letter formation from one alphabet to the next. This is a natural result of a letter that lends itself to a variety of treatments, and each man is inclined to give it the design that satisfies his own bent or taste. See figure 15.

For those of you who have had no lettering experience, I suggest that you learn the simplified Old English alphabet shown here first. The basic construction is quite simple, and there are only a few exceptions. The guide lines should be used, and they consist of the vertical lines and the 45 degree diagonal lines each way, see figure 15D. The stems are heavy and

ABCDEFG
HIJKLMN
OPQRST
UVWXYZ&

abcdefghijklmno
pqrstuvwxyz

FIGURE 16

The letters B and R can also be improved by not following the 45 degree guide lines. See illustration of the letter B at figure 15. The diagonals at which the arrow is pointing should also be made at an angle that is more acute than the guide lines.

The simplified alphabet shown here has been cut to follow the guide lines; that is the vertical and diagonal lines are cut straight. As stated before, there are many variations to this alphabet and as you acquire the knowledge and skill these will show in your finished work. Your diagonal cuts, both the light and the heavy, may take on a slight curve which relieves the monotony of all of the straight lines. Shown at figure 16 is an Old English type face used by printers in which the diagonals show this slight curve. Also you will notice that some of the letters such as the B, E, F and so on, have in the main stem a double line. This makes for a letter that is a little more decorative and which can be used to advantage in initials. However the simplified alphabet retains this character and to the average individual this difference would scarcely be noticed. The letters G, M and S in figure 15 show a treatment of the Old English letter as it might be used in a set of initials.

parallel to the vertical guide lines. As with the Roman letters, the up strokes are thin and the down strokes are heavy. So, a stroke that is going up to the right is a light, or element, while the stroke that goes down and to the right is a heavy, or thick stroke.

As with most rules, there are a few exceptions where it is best to deviate from the guide lines in order to improve the appearance of the finished letter. Two of these changes have to do with letters that are not too often used, namely the X and the Z along with the ampersand "&". If the diagonal elements in these letters were to follow the guide lines, the resulting letter would be too extended and would appear as lighter spots in the line of lettering. The diagonals of these letters should therefore be drawn at a more acute angle; approximately a 60 degree angle will give the desired result.

FIGURE 17

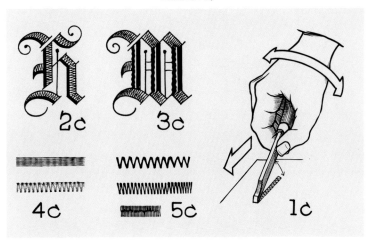

Before leaving the subject of Old English letters let's look at one of the tools used in cutting this letter, often referred to as a "wiggle tool" or "wiggle cut." Figure 17 at 1c shows a flat tool making a coarse wiggle cut. The lift, or angle at which the tool is used is indicated by the arrows directly underneath it. This angle is greater than that of the regular cutting tools, and may be anything between 35 and 60 degrees depending upon the coarseness or fineness of the pattern that you want. The steeper the angle of the tool, the finer the pattern will be, see figure 17-5c. A combination of the forward pressure, the amount of rotational movement and the degree of lift will determine whether the cut is a coarse, medium or fine wiggle.

Figure 17-1c shows the mechanics of the cut. As pressure is applied to the tool, the hand rotates back and forth, forcing the tool to cut alternately from one side of the tool to the other. When first trying this cut, rotate the hand only (without any side to side movement of the handle) while maintaining a constant angle and pressure. If a still coarser cut is wanted, the handle of the tool can be tilted a little from side to side at the same time the tool is being wiggled. It is a matter of coordinating all of these movements. You may find that it helps to count 1-2, 3-4, 1-2, 3-4 to help maintain a uniform tempo which along with a constant angle and uniform pressure, results in a good, even cut.

At figure 17-2c and 3c are shown two treatments of the Old English letters by wiggling the flat tool. As you build up your files and read other books, variations of this engraver's wiggle will be added to your repertoire. Figure 17-4c shows the use of a lining tool as a wiggle tool and the unusual pattern that it will give you. (The illustrations shown here are made with a wider tool than you will normally use, and was done to illustrate clearly the character of the cuts.) In actual use, most of your wiggle cuts will be made with the flat tools, sizes 37 to

FIGURE 18

41 or 42. However, do not take this as an iron-clad rule, for if a wider tool, a round tool or a square one will get the effect that you are trying for, do not hesitate to use it. You will find such experiments fascinating and often you will come up with something that you can use and will be one of your own identifying characteristics. In your experimenting, you will find that this wiggle technique can be used effectively as a background texture for scroll work also.

The subject of initials and monograms is one that could go on and on because of its unlimited variety. In the good old days of jewelry engraving, when the pocket watch was the common timepiece, many of these watches were marvelous examples of the engraver's art. In fact, on many of these watches, the design was so intricate and involved that it was almost impossible to recognize the letters. The very fact that they were so difficult to read would have seemed to defeat their purpose, aside from ornamentation. So, let us do our designing on the assumption that if a man wants his initials engraved on his pet firearm, he would prefer them to be easily discernible. The initials "TAB" shown at figure 18 were cut in the manner of some of the old pocket watch monograms, although they are quite simple when compared with some of the more elaborate old-style examples. The main stems are high-lighted and cross-lined, with the leaves close-lined. The initials "FGD" is another style of treatment that was quite common to this period, and was referred to as "ribbon monogram." The book by Albert Winters, previously mentioned, goes into this style of engraving with detailed instructions and illustrations. The initials "JSM" can be cut with the main stems close-lined if you want to emphasize them. After careful observation, it is quite evident that all of these monograms are basically vertical script letters.

In most monogram engraving where three initials are designed in a geometric form such as a diamond or circle (for example the initials "TAB") the shape dictates that the center letter must be larger. This larger letter is commonly the initial of the family name or surname, with the two initials of the given names smaller on each side. When all of the initials are of the same height and in a row, they appear as they would naturally with that of the surname last.

In addition to the two books on engraving that have been mentioned, there are several that are a fine source of information for the person who is beginning in the lettering field. One of these, **Decorative Alphabets and Initials** edited by Alexander Nesbitt, is published by Dover Publications and is available from Dick Blick. It contains 123 plates, 91 complete alphabets and 3,924 initials. There is another book, **Calligraphy** by Johann Georg Schwandner, which was first published in Vienna in 1756 as a collection of continental calligraphy. Containing 150 extremely ornate frames and panels, it also has many ornamental initials and figures, and is available from Dover Publications. There are many more books covering this part of the engraver's art, and should your interest lean this way you will find a great deal of pleasure in searching them out.

However, if you are beginning, your aim should be toward simple legibility rather than over-elaborate and involved initials. Your de-

signs may still be based on one of the four basic alphabets, Gothic, or block letter, Roman, Old English or script. They can be placed simply, one after the other as they would appear, (for example see the initials "RTL" at figure 19) or they might be placed one beneath the other as on a trigger guard, see "FRB". Slanting the monogram as in the "GSM" may be used to advantage in occupying a space both vertically and horizontally. With the letters designed in panels of various shapes, such as squares, diamonds, ovals, circles, triangles and so forth, you can envision the endless possibilities that are available.

When designing initials within a triangle, square or diamond panel, I should like to again emphasize that the letters must remain easily recognized. Where the letters are made to conform to the shape of the panel some weird effects can result. For example, the P in the "PGK" monogram in figure 19 could be a lower case e, and it is scarcely recognizable as a P

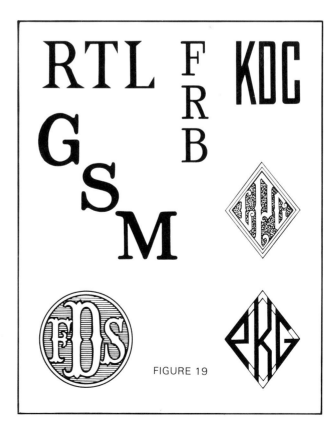

FIGURE 19

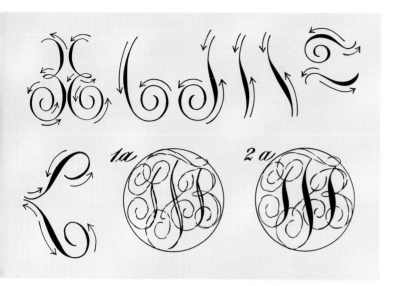

FIGURE 20

These basic cuts are self-explanatory and are easily recognized as portions that make up the various letters. While these vertical letters might be considered normal for script monograms, there is no reason that the slanted script cannot be used; although usually with a little more embellishment in the way of loops and scrolls. A few examples are shown at figure 21.

When designing and cutting the vertical script letters, give particular attention to the main stems. Let us take the initials "GBF" and design a monogram to fit a circle, see figure 20-1a. Scribe your circle on a piece of paper and lay out the monogram lightly for chances are that you will want to change it in places. Should you want to make some drastic changes, use a new piece of tracing paper! By using fresh tracing paper, your design will remain a direct statement and you will not be confused by a jumble of erasures and multiple lines.

As mentioned before, pay close attention to the spacing of the main stems (figure 20-1a) as they are the elements that will determine to a large degree the legibility of the monogram. In cutting the letters, engrave all of the main stems first, as in figure 20-2a. On small monograms these can be bright cut. With larger letters, the main stems can be cut by close-lining. Figure 20-1a shows the corrected and finished layout with the emphasis on the main stems. Figure 20-2a shows the main stems cut,

since for all of our lives we have been accustomed to a P in which the main stem is a straight line. The K and the G are easily recognized but you can visualize what might happen should you require an H, J or F in place of the G. Therefore, I think that it is best to outline the shape of the panel so as to present the definite figure desired, then design the letters within this area with reasonable clarity. Giving the background a texture using punch work, Florentine finish or cross-lining will further separate and distinguish the letters, as in the monograms "LGP" and "FSD" in figure 19. For purposes of clarity and study these monograms are shown somewhat larger than they would be made in normal use.

In designing script monograms the basic cuts are closely related to the script alphabet cuts, see figure 20. The curves are fuller and the scrolls are carried out further. However, the cutting is counterclockwise as in regular script. You will notice that these examples are cut as vertical letters. After you have practiced script cuts, you will find these vertical script basic cuts to be practically the same motions.

FIGURE 21

while figure 21-3a shows the completed monogram. In the monogram "EMA" at figure 21-4a, several small additional scrolls were added in some spaces that appeared too blank. The scroll was added above the E, and the cross-bar of the A was extended to fill the blank space above the M. In adding these scrolls, keep the cuts very light.

Figure 21-5a shows a treatment that can be used when the letters must fit a vertical space. For this, you can lay out three circles, placing the compass point on a vertical line. Let the circles overlap, so that the loops of the letters may be interwoven. Figure 21-6a shows slanted script with some added embellishment in the way of scrolls. The monogram at figure 22-7a "WES", shows some added scrolls with a slightly different treatment. The "MEM" initials at figure 22-9a returns to the classical Roman alphabet, a letter that is always dignified and legible. The "DSR" monogram at figure 22-10a is basically a Roman alphabet, but slightly more decorative, and it makes an excellent choice of style. Figure 22-11a shows a different treatment of a condensed Roman letter that is good where space is restricted, and the letters must be designed more tightly. The initials "NTW" at figure 22-12a shows a Gothic letter

BY PERMISSION OF LYNTON McKENZIE

A splendid example of fine craftsmanship in every detail. A large cased Colt set engraved by Lynton McKenzie. The pistols and knife mounts both have raised gold work and gold borders as well as rich, fine English engraving. The knife blade was first engraved (with considerable tool breakage), then the background was etched to heighten the effect. The frame of the .41 derringer is heavily gold plated and engraved.

with serifs. Note the liberty that was taken with the outside slanting members of the W. Since it was the surname initial, and could logically be made larger, these bars were extended up to occupy some of the blank spaces on each side of the stem of the T. This is part of the fascination in designing initials, which have variety and limitless possibilities of combination. For those whose interest prods them on, the books mentioned have much additional information.

The tools most used in lettering are the flat, the round and the square. When sharpening the square tool, which is the one most used in cutting the script alphabet, there are several forms this tool can take and each form results in a different shape of cut. Basically the sharpening steps are the same, the only differences

FIGURE 22

being in the angles at which the different planes are sharpened. So this explanation will deal with sharpening what would be considered the normal tool.

These tools may be sharpened by hand. However, the engraver has available a tool holder with which the planes can be sharpened at definite angles, and these planes can be maintained perfectly flat. This may seem to be going to great lengths, but that slight rounding of the edges when sharpened by hand can make a difference in the cutting characteristics of the tool. For bright cutting of script, the tool must have a very keen edge and the cutting edge must have a good polish to get the mirror-like finish that is such a distinguishing quality of well-cut script. This tool is shown in the accompanying photographs at figure 23-3b, 4b, 5b & 6b. The graver, when it is in the holder, can be rotated a full 360 degrees and locked at any setting

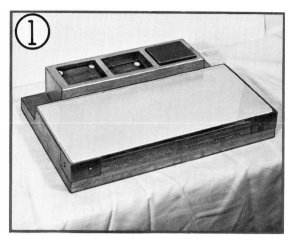

FIGURE 23-1

since all three adjustments are calibrated. Once you have determined the angles that seem to work best for you, the graver can be placed in the holder and, by setting these angles, you can be sharpening the tool in a negligible amount of time. In this way, only enough metal need be removed to restore the cutting edge, generally on the face of the tool. If the point has actually been broken, then it is best to touch it lightly to the grinding wheel for the rough removal of metal, using the stones only to restore the correct planes and cutting edge.

In order to take full advantage of the potential of the tool holder, the base and stone holder shown in figure 23-1 was made. The base is two pieces of plywood for warp resistance and flatness. The piece that holds the stones was made from a piece of 2"x4" hardwood. On top of the plywood was placed a piece of plate glass to provide a flat, smooth surface over which the tool holder can glide freely and smoothly. The holes for the stones were countersunk to a depth that would leave about 3/16" of the stones projecting above the surface of the wood base. A hole was drilled and tapped in each corner under each stone, as shown in figure 23-1. In threading these holes, do not thread them quite all the way through but let

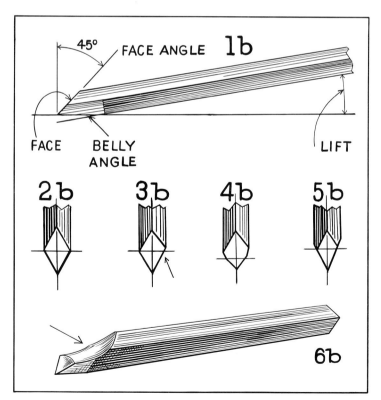

FIGURE 23

the screw form the last small amount of thread, so that the screw will be held firmly. A piece of 3/8" x 16" threaded rod was purchased at the hardware store and cut into approximately 1-3/4" lengths. One end of the screws had a screwdriver slot cut into them with a hacksaw, so that each screw could be adjusted up or down to get the correct height to level each stone.

Before going into the levelling of the stones, I should like to mention a few suggestions about the stones themselves. The stones most commonly used are India and hard Arkansas stones. The India stone is a fast cutting stone, but it is somewhat difficult to keep a flat surface on it because of wear. In the center of my stone holder I use a manufactured white polishing stone, bonded to extreme hardness. It cuts and wears like a hard Arkansas stone but it is much less expensive, and it actually cuts faster than the hard Arkansas stone. Available in medium for cutting and fine for polishing, it has a hardness of 9 on the Mohs scale that uses 10 as a maximum hardness figure, which is the hardness of a diamond. Upon receiving these stones I cut them in two, using only half of the stone. With the growing hobby of rock polishing I am sure that you will have no problem in

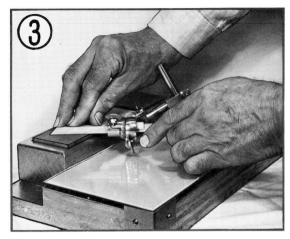

FIGURE 23-2

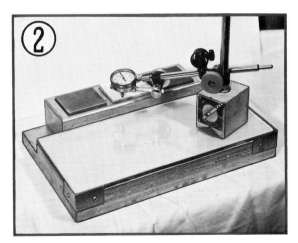

FIGURE 23-3

locating someone whose hobby is rocks, or almost any rock shop would saw them for you. The reasons for sawing it in two are: first, you do not need the larger size which would make the base and stone holder quite unwieldy, and secondly, in order to maintain the original flat surface of the stones, you need two stones. We have used these stones for about a year and so far they show no appreciable wear. However, should the stones in use develop an unevenness we would switch to the second half of the stone and use it until it too was uneven. At this time these two uneven stones would be rubbed together, being flooded with water to carry away the cuttings. A sprinkling of Boron Carbide powder will aid in the process of returning the stones to flatness. The two darker stones in the photographs are the Ruby Bench stones. Both of these stones are imported, and were purchased from Paul H. Gesswein & Company, Incorporated.

Having a dial indicator and a surface gauge available in my shop, I used them to level the stones. If you do not have these tools at hand don't worry, for they are not absolutely necessary; they only make the job easier and more fun. The stones can be levelled by eye, using two straight edges. In photograph 23-2,

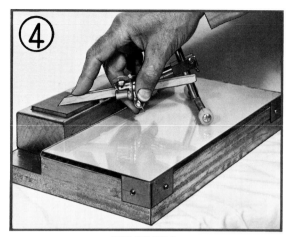

FIGURE 23-4

the first stone that shows completely un-obstructed is the medium ruby stone which has already been levelled to be slightly higher than the other two stones (actually .010" higher). A piece of paper was used to cover the stones while they were being levelled to protect the plunger of the dial indicators, and the same piece of paper was used on all three stones. The first stone was brought to the desired height and levelled, using the screws. Being made of wood and glass, toolroom accuracy was not to be expected, however, it did level up surprisingly close. Figure 23-2 shows the second stone being levelled. The surface of this stone was set to be levelled at about .020" below that of the first stone. This was done to insure that in spite of any inaccuracies in the base and stones, the front portion or cutting edge of the tool would be making contact with the stone. After the second stone was set, I placed the last one, the ruby fine stone. This stone was set lower than the second stone by about .025 inch. It puts a remarkable polish on a tool, and with a minimum of stoning a very keen edge can be gotten. After the last stone was set, small wooden wedges were pushed into the crack between the stone and the wooden base on one side and one end of each stone. These wedges hold the stone in place and prevent any

movement of the stones while sharpening the gravers. All of this set-up may look involved and more trouble than it is worth, but in actual practice it pays off in a better cutting tool, and a tool that will last longer between sharpenings.

Figure 23 shows the nomenclature that will be used in talking about the sharpening of the square tool which will be used for the cutting of the script letters. As mentioned before, this sharpening results in a tool that is a good starting tool for the beginner. The face angle is normally 45° to the belly. As shown in the illustration, the belly angle and the lift are the same. However in the process of actually making a cut, this lift angle will be slightly more because we must have some clearance if the tool is to cut freely. The belly angle (plus the clearance angle) must be enough to allow room for the fingers to clear the work when using the graver. Before starting to stone this angle, see figure 23-3. Fasten the graver into the holder securely with the edge of the graver that has the point on it, at the bottom and opposite the holding screw. Loosen the screw that allows the securely held graver to rotate in the holder and turn the graver until one of the flat bottom sides lays flat on the stone. While holding it firmly with the right hand (see figure 23-3), turn the locking screw at which the finger of

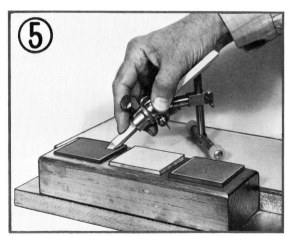

FIGURE 23-5

the left hand is pointing to lock the tool in position. The holder is now set to maintain the 90 degree angle. Loosening the locking screw on the top of the main arm will permit the graver holder to turn, so that the back end of the graver may be raised up off the level of the stone, see figure 23-4. Raise the back of the tool up until it makes an angle of about 7 degrees and lock the holder. With the graver now held firmly in position, stone the graver back approximately 1/8 inch from the front edge. This plane is stoned on all three stones successively, with the last stone putting a nice polish on the graver. Note the calibrations on the holder, unlock and rotate the holder to the same mark on the other side and lock it again. You will note that the belly angle adjustment is not changed. Only the tool in its holder is rotated, so that the other bottom side is presented to the stone. It is now stoned back until it reaches the exact point on the bottom edge to which the first side was stoned. If one side is stoned back farther than the other, the two planes will not meet in the center, and the tool will not track properly, making it want to cut off to one side. The belly angle is the result of the two planes that you have just completed. This finished belly angle of the bottom edge is a little more than the angle at which each indi-

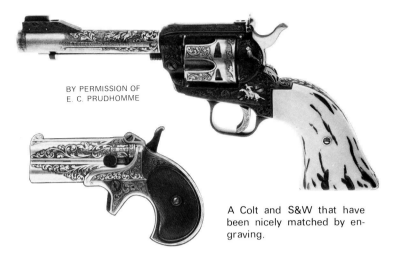

BY PERMISSION OF
E. C. PRUDHOMME

A Colt and S&W that have been nicely matched by engraving.

vidual side was set, and by setting the stoning angle for each side at about 7 degrees, the finished belly angle will end up more like 9 degrees. These degrees need not be adhered to precisely down to the last minute of angle. Their importance lies in the fact that you can go back and sharpen the same tool, or other tools, to the same shape later. So, if you hit on a tool that seems to work better for you than others, make a note of the settings to which it was stoned so that you may use them on other tools. This belly line that you have just finished is the line from which the face angle will be determined.

You should experiment with these belly angles to determine for yourself which one works better in a given situation. Consciously study the effects of the different angles as you experiment. In general, on both convex and concave surfaces, a tool with more lift will be more easily controlled than one that has a lower lift and works well on flat areas.

The face will be stoned next, and the graver is set so that it will be stoned at a 45° angle, see figure 23-5. This shows the tool set to be sharpened perfectly flat and square with the axis of the graver, at the 45° angle. The result of this stoning is shown in the drawing in figure 23-2b, where the face is shown to be symmetrical and square with the length of the

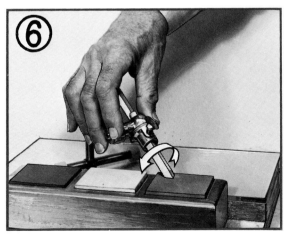

FIGURE 23-6

tool (except of course for the 45° angle). This makes a good tool for fine lines. However, this angle can be improved for the cutting of a line that must start out fine, become broader and then thin down once more. Look at figure 23-6, and by studying it you can see that by rotating the tool in the holder so that it is no longer perfectly flat there will be more metal removed from one side than the other before you attain a flat surface all across the face. This will be taking more metal off of the left side of the tool as you look down over it, while holding it in readiness to make a cut. This in effect moves the cutting edge a little forward, which makes the tool more effective in going into a broader line and back out again. You will remember that all of your cuts are counterclockwise when cutting script. So putting this edge a little forward results in its meeting the metal a little more squarely, and with improved clearance. See the illustration at figure 23-3b and compare with 2b. Setting the holder off center 8 to

10 degrees will give a good edge. Beware of carrying this edge too far forward, since this results in a tool that is difficult to control. For the beginner, the tool just described is a good one to start with.

There are two variations of the tool just mentioned which are accomplished by using different angles when setting up the tool for stoning the belly. Look again at figure 23-3. Here the tool is held perfectly flat on the stone. The finished angle of the belly is the same as that of the square tool itself, 90 degrees. If the tool is rotated so that the bottom edge of the tool contacts the stone first, instead of being held flat on the stone, then more metal is going to be removed from this edge, and the tool is going to end up with an angle of say 105 degrees instead of 90 degrees. This second tool will make a broader cut without the necessity of cutting as deeply. Here again, extremes are to be avoided. As the angle becomes greater, the more difficult it becomes to control the tool. So on your first try, aim for a tilt on the tool of about 7 or 8 degrees. This will give you a tool similar to the tool shown at figure 23-4b.

The last tool variation is one that may be used for fine lines and for close-lining letters. With the graver flat on the stone, as in figure 23-3, rotate the tool so that the outside edge of the tool contacts the stone first. By so doing, the outside edge of the graver is removed, and the resulting angle is less than the 90 degrees. The angle of tilt may again be 7 or 8 degrees, which will give an included angle of approximately 75 degrees instead of the normal 90 degrees. With this sharp an angle it is well to

Another detail of the R. Q. Sutherland pistols. Note the solid gold butt cap and checkered ivory grips - made completely by A. A. White. Courtesy of A. A. White Engravers, Inc.

have enough lift so that the tool does not tend to cut too deeply. The finished tool is illustrated at figure 23-5b.

When using the flat tool, a slight lift or belly can be given this graver quite easily, and it can prevent a sharp tool from having the tendency to cut too deeply. On your first trials it is better to try the lower lift angle, gradually increasing the angle if you feel that more lift is needed. Obviously, this angle can be sharpened easily and accurately with the tool holder and stone set-up.

The round graver can also be given this lift angle, but in this case it must be done carefully, and by hand. Once again, it is not necessary to remove a great amount of metal to get the desired result.

One point that has been ignored in these descriptions and illustrations is shown at figure 25. Seldom will tools that you will be sharpening be as large as the ones shown in the photographs. These are actually pieces of wood that were made larger for purposes of clarity and photographic reproduction so that we

FIGURE 25

might give you pictures with better detail. For this reason the tools were left a full square all the way to the face of the tool. In actual practice, you may want to grind off much of this extra metal so that the stones will be used only to produce the correct angles and keen cutting edge. When you place an actual graver in the holder for sharpening, it will look more like the drawing at figure 25 than the tools shown in the photographs.

For additional study of the art of engraving letters, the two manuals recommended at the beginning of this chapter are suggested. And, I sincerely hope that the information discussed in this chapter will make the way easier for those of you who are beginning this very interesting phase of the engraver's art.

Chapter Five
The Camera, Another Tool

he engraver has only his talent and his time to sell, and nothing is more true for him than the old aphorism, "Time Is Money". So, anything that he can do which will shorten the work, or make it easier, is well worth serious consideration. The camera is not going to replace the artist, but for the person who can work carefully with some artistic judgment and appreciation, the camera will enable him to accomplish results that his talent alone could not produce. So, for the beginning engraver who is not averse to being commercial, I should like to point out some of the methods, and the benefits that he can expect, from the use of the camera.

Many artists take a dim view of using a camera, feeling that it is an insult to their talent; a form of cheating. However, there are many things that a camera can do in an instant, that would require a great deal of time for an artist to record. In fact, many phases of certain animal actions occur so rapidly that it is impossible to visually record these sequences. A movie camera can catch this succession of actions, and any particular phase can be chosen to be studied at leisure and in detail. Any artist can take advantage of the camera, whether he be an accomplished professional or an amateur. Naturally, the better the artist (and photograher), the more complete will be his understanding of the interrelationship of the focal length of the various lenses to perspective, and of visual perspective. Should the engraver become

interested in using the camera to increase his understanding of the animal and bird life around him, he will, as a matter of course, study these details in order that he may get the best possible results from his equipment. However, as we are going to use the camera primarily for copy work, we will be working in a single plane (the copy board), so that perspective will not be a factor in our use of the camera.

Before going into the use of the camera, I should like to generalize a little on the camera and the artist. (This is aimed at the beginner, so the professional artist and accomplished engraver can pass over this lightly.) When the artist records something, it is the result of a visual impression that is seen by two eyes and sent through the brain which then also directs the actual drawing. Each individual artist is an emotional creature, and each may react somewhat differently to the same subject. The two eyes, seeing the object from two separate viewpoints, give us a depth perception that influences our concept of the subject being drawn. This is one reason that a person, when shown a photograph of a friend, may say "That certainly looks like John"; while the next friend may react with, "That's John?". Each knows John, and has reacted to his own visual and emotional impression of John. The camera, on the other hand, has only one lens or point of view. It is completely impersonal, and under proper lighting conditions will record precisely and in minute detail everything before it.

Cameras, like cars and many other products, may be had in a variety of styles, makes and prices. For our purposes, only a camera with a ground glass viewing back will do the job that will be required of it. Of the cameras with this type of back, our interest will center

mainly on the press camera or the view camera. There are several photographic magazines that carry advertisements for new and used camera equipment and cameras of this type can be purchased at reasonable prices. If you are unacquainted with cameras, perhaps you have a reliable camera store, or a good friend who can advise you. Both types of cameras will be available in different sizes. The camera that I use is a 4"x5" Linhof press type camera, and I have found it capable of handling any size of job that has come up so far.

To demonstrate some of the possible applications of the camera for an engraver, I shall use a model 94 Winchester that has had the scroll engraving and the gold inlaid borders completed. Space has been left into which will be put the major scene with its gold inlaid figures. Drawings for this area can be made actual size and transferred, though it is much

easier to work in a larger scale. By working larger, the proportions can be more accurately compared, and the smaller details can be studied and drawn with more exactness.

Beside the advantages of doing the drawings oversize as mentioned, there is an added bonus when using the camera to reduce this drawing back to actual size for transfer to the gun. Say that your drawing was made three times larger than the size of the finished job. Also assume that you made a slight error in proportioning, for example, the size of a revolver in a man's hand compared to the size of the holster into which it is supposed to fit. If this error is only slightly noticeable in the oversized drawing, when the drawing is camera reduced to one-third this size on the ground glass this small discrepancy is also going to be reduced by this same amount. This is one reason that much of the commercial art work is drawn larger than it will actually be reproduced. Small irregularities and imperfections will be reduced until in the finished product they will be unnoticeable.

With the preliminaries out of the way, look at figure 1. A piece of acetate sheeting has

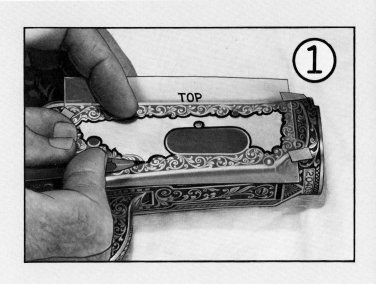

been taped firmly in place to prevent any shifting while tracing an outline of the area into which your drawing must fit with a good black pencil. (Tracing paper can be used instead of acetate.) It isn't necessary to be too exacting with every little crook and turn recorded. It is good to have this outline as black as possible, even to drawing it with pen and India ink, should you not have a real black pencil because you will want a good contrasting line when it is viewed through the camera on the ground glass. Also, it is well to indicate "top" which will aid in determining at a glance whether the acetate is right or wrong side up.

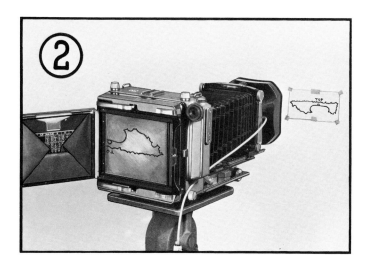

This outline that you now have is actual size, and the enlargement of this outline to the size you wish to draw at can be done in two ways with the camera equipment. Figure 2 shows the tracing set up before the camera, well lighted, and focused so that its image is reproduced on the ground glass. Unless your camera has an extra long bellows extension, you may not be able to get as much enlargement as you want. In this event, simply trace the largest image that you can get on the ground glass. This can be done in a few minutes. Now place this second tracing on the copy board, and focus it to the size that you want, and trace it off. This sounds like a great deal of tracing, but very little actual time is required. For those of you who are unacquainted with cameras, especially those with ground glass viewing, you will notice that the image on the ground glass is not only upside down, but also reversed from side to side.

Those among you who have a 4x5 camera, also no doubt have an enlarger for your 4x5 negatives. This is the second means by which an enlarged tracing can be gotten. Tracing on the baseboard of an enlarger is much easier than doing so on the camera back, because you are working on a flat surface. Also, a greater enlargement is generally available from the enlarger than from the camera. This means that you will be able to get the size that you want with only one tracing.

There is an alternative method to the two just mentioned. It consists of making your drawing of any size, medium or manner that you choose. You may make an oil painting, a water color, work in pastels, make a charcoal study or do your drawing in pencil using the medium in which you work most freely and easily. You should, however, use the tracing that you make, as in figure 1. When you have your preliminary layout made for your drawing, place it before the camera and reduce it down to see that it will fit within the boundaries of your original tracing. In a few minutes you can be certain whether the drawing is the size and proportion you need, or whether it must be changed. This technique opens up unlimited possibilities for the person whose artistic training is limited, but who has a natural talent. With the wealth of animal and bird subjects on calendars, in books and magazines waiting to be put before the camera and transferred to metal, there is enough material to

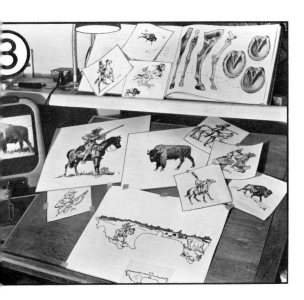

keep the amateur busy from now on. And, these are in addition to the animals and birds that he may capture himself, with his camera or pencil.

After you have decided what the subject for your engraving is to be, assemble the material that you have to work with. This will include various sketches you have made to consider different actions or placement of figures, photographs of the subject that you have taken, and manuals on anatomy for studying specific detail. With all of this information at hand, you can make a drawing that will be accurate and convincing. Let us do this drawing with the direct purpose in mind of transferring it to metal. You may find later on that you have a talent for painting outdoor scenes and subjects, in which case you can make a painting that will not only serve your engraving needs, but when neatly framed, will find a ready market among your sportsman customers. For this demonstration, however, our drawing should be made to be transferred to metal.

Normally when an artist makes such a study he looks for the forms and how they go together. These forms he may indicate with variations in the pencil lines, the lost and found edges being drawn as lighter or heavier lines, in addition to being narrower or wider. The book **An Atlas of Anatomy For Artists** by Fritz Schider (previously mentioned), has a number of drawings by Ingres, Michelangelo, Cloquet, Rubens, Leonardo Da Vinci and others, that are clear examples of how to get the most from your pencils.

Figure 3 shows the oversize drawing completed plus two serious, in-detail studies, and a number of action sketches that were made to help in arriving at the final subject and pose. The template that was traced of the area to be engraved as it is illustrated in figure 1 is shown actual size in relationship to the rest of the drawings. The line drawing immediately above it was made three times larger than actual size. From this you can see the advantage of being able to study the detail when a larger area can be used for the drawing. The slide viewer on the left side of the illustration shows the slide that was finally selected for use. The viewer contains a number of slides that were shot of the herds, as well as individual studies, many of which were used as sources of information. These herds in the Black Hills are an excellent source of material for anyone with a camera. The herds are often near the highway, so that good close-up shots can be gotten without special lenses. If you do have telephoto lenses, so much the better, since you can then get excellent detail studies. At the time these shots were made, there must have been between two or three hundred animals in the herd. The total number of buffalo in the park was about fifteen hundred, according to the park literature. General views of the herd should be taken also. These will provide an unlimited variety of natural poses, from almost every angle, and will make a good record for future use. In many of your nature shots, there will be some details that may be missing, or information that isn't shown clearly. For example, the feet of the buffalo on the slide viewer are concealed in the grass. For this reason you may have to rely on your library, or other shots to supply these details. In this particular instance, there were other shots that were of help, as well as animal and anatomy books. The result is shown in the finished study of the buffalo at the top center of the drawing board. Shown in the upper right hand corner of the illustration is a book of anatomy that is turned to a page on the construction of a horse's leg and foot. The finished study of the horse and rider is shown at the upper left corner of the drawing board.

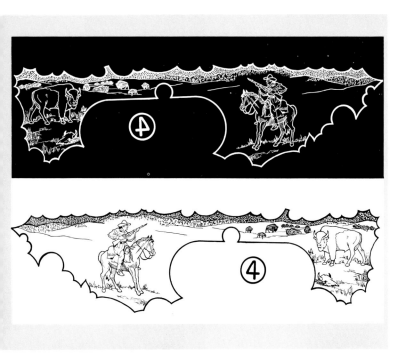

Figure 4 is the finished, actual size reduction of the line drawing of the studies. Before going any further, let me briefly explain a few of the elementary facts about photography for the

benefit of those who are completely unfamiliar with it. When an illustration such as figure 4 (which is black lines on a white background), is placed before a camera and a piece of film is exposed and developed, the resulting film is referred to as a "negative" because it is exactly the reverse of the original drawing. The background which was white on the drawing, comes out totally black on the negative; and the lines that were black on the original, come out clear (in effect, appear white when held up before a light). The only exception to this procedure is, of course, the Polaroid cameras in which the end result is a positive print. In order to obtain an image that duplicates the original drawing (black lines on white background), another exposure through the negative must be made onto either photographic film or paper and developed. Figure 4 is shown both as a negative would appear (black background), and as a positive.

For the most accurate method to transfer an image to the metal, the first step is to get a good black outline. This can be your own drawing, a tracing from a photograph, calendar, magazine cover or an illustration. With this good black outline placed before the camera on a white background, and well lit, reduce the outline on the ground glass to the exact size that you want your design to be. In shooting this outline, a high contrast film, such as Eastman's Kodalith Ortho, gives superior results since it is made for the reproduction of line drawings. Eastman's Plus-X or any of their continuous tone films may be used if necessary. Figure 4 shows both the negative and the positive of such an outline. These are pictured the exact size of the finished panels.

Once you have a sharp, clear negative of your design to size, the most simple and direct course is to use it to transfer the drawing. Should you wish to keep the negative for use in the future, a tracing can be made by taping a piece of clear acetate sheeting over the negative and making the scribed outline on it. An-

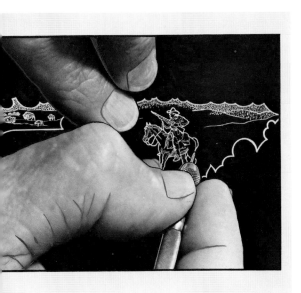

sure, and for maximum stiffness, the needle can be clamped in the pin vise as close to the point as desired. A fine line will hold and transfer enough ivory black to make a definite line. A scribed line that is too coarse will turn up such a large burr that too much ivory black is held in the line, and will transfer a line that is so broad and coarse that much of the accuracy is lost.

The powdered ivory black may be applied to the scribed negative before it is taped in place on the gun or after it has been taped down. Ivory black is an artist's pigment that is used frequently because it doesn't yield such cold blue-greys as lamp black. Lamp black is the more common powdered black, and might be more easily obtained. For this purpose it will work equally well. If you are making a transfer to a dark surface such as a blued firearm, you would use a white or yellow pigment. In an emergency, talcum powder, whiting or almost any other white powder can be used. In figure 6, the negative has been taped securely in place, and has been folded back, ready for the pigment to be applied. The finger is dipped

other possibility is to make a film positive which is simply and easily done. Figure 5 shows the outline of the figure being traced with a needle in a holder on the negative. You will note that the negative has been turned over and the tracing is being made on the wrong side. If you were to lay the negative down with the horse facing in the direction that it was drawn originally and traced your outline, when you turned the negative over to make the transfer the horse would be facing in the opposite direction. The burr cast up by the needle scriber holds the ivory black powder onto the tracing, and it must be turned over to come in contact with the varnish on the surface of the metal into which the design is to be made. So it is obvious that if the horse is drawn originally facing to the right, in order to transfer correctly, the horse must be traced facing to the left.

When making your tracing, whether it be made on negative material or acetate sheeting, make sure that the point of the scriber is very sharp. I use a Starrett pin vise to hold a needle for scribing on acetate. This scribes a fine line, is fairly easy to control without too much pres-

into the black powder and rubbed into the burr cast up by the scriber. Make sure that all parts of the line are carrying the powder. Remove all excess powder with a clean finger tip or with a soft cloth. The finer the transferred line (as long as it is legible), the easier it will be to work to it precisely.

After the pigment has been applied to the scribed lines, get out the damar varnish. This is an artist's varnish, and can be bought in two-ounce bottles in art stores. Many of the present quick-drying varnishes might be used, but I have found the damar varnish works perfectly. It is quick drying, and if it gets a little thick in the bottle as you use it, it may be thinned with turpentine. The two-ounce bottle will last you for years. Make sure that the scribed and pigmented negative is in the exact place you want it to be, and that it is securely taped. Swing it back out of the way, as shown in figure 7. Tip the bottle of damar varnish over until you can pick up a small amount on the end of the finger. Apply a thin coat to the area that is to accept the pigment from the scribed lines. If it is flowed on as a heavy coat of varnish might be applied, the surface will get tacky, and when the negative is burnished down to

transfer the pigment, the tacky surface will come away on the negative, because there was an undried coat of varnish underneath the tacky surface. So make sure that the coating is thin enough to get tacky all the way through, which only takes a few minutes. It can be tested by touching it lightly in an area near the edge where none of the lines will transfer. When you decide that the varnish has reached the right degree of tackiness, the negative can be hinged down and burnished firmly to bring the black pigment into positive contact with the varnish. If the varnish hasn't become too dry, the pigment will be held in the tacky varnish. It is wise to check the taping to be sure that it is not only in the right place, but to be positive that it is fastened securely and will not move while the negative is being burnished.

There are a number of burnishers available to the engraver, usually from the same source that supplies the gravers. Should you not have a regular burnisher, you can use any hard, well-polished material such as ivory or bone. The side of an onglette or point graver that has been polished serves very well. Almost any piece of hard, polished tool steel that has no sharp edges can be used. The burnishing

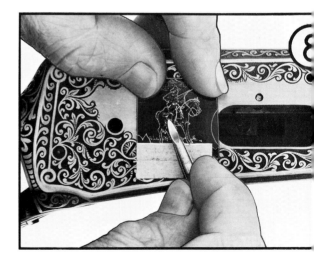

does not require a great deal of pressure. All that is needed is a definite, positive contact between the burr that is holding the ivory black and the tacky varnish. The burnisher shown in figure 8 is homemade from a piece of drill rod and hardened. It was left very hard when it was tempered, being drawn only to a light straw color.

Figure 9 is a picture of the transferred outline. On the first few transfers at least, it would be safer to go over this newly transferred outline with a scriber to insure that your outline will not be accidentally destroyed. When the outline is safely scribed into the metal, you can remove the varnish with a rag dampened with alcohol. This particular design is for two gold inlays, and later in the book we shall complete this project with pictures and a description of the cutting and inlaying of the gold.

The first method, described as the most accurate way of making a transfer, is not the only way in which the camera can be used for this purpose. The second method eliminates the darkroom processing, and all of the tracing is done on the ground glass back of the camera. The ground glass is the viewing glass on the back of the camera on which the image is

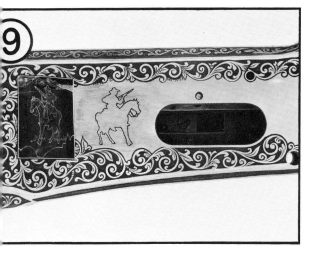

brought into sharp focus. The ground glass occupies exactly the same plane as the film when the exposure is made. So if the image is clear and sharp on the ground glass, it will also be sharp on the negative when it is exposed and developed.

The ground glass, as the name implies, is a piece of glass that has had one side roughened (as with a very fine sand blast). This is done to break up the light rays coming through the lens, so that unless the distances from the object to the lens and that from the lens to the ground glass are exactly right, the image will appear blurred. Once these distances are adjusted correctly, the rays are brought into focus on the ground glass, and the image appears sharp and clear. This roughened side of the glass is on the inside of the camera, which means that there will be not only the thickness of the acetate upon which you will be scribing the lines but also the thickness of the ground glass through which the image must be scribed. You will have to be aware of this parallax, and concentrate on keeping the point of your scriber directly over the point that you are tracing. This does require quite a bit more attention, and is the big reason that you should make your camera set-up in such a manner as to allow yourself to be completely at ease while you are making the tracing.

The diagrammatic silhouette of the little figure making a tracing is a suggestion for the placement of the camera and copy to permit you to make your tracing in a relaxed manner.

118

originally. In order to get an outline that can be transferred either way (there will be times when you will want to reverse the direction that a figure is facing), make a tracing in ink of the outline of the buffalo only. With this black outline drawn on the transparent sheet of acetate, the figure may be traced from either side, and can be transferred in whichever direction you want the figure to face. In looking for animals to copy, you may find a picture that you want to use in which portions of the animal's outline are almost lost in the background. These outlines should be studied and strength-

If you are trying to hold an awkward position while making the tracing, you cannot concentrate your full attention on the copying and the tracing will suffer. Make your set-up so that you can be completely relaxed and the tracing can be given your undivided effort to achieve the utmost accuracy.

I would like to point out that the camera can be used for this purpose by anyone who can work meticulously and deliberately. It will be of great help to those whose artistic talents are not yet developed, but whose interest is genuine. Every time a figure is completed, even with the use of the camera, something will have been learned; and that is far better than just fumbling along producing inaccurate, badly-formed animals and figures.

For an example of this tracing technique, I have taken the buffalo that is shown on the drawing board in figure 3. It is shown placed before the camera, reduced to the desired size, and being traced off directly. When this is done, the resulting tracing, when charged with ivory black and turned over to make a transfer, would be reproduced with the buffalo facing to the right instead of to the left as it was drawn

BY PERMISSION OF LYNTON McKENZIE

An unusual and attractive evening scene engraved by Lynton McKenzie on the floor plate of a double Westley Richards. Unfortunately the photographer's lighting burned out much of the fine detail in the elephant. The effect acheived by McKenzie on the trees, birds and clouds is excellent.

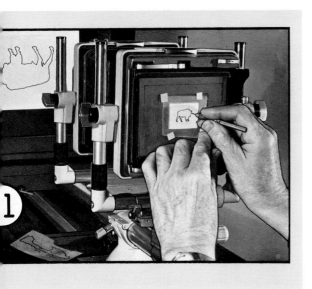

adjusted to the correct size and the tracing being made. After the tracing is completed, it is transferred to the gun in the same way we did the negative earlier.

In going to such lengths in describing the use of the camera as a tool for the engraver, I've tried to keep in mind those who might particularly benefit from its use. For example, it can be an aid to the novice who has talent, but has not yet had the opportunity or the time for training that talent. For the man who has no driving ambition to become an artist but who is intensely intrigued by the craft of designing in metal, the camera can become a big

ened so that there will be no question about the outline. An outline that is vague on the original (if you were tracing from the original), will be even less discernible on the ground glass.

In figure 10 an outline has been drawn in ink on the clear acetate. This outline is drawn slightly heavier than it need be because I wanted it to show up clearly and photograph well for the book. A small piece of tracing paper has been inserted between a portion of the drawing and the clear sheeting in order to show the outline more clearly. One other point to keep in mind when doing reductions to size for future inlays: the outline that you are drawing is going to be cut into metal, and undercut. Do not get carried away with minute details for these small parts for these small parts will be carried out on the gold inlay after it is securely fastened into the gun.

With the outline of the buffalo that was just traced placed before the camera (remember that this outline must be turned over if the tracing is to transfer and face the way that the original is facing), you can take the tracing that was made in figure 1 and reduce the image on the ground glass until it fits into the space you allotted for it. Figure 11 shows the camera

Another of Arnold Griebel's examples for the student to study is this simplified treatment of leaves with an occasional scroll added.

help in the design and drawing field, especially if he is a patient and careful craftsman. Even the accomplished professional could make good use of it at times should he want to.

Naturally the best engravers (those who can rightfully be called master engravers), are men whose interest has always been along the lines of art and decoration. Many of these men have studied in art classes to develop their knowledge of anatomy, their powers of observation, and their talent as draftsmen. With the years of observation, study, and the actual practice of their craft, they have developed skills and their confidence to the point where they can make their layouts (which are sometimes minimal) directly on the metal with no doubts as to the excellence of the finished job. As an old instructor at the Chicago Art Institute used to say, "It would be nice if we could all start in where Michelangelo, Velasquez or Rembrandt left off". However, since it doesn't work that way, and we all start in more or less the same place, it is up to each of us to go as far as we can. In doing so, we should take ad-

vantage of any means to improve our work that presents itself.

Regardless of the degree of accomplishment that an engraver may have attained, the camera can become another important tool. It can reduce the time required in transferring drawings. It can enlarge, reduce, and/or reverse layouts, designs or drawings accurately, and in a minimum of time. It can record details and information for future reference. It can build up a library of facts on animal and bird life that would take years to accumulate if it had to be done with sketches and drawings.

I believe it is the finished job that should receive severe and critical judgment. Examine the work carefully to see if all of the cuts are clean, the design well organized, the straight lines cut straight and to a uniform depth, the curved lines clean and flowing, and the figures well proportioned, with good detail and accurately inlaid. If all of these details are well done, then the job is a work of art, and it should be enjoyed to the fullest...regardless of how the engraver accomplished the results.

Chapter Six
Beginning to Engrave

he preceding five chapters have given the beginner information on design, materials and tools to help prepare him for the time that he will pick up a tool and begin to engrave. A number of beginners have come to me for help in getting started, for invariably they are confronted with situations that seem to unloose a flood of questions. So in this chapter, I would like to take a little more time and answer some of those questions that occur most frequently.

Many phases of the engraver's art comes down to a matter of personal preference, for instance, whether the work is done while standing or sitting. While visiting in Germany recently, a friend told about a visit that he had with an older German engraver who was unquestionably a master. This engraver did his work standing, driving the chisel with his hammer and moving his body and hands to follow the cutting while carrying on a running conversation. An illustration in my files shows Browning's engraving room where many of the engravers are women and all are standing at their work. On the other hand, there are perhaps as many examples of those who do their engraving while seated. One article about an engraving firm in Texas shows five engravers at their tables, all seated. My own work is done while seated, with the exception of some occasional barrel and action work where it seems more convenient to hold the piece in a heavier

vise and to do the work standing. Each engraver will simply have to choose the method most comfortable for him.

Another question that often comes up is the choice of tools, and whether the work is done with hand gravers. The fine old English scroll engraving and much of the finer German engraving were done with hand gravers. Bear in mind that many of these guns were engraved before any of the case hardening or heat treating was done, so that the steels were comparatively mild and easily cut. This applies also to our own early factory-engraved Parkers, L.C. Smiths and Ithacas. As to the choice of tool, the onglette or point graver is the tool that I would recommend using for your beginning efforts. It makes a cut that is quite similar to the square or lozenge graver, and you may find yourself using any one of these as the hand graver that you eventually prefer.

In cutting by hand as well as with hammer and chisel, I use a lubricant on the tip of the tools. I think it not only makes the cutting easier, but also lengthens the time between sharpenings. I use a mixture of kerosene and a machinist's sulfur cutting oil, increasing the proportion of cutting oil for the tougher steels. On gold and silver, add a few drops of kerosene. For a convenient oil dispenser, I took a fired 20mm shell casing and sawed it off about one inch above the primer end. Into this casing, which has good weight and doesn't tip over

122

easily, I put some cotton moistened with a few drops of kerosene and a few drops of sulfur cutting oil. Do not get too much oil in the cotton. If you can see the oil in the cotton, too much has been put in. When the graver point is dipped into it, the tip will come out carrying a drop of oil, and when the tool touches the work this drop of oil will spread all over the area that you are working on. All that is needed is a film of oil over the tip of the tool. If there is too much oil in the cotton simply absorb some of it with a paper towel or rag. The kerosene eventually evaporates or is used, and should be replaced with a few drops at a time. This dispenser should be kept close at hand and dipping into it will soon become a habit. I find it is especially beneficial when using hand gravers.

One of the problems that seems to plague the novice is keeping the point intact. They frequently remark on how often they must stop to sharpen the tool. The most important thing (beside practice) is an understanding of why the points are breaking. To state it as simply as possible, the center line of the tool must be headed SQUARELY into the cut at all times. This applies especially to any changes in the direction of the cut. Assuming that the onglette has been ground to the correct angles and that the face of the tool is square with the sides, this is most apparent in cutting a straight line. As long as the tool is cutting squarely into the work (neither tipping, turning, raising or lowering), the line must come out straight. This

is true of a straight line and it is even more important on the curved lines if the point is to be preserved. It also applies to the long slow curve as well as to the fast, tight scroll. In figure 1 is a diagram that may help you to visualize the relationship between the position of the tool and the curve that you are cutting. As the scroll progresses inward, this same relationship must be maintained. You will note in the diagram that the top edge of the graver is tipped slightly outward (or to your right) as it is driven around the scroll counter-clockwise. In going around a curve clockwise, the top of the tool would be tipped outward (which in this case would be tipped to your left). The important part of the illustration is the fact that the tool must be at a right angle to the radius of a circle if it were to be drawn exactly at the point where your tool is cutting. It is when the tool is turned or twisted and it is not meeting the cut squarely that the broken points occur. As you practice, especially with the hand tool, you will develop a feel for the tool to a point that when the cuts are going well you will know it.

The onglette or point graver die sinkers chisel that will be driven with an engraver's hammer is a good tool with which to start your practice. You can make up handles for the hand

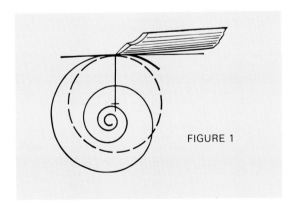

FIGURE 1

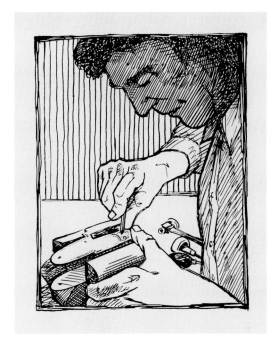

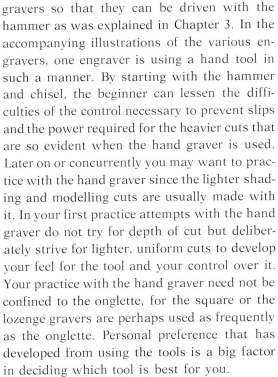

gravers so that they can be driven with the hammer as was explained in Chapter 3. In the accompanying illustrations of the various engravers, one engraver is using a hand tool in such a manner. By starting with the hammer and chisel, the beginner can lessen the difficulties of the control necessary to prevent slips and the power required for the heavier cuts that are so evident when the hand graver is used. Later on or concurrently you may want to practice with the hand graver since the lighter shading and modelling cuts are usually made with it. In your first practice attempts with the hand graver do not try for depth of cut but deliberately strive for lighter, uniform cuts to develop your feel for the tool and your control over it. Your practice with the hand graver need not be confined to the onglette, for the square or the lozenge gravers are perhaps used as frequently as the onglette. Personal preference that has developed from using the tools is a big factor in deciding which tool is best for you.

I have gone through my files, and the illustrations shown here are some sketches that have been made from photos of various engravers at work with their own work-holding devices. In addition to the regular engraver's ball, you will find swivel bench vises, several kinds of adjustable vises, and clamping fixtures of ingenious design being used to hold the work. Holding and clamping fixtures can be made of hardwood to be used in your bench vise or engraver's ball. In clamping some receivers and parts, considerable care should be used to prevent bending or deforming the part to be engraved.

The hammers that you see used in most of the illustrations are the chasers hammer. These have a large face, are usually comparatively light in weight, and are available in three different sizes: 1-1/8", 1-1/4" and 1-5/16" diameters. The hammer that I use most frequently has a 1-1/8" face. I have the two heavier hammers, and use them when heavier cuts are required and more metal has to be removed. The lighter hammer is an excellent choice to begin with, and the heavier sizes can be added when you feel the need for them. Naturally, any comparatively light weight hammer that you may have can be used, but the chasers hammer is the design that has evolved as the one most suitable for this work. One feature of the chasers hammer that will not be found in the lightest of machinist's hammers is the thin, springy handles. These light handles give a resiliency and life to the engraver's hammer that makes the common hammer handle feel stiff and unyielding. So, if you are using a small regular or machinist's hammer, at least you can thin down the handle so as to get some of this springy quality.

When you have decided to try your hand at engraving, you will want to buy equipment slowly as a matter of prudence. For example, several (or even only one) die sinkers onglette chisel and one or two hand gravers in the ong-lette and square shapes are all that is needed to give engraving a good try. If you have a small bench vise (preferably of the swivel type) you can forego the expensive engraver's ball. After you have given it a try and find that you have the ability - and especially the desire - to engrave, then you can add the other tools that you may need. Should you decide that you really want to put some time and effort into engrav-ing, you will find that as your skill and expe-rience increases, so will your accumulation of tools!

Let us assume that you decided to take up engraving seriously, and that you now have three or four years of experience back of you. You will also have acquired quite a large assort-ment of tools. As this array of tools grows, some thought should be given to arranging them so that a specific tool can be located quickly without instituting a lengthy search for it. Some men are naturally methodical, while others may work in a helter-skelter fashion. The end results may be equal, but the odds are good that the one who works with care will accom-plish his job with less distraction and lost motion and as a consequence will finish his job in less time. The arrangement that I have made for my tools is shown in some of the ac-companying illustrations. There are doubtless

to the frustration, confusion and the time lost in a sometimes futile search on a cluttered bench for a particular tool. While I have quite a number of gravers, punches and files, I still have many holes available for additional tools. So, for those of you who are starting out, you should organize your tools to make them as orderly and easy to find as possible.

For your first practice attempts you will want some flat pieces of metal. The Southwest Smelting and Refining Company sells practice

other plans that might suit your ideas better, but this has worked out quite well for me. It is simply a lazy suzan, 13 inches in diameter, with 404 holes for holding the tools, and requires only slightly more than one square foot of bench space. The holes for the flat and the round gravers have the number of the graver beside each hole so that any specific tool can be chosen instantly. The lining gravers are identified as to size and number of lines, and the set of beading tools is numbered from one to ten. This orderliness costs little in time compared

plates for engravers. These are copper and are supplied in a small size of 2 x 3-1/2", and a large size is of 2-3/8 x 3-3/4". I also always have some steel practice plates around, either hot rolled or cold rolled, from 1/16" to 1/4" thick, depending on what is available. The surfaces of the steels as they come from the mill are not good for engraving for the hot rolled steel has a rough, hard scale formed during the processing. The cold rolled steel is cleaner and smoother, but it too has a rather tough outer skin which is a result of the final rolling operation. For my own use the plates are surface

ground on both sides until this objectionable surface is removed and the plates are perfectly flat. If you have a machine shop available where you can have this done, it is the easiest and most satisfactory way of having your plates prepared. These surfaces can be filed and polished by hand but this is a time consuming and disagreeable task. A belt sander could be used for an easier and faster job. In any case, the flat plate will minimize the difficulties of your first attempts at engraving. If you do not have an engraver's vise, screw the plate to a fairly thick block of wood (at least an inch thick) a little larger than the plate. With the plate attached to the block of wood, it can not only be held in your vise but you can try your hand gravers by resting it on an engraver's pad, a sand bag or even on the bench top. A word of caution is in order: when using your hand tools in this fashion, be sure that the hand which is supporting the block is below the surface of the plate (this was the reason for the thickness of the block of wood). Slips are going to occur and if the hand that is supporting the block is directly in the path of the tool, you are going to stab yourself.

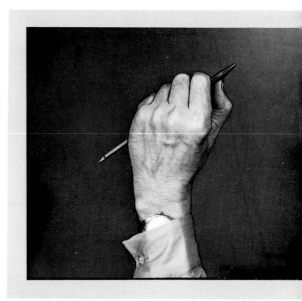

FIGURE 3

After reviewing the instructions on sharpening the tools, make sure that they are correctly shaped with all traces of the coarse stoning removed so that the edges are really sharp, with no burrs or roughness. This first plate can be simply a means of getting acquainted with the feel of the gravers and the handling of the hammer. At first, you will find yourself watching the hammer part of the time to be sure it is making contact. This tendency will soon disappear and all of your attention can then be concentrated at the cutting end of the tool.

Now let us take our first practice plate, fasten it in the vise and try some actual cutting. By examining some of the sketches of various engravers at work, you can see how the die sinkers chisel or graver is grasped in the left hand (all instructions will be given for the person who works right-handed). A real tight, rigid grip is not necessary or desirable when working on average materials. Occasionally some extremely tough, hard material may be encountered where a firm, rigid control will be required, but normally, a firm hold that can main-

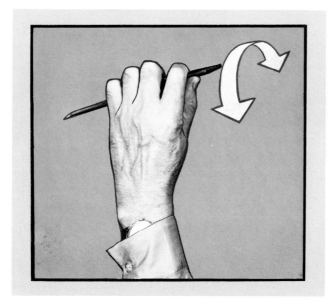

FIGURE 2

There is one other movement of the tool that is very important: the vertical movement at the hammer end of the tool to change the angle of the tool in relationship to the work. Raising the back of the tool while striking it with the hammer will cause the tool to enter more deeply into the work. Lowering the hammer end of the tool while it is being struck will cause the tool to emerge from the work. The beginner usually finds that cutting a straight line to a uniform depth is one of the more difficult cuts to achieve. The difficulty arises when the hammer end of the tool deviates from its vertical position in relationship to the surface of the work. Once the tool changes from this uniform position ever so slightly (in any direction), its tendency is to continue this new course until it is consciously corrected. In contrast to a straight line of uniform depth, there will be cuts where the line starts out thin and shallow, becomes wider and deeper and then gradually return to a thin shallow line. In this case quite a lot of vertical movement of the hammer end of the tool may be used. Determining how these different movements effect the cut is, of course, the purpose of your practice. But before taking up the tool, there are a few remarks about the hammer that should be made.

tain complete control of the tool is all that is needed. You will note in figure 2 that the tool is held between the thumb and forefinger, and in the fingers so that the tool is at the end of the palm to permit the most flexibility in the use of the tool. If a tighter, more rigid control is called for, the forward end of the tool may be dropped back until it rests under the outside of the palm as in figure 3. There is another movement that will be given to the tool and this is shown by the arrow in figure 2. By rolling the tool between the thumb and forefinger, the top edge of the tool may be tipped to the right or the left as has been referred to previously. When cutting a scroll counterclockwise the top edge of the tool will be tipped to the right, and when cutting the scroll clockwise, the top edge of the tool will be tipped to the left. When filling in the decorative part of the scrolls with the small tight curves, this rolling of the tool will be used a great deal. In cutting large scrolls and long slow curves, the wrist may be used to roll the tool. Lowering the wrist will bring the tip edge of the tool toward you, while raising the wrist will tip the top edge away from you. It may be some time before you will take full advantage of the wonderful flexibility and control that the wrist provides. Eventually, however, you will be using all of these wrist and rolling movements in various combinations to produce the cut that you want.

To the average beginner, a hammer is for driving nails. The harder the blows, the quicker

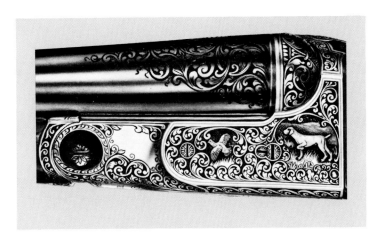

the nail is driven. To do this, a full arm movement is usually employed to develop as much power as possible. In engraving, very seldom (in fact, you could say never), is a die sinkers chisel or graver attacked as one would drive a nail. The chasers hammer has a light springy handle, as previously described, and is not made to deliver the heavy blows for which the carpenter's and machinist's hammers are designed. In driving a nail the hammer may be raised a foot or more from the nail to gain power and momentum for the stroke; the engraver's hammer may be withdrawn as little as an inch, and in many cases only fractions of an inch in its tapping action. When starting, this distance will probably be greater than it will eventually become when you have learned to use the hammer properly. It is desirable to increase your strokes per minute as this is one factor that will contribute to the smoothness of the cut. One way of doing this is to shorten the back stroke of the hammer.

FIGURE 3a

In figure 3a are shown three scrolls magnified three times. The same tool was used in cutting all three scrolls and the same hammer was used on scrolls 1 and 2. On the number 3 scroll, the tool was powered by a pneumatic hammer, which will be described later in the book. This illustration shows graphically the relationship that the power of the stroke and the strokes per minute have to the character of the resulting cut. In scroll number 1, the blows were relatively heavy and the backstroke quite long. There were about sixty strokes used in cutting this scroll and each stroke is readily distinguishable under magnification. If you can visualize the hammer end of the tool as it went around the rough scroll (in a much wider arc), you can see that the intervals between hammer blows along that arc are quite long. This results in each heavy blow appearing as a straight segment of the curve. Scroll number 2 used approximately seven hundred strokes to complete. The length of the back stroke was shortened, the individual blows were much lighter, and the strokes per minute were greatly increased. Due to the increase in the strokes per minute, the time required to cut the two scrolls was about the same. You can now see what happens when you break each one of those segments in scroll number 1 into a greater number of smaller, lighter cuts. With each lighter cut blending into the following one you can understand why these cuts have resulted in

The two sides of the Parker on the preceding pages and this illustration were engravings done for Lloyd Thompson of Boone, Iowa. The dog is in 24k gold with the quail done in silver. The gun was a light weight bird gun with a straight English style stock in the VH grade.

a smoother curve. To repeat, the smoother cut is a direct result of an increased number of lighter hammer blows. In scroll number 3, the machine was set to deliver 1200 strokes per minute, and it was set for lighter blows. The resultant cut was an even cleaner scroll. With this explanation, you can increase the scope of your practice cuts to include experiments with longer and shorter back strokes, increased strokes per minute and lighter or heavier hammer blows.

In the first wrist action technique, start with the forearm parallel to the floor and the palm down. Take the hammer in the left hand as shown in figure 4, and place the handle of the hammer into the palm of the right hand naturally, with the thumb along the shaft of the handle. The palm of the hand and the face of the hammer are both parallel to the floor. Grasp the handle easily and naturally. Now, if you flex the wrist up until the palm is nearly at a right angle to the forearm, you will find the hammer face in a vertical plane. If the hand with the hammer were facing an imaginary clock with the hand holding the hammer at the center of the clock, the face of the hammer would be in a position about opposite 10:30 o'clock and parallel to the clock face.

With the hand remaining in this position, try moving the wrist forward and backward so that the hammer head travels in an arc about 1" in length. Take a pencil in the left hand and hold it in front of the hammer head. By moving only the wrist, tap on the pencil and see how natural the movement seems, see figure 5. With the forearm still parallel to the floor and the wrist still bent at a right angle, rotate the forearm and hand with the hammer to the right, and then to the left as far as you

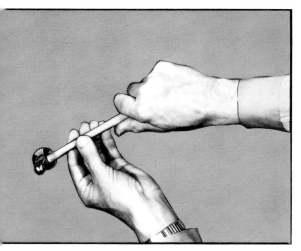

FIGURE 4

I want to reemphasize the fact that you will develop an entirely different method of handling the hammer than the one that you use to drive nails. Instead of the full arm swing, you will be using only your wrist and forearm, and it will be the wrist that develops most of the action. There are two distinct actions of the wrist that can be used in your beginning practice. Also, there is another method where an extremely light, short, rapid stroke is achieved that employs only the fingers of the hand to supply the action. Scroll number 2 was cut using this technique.

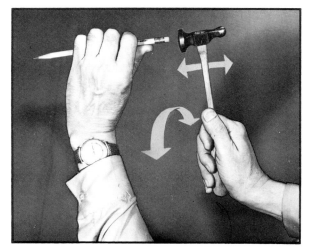

FIGURE 5

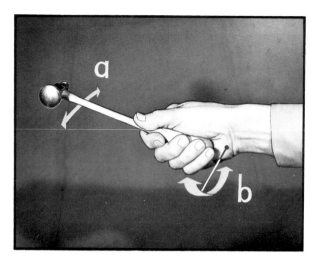

FIGURE 6

can comfortably. You will find that you can rotate the hammer face in an arc of about 120 degrees with no strain, and that the hammer face remains virtually parallel to the clock face. Also you will notice that any place along that arc, from about 9:30 to 2:30 o'clock, there is no restriction on the tapping movement that you can give to the hammer, simply by moving the wrist forward and backward. By moving the body and the arm, in addition to the rotation of the forearm, the range of the hammer's travel can be increased beyond the 120 degree arc.

In the second wrist action technique, place the hammer in the hand as you did in figure 4, with the palm of the hand and the face of the hammer parallel to the floor. Now, rotating the forearm, turn the hand until the palm of the hand and the face of the hammer are in a vertical plane as shown at figure 6. From this position the head of the hammer can be driven either by flexing the wrist as at figure 6a, or by rotating the palm back and forth as at figure 6b. Not only can you use either of these movements but you can go from one to the other smoothly. For the purpose of describing them more clearly, we have shown the action at figure 5 and at figure 6 as two different actions. In actual

practice these actions will merge from one to the other, as you work on varying contours and shapes.

The final hammer technique is especially good on light cuts, and I find it exceptionally useful on fine, delicate cuts for the extra light taps gives time for excellent control of the tool. This method was used in cutting the scroll number 2, in figure 3a. This action is shown in figure 7. Note that the hammer is grasped fairly close to the head. For lighter blows move the hand closer to the head of the hammer, and for somewhat heavier taps move the hand a little farther down the handle. The hammer is held firmly between the thumb and the forefinger, and this point becomes the fulcrum for the movement of the hammer. The second finger limits the forward motion of that part of the handle. The third and little fingers limit the backward motion of the handle. By moving these three fingers forward and backward as shown at A in figure 7, a very short, rapid backstroke with a light tap can be achieved. The wrist and hand should not be held rigid, and may contribute a small amount to the action; however, the principal action will be in these three fingers. This technique works very well for me when light, delicate cuts are to be made.

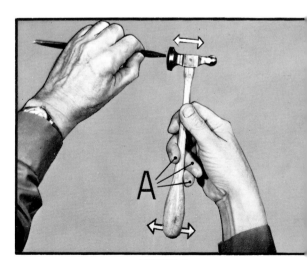

FIGURE 7

The descriptions given here are not to be taken as rules, but as an aid for the beginner who has no idea how to use the engraver's hammer. It would be well for the beginner to study these instructions and use them on his practice plates, rather than taking a hammer and striking out in a hit-or-miss fashion. The wrist and forearm action may seem strange at first, but with persistence a fine control can be developed. Examine closely the sketches of the various engravers at their work, and see how

When cutting the counter-clockwise curves, the top edge of the tool is tipped to your right. When cutting a clockwise curve, tip the top edge of the tool to your left. In practicing, try tipping the tool to different angles on different cuts and determine what the results are. If you cut a curve in which you do not tip the tool, you will find that the outside edge is not cutting well because it lacks the clearance on the curve that the inside edge of the tool has. As the tool is tipped, this clearance on the outside edge is increased which improves the cutting quality. As the tool is tipped increasingly to the outside, the width of the line will be increased. There is a practical limit to how far this tipping can be carried, and with several cuts you can determine this limit. Figure 10 shows a practice plate with scrolls cut to the left, to the right and in a variety of sizes.

When starting your cuts you will find that applying a little extra downward pressure at the point of the tool will aid in getting the tool to enter the steel, instead of skidding across the surface. As soon as the tool has entered the cut, this pressure at the point can be relaxed, and the tool will stay in the cut naturally as long as the correct angle is maintained. Also, raising the hammer end of chisel a little higher than is necessary for the main

FIGURE 9

they are holding and using their tools. In practicing and experimenting, you will develop the technique that works best for you. But you will discover that you are using one or a combination of the basic movements that have been described here.

Now, to the practice plates. This first practice plate is an exercise to get the feel of the hammer and the graver. The illustrations show the onglette being used. Figure 9 shows straight cuts and various curves to be practiced. In making the straight cuts, the top edge of the tool is held squarely above the cut.

FIGURE 10

132

part of the cut will help in getting the cut started. If this is done, make your taps lightly and drop the tool gradually to the position that it will assume while the main part of the cut is being made. The tapping should continue while the tool is being lowered. Normally you will experience no difficulty in getting the tool to enter mild steel.

How many practice plates should you cut? Cut as many as required to develop enough confidence in your hammer and graver that you can cut a straight line which is reasonably straight and even, and a curved line that is fairly smooth, both in the curve and in the cutting. It should not be expected that these practice cuts will be perfect before you actually start to engrave patterns. Actually, from the time you first pick up a tool, each cut that you make will be a "practice" cut. When your cuts become well done and are cut with no conscious effort, you might say that your days of practicing are finished. From the start, you should try to appraise your work with as detached and critical judgment as you can. One good way of attaining this degree of detachment is to occasionally view your drawing or design in a small mirror which doubles any irregularities, and makes them immediately apparent. It helps too, if you have a goal ahead of you. With all of the good reproductions of engraving available in

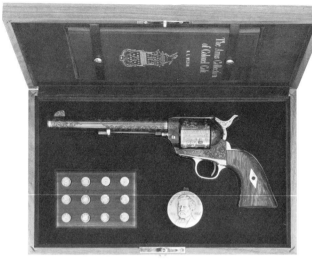

A Thousand Dollar grade custom deluxe Colonel Samuel Colt Sesquicentennial. The entire production of 50 of these pistols was engraved and gold inlaid by A.A. White. Courtesy of A.A. White Engravers, Inc.

books and magazines, keep some of the best close at hand where you can study and compare them to your work. From this comparison you will get ideas, and the incentive that will bring an improvement to your work.

When you feel that you have cut enough practice plates to be able to achieve a reasonably smooth cut, look at the basic scrolls in the chapter on design and begin to cut them on new practice plates, filling them with scrolls, as shown in figure 10. When practicing scrolls be sure to cut them both clockwise and counterclockwise. If the cutting seems more difficult going in one direction than the other, practice the more difficult one the most until you are equally at ease going in either direction.

Assuming that you have practiced diligently and that both your straight cuts and scrolls are acceptably well cut, let us take a practice plate and carry a design from start to finish. We shall take a Springfield floorplate and start with a conventional scroll design. This design (or any other that you might prefer) can be used to cut a Springfield plate, practice plate or even a different floorplate. I want to introduce this method to the beginner because it is one that will allow you many chances to alter and experiment with the de-

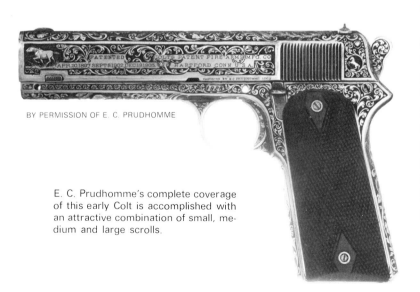

BY PERMISSION OF E. C. PRUDHOMME

E. C. Prudhomme's complete coverage of this early Colt is accomplished with an attractive combination of small, medium and large scrolls.

sign, before you finally commit yourself to one plan. However, after you have put a great deal of time and thought into making your plan, do not allow yourself to deviate from it. Any extemporaneous cuts or improvements are almost always regretted. Save your improvements for the next design. After you have gained experience, there will develop an affinity between your designing and your cutting that will make possible the freehand cutting of certain areas, with an assurance that they will be well cut. But, in starting out, stick to your design.

FIGURE 11

To begin, we need an accurate outline of the floorplate. Attach a piece of tough tracing paper a little larger than the plate to the plate with masking tape as shown in figure 11. Make the tracing paper of such size that it will wrap around the face of the plate and lap over the back about 3/8''. Fasten a piece of masking tape to this edge so that the paper can be pulled taut across the face of the plate, and tape it down firmly. Your plate should now look like the one in figure 12.

For the next step, a pencil with a hard

lead is preferred (a 7H pencil was used in this instance) since it will make a sharper, more accurate line. The pencil is held at an angle as shown in figure 13, and an outline is made of the outside edge of the plate. Being taped down securely, the two outside edges are easily marked. At the two ends, however, the contours being different, the paper will need to be held down as the pencil traces around these edges. Also mark around the plate release hole at the end of the plate. Figure 14 shows the finished tracing, actual size. Note that a center line has been established, and several lines drawn at right angles to it. On each side of the center line equal parallel lines have also been drawn to keep the design centered. As many of these guide lines can be drawn as you think will help you in your designing. Our design can be drawn directly onto this tracing of the plate that you have just completed. However, I prefer to keep this tracing intact for future use, and by fastening this tracing to a piece of cardboard it can be used repeatedly. Figure 15 shows a piece of tracing paper taped over the original outline, and a design being finished. Also shown are a number of pieces of tracing paper that have been cut to size to be used in the development of the design. If the design

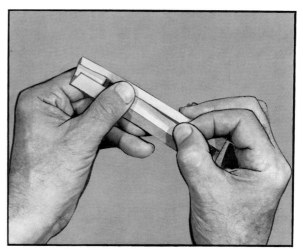

FIGURE 12

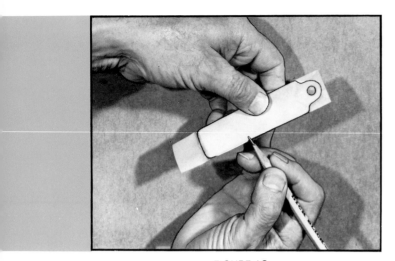

FIGURE 13

sign that is underneath. With the cleaned-up new design in place, you can carry it forward or make any changes in it that you desire. This process can be continued as many times as it is necessary until you are satisfied with the final effort. Figure 16 shows the final design, at actual size, for a Springfield floorplate.

With the design completed, its transfer can be done with the matte acetate, ivory black and damar varnish technique as was described in Chapter 6. However, I would like to demonstrate a different procedure here to give you some choice as to the method of transferring the design. Since the design was made to be

becomes indefinite and messy, put a clean piece of tracing paper over it and lift off any part of the design that you might wish to keep, with clean pencil lines, then remove the untidy de-

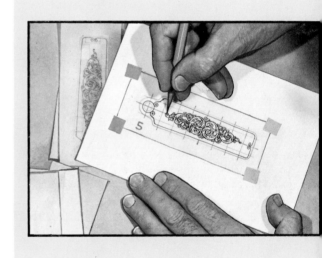

FIGURE 15

applied to a Springfield floorplate, we shall do our transferring and cutting on one of these plates. First polish the plate so that you have a good surface. (This design can, of course, be applied to a practice plate, or another floorplate if you prefer.) Take the polished plate and clean it thoroughly. I use an industrial solvent, trichlorethylene, sold under the label

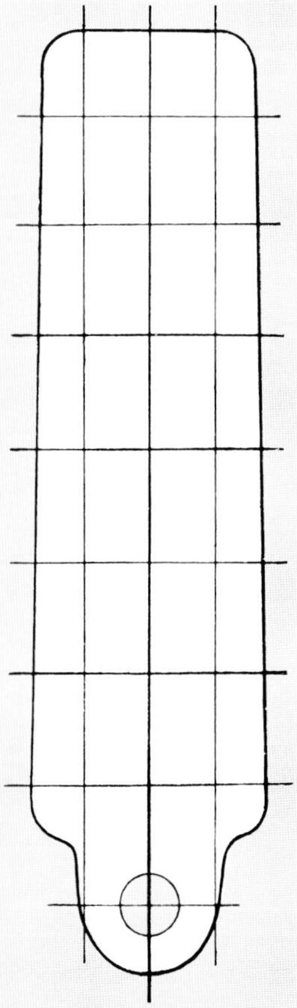

FIGURE 14    FIGURE 16

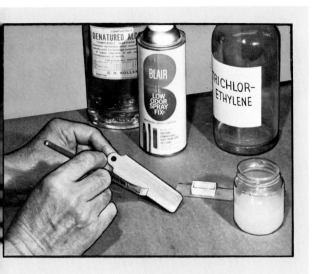

FIGURE 17

rub the brush over the cake of Chinese White. The bonding agent is dissolved and the brush picks up the pigment and some of the bonding agent. The longer the wet brush is applied to the cake, the more pigment is loosened and picked up by the brush. It takes only a few minutes to apply this coating, so you can try it and if you have applied too much or too little, you can wipe the plate clean and try it again. After a few experiments, you will be able to judge the amount that you will want to apply. As you are brushing the color onto the plate, you can blow on the plate to hasten the drying time. Any slight tendency of the coating to crawl can be corrected by continuous brushing as the coating dries. Before the coating becomes so dry that the brush wants to drag and roughen it, stop brushing. If everything has gone well, you will have a smooth, thin coating on the metal which is not white, but a shade of gray. If it does show up white, the coating is much too thick and it will quite likely tend to chip off when it is worked on. The shade of gray that a thinner coat produces will show a pencil mark or tracing very well. To strengthen the coating of water color and make it more resistant to scratching and abrasion while transferring and cutting the design, a light film of an artist's fixative spray used to fix pencil

"Trichlene D" and manufactured by du Pont for use in degreasing operations. Any other solvent that will dissolve the grease could be used, such as naptha, acetone, alcohol, or lacquer thinner (which is very effective). These must all be used with the proper precautions as to ventilation and fire hazard.

We must have the plate free of grease because we are going to cover it with a coat of Chinese White, a water soluble artist's color that will not adhere where any grease is present. To insure that our Chinese White is going to adhere to the plate, take the plate that we have cleaned with the solvent and give it a good washing with soap and water. If the plate is thoroughly clean, the water will cover it with no tendency to bead up or crawl. Figure 17 shows the plate being coated with the Chinese White. The brush is a red sable "Brights" for oil colors, about 5/16" wide. Almost any available brush could be used, but a red sable hair brush is best because it retains its life very well when it is used in water. A thin coat is enough to dull the reflective quality of the metal and to hold a pencil mark. To apply this thin coat, dip the brush into clean water and

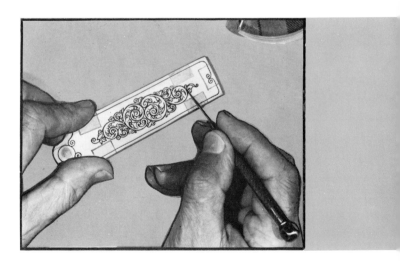

FIGURE 18

drawings to prevent smudging can be sprayed onto the Chinese white. With a thin coating of the water color and a thin spray of the fixative, the cutting can be done right through this coating without the necessity of scribing the design into the metal.

With the design and the plate prepared, we can transfer the drawing. Rub the back of the design with the broad side of a soft pencil to cover it with a coating of graphite. Then rub it with a piece of cloth or a paper towel to distribute the graphite evenly and smoothly over the surface of the paper. If the excess is not removed, accidental pressure on the design can result in a blurred transfer.

Next, cut away the excess tracing paper so that the design will lay down on the plate with no paper projecting beyond the edges of the plate. I use transparent tape to attach the design to the plate since it will interfere with neither your vision nor the tracing. Exercise care in placing the tracing so that it is centered precisely fore and aft and from side to side. With the design taped securely in the correct position on the plate, we can trace the design. A sharp pencil is generally used in making a tracing; however, I prefer to use a standard Starret scriber point that has been made into a

FIGURE 20

stylus by stoning the point to a rounded end. After shaping, the point was given a high polish. A pencil will lose its sharp point quickly, but this steel point will last for many tracings and will make a uniform line. Figure 18 shows the design taped to the plate and the stylus making an impression. As the stylus goes over the design, it leaves a shiny surface where the dull pencil line was so you can see the parts that have been traced. Since you covered all of the surface on the reverse side of the design with graphite, any place that the stylus strays from the design will register. Sometimes, instead of coating the entire reverse side of the design with graphite, I prefer to trace the reverse side of the design carefully. The advantage of this method is that the stylus cannot transfer anything except the design. If the stylus should stray from the design, nothing will be transferred. This being the case, the design need not be retraced line by line, but simply transferred by burnishing over the whole design with a steel or ivory burnisher. If this method is used, be sure to omit spreading or smoothing the graphite with the cloth as you will wipe out all your careful tracing.

After going over the design with the stylus, remove the tape from the two ends and one side of the plate. Leave the design attached by one side as shown in figure 19. Check your tracing, and if there are any places that were missed, fold the design back onto the plate and complete the tracing. Note in figure 19 that no attempt was made to trace the border lines

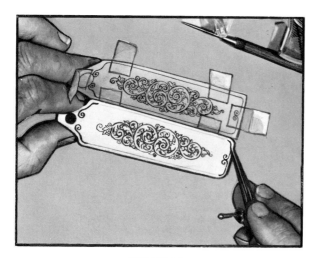

FIGURE 19

along the edges of the plate or around the plate release hole. These lines are more easily and accurately done with a pair of dividers by placing one leg inside the hole, against the outside edge. The inside, or guide, leg will follow around the edge of the hole, keeping the scribed line (outside leg) equidistant from the edge all around the hole. Next comes the actual cutting of the plate. Figure 20 shows the transferred design with the main lines cut. When the engraver makes his design, he begins with the

there is an order to the cutting, and as it was with your designing, the main lines will be cut first. After you have become experienced, the designing and cutting of these basic lines will present no problem. However, the degree of perfection with which these main lines are designed and cut will determine how you will be rated as an engraver, so it is imperative that your best efforts go into their execution. Just how diligently you have done your practicing and how far you have come will be easily

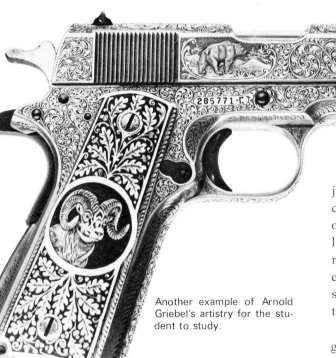

BY PERMISSION OF ARNOLD GRIEBEL

Another example of Arnold Griebel's artistry for the student to study.

judged in your cutting of these revealing principal lines. After you have completed cutting of the main lines, you can continue cutting the larger and more important of the lines that remain to be cut; or you can cut and complete each part of a scroll as you prefer. Leave fine shading lines until last, for they are done after the design has been completely cut.

You will see in figure 21 that the background of the scrolls has been cut away, which in effect raises the scrolls. In cutting away this background, do not work over the scrolls and across them, but start your cuts in the corners and work with the scrolls to avoid leaving unsightly tool marks on the scrolls. The beginner might find it easier (instead of removing the metal) to simply give a texture to the background metal with punch work. A beading punch is quite often used for this purpose, and each punch mark leaves a small raised dot that is a portion of a sphere in shape. This makes an attractive background that is easy to clean.

big things first, such as the size of the scrolls and the way in which they flow together or intertwine. The details will fall into place easily after the big design is completed. If the large over-all design is not pleasing, all of the fine detail that is added will not cover up the lopsided scrolls and the uneven transitions from one scroll to the next. So it is with the cutting:

138

However, since the punch is a little difficult to make, I would suggest that the beginner give the background a matte texture with a center punch since these are readily available. The point should be ground to a fairly slender taper so that the tip can be easily seen, and the very tip can be ground or stoned to an included angle of from 40 to 60 degrees as a sharp, fine pointed punch will make impressions that are unnecessarily deep. A punch with a more obtuse angle will require fewer contacts to cover a given area and the burrs cast up by this punch will not be so evident. Also, with lighter taps of the hammer, the marks will be shallower, making the matted surface easier to clean. The punch should be held just off the surface of the metal with the weight of the hammer driving it lightly into the metal. The finished Springfield floorplate is shown in figure 21.

FIGURE 21

In order to give the beginner a choice, I am including designs for a Mauser 98 and for an Enfield Model 1917 floorplate. Let us try another scroll with only minor changes, making this design for a Mauser 98 floorplate. Since the same method of transferring the design will be used, only the basic outline of the plate and the layout will be shown. Figure 22 shows the outline of the Mauser 98 floorplate at actual size so you can draw your own layout from it if you want a design that is completely personal from start to finish. In designing this plate, let's extend the range of our experience by using smaller scrolls. You will want to master the use of various sizes of scrolls so that you will be prepared to present a variety of effects to prospective customers. Naturally, the smaller scrolls will require a different touch when it comes to cutting the design. The lines will be cut finer and less deeply incised, but they should be cut with all of the boldness and control that goes into cutting heavier scrolls.

Figure 23 shows the completed layout. Note that the panel is designed so that it may be left clear for an initial or a monogram to be cut into the center area. The texture applied in this open area is a common pattern consisting of crossed lines with a punch mark set in the center of each square. Sometimes the punch mark is done with a beading punch at the intersections of the lines. One German shotgun in my collection has the butt plate treated in this fashion, and each small square has a punch

FIGURE 22 FIGURE 23

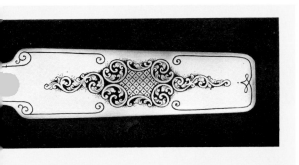

FIGURE 24

mark in the center in the form of an asterisk. In general, these lines are approximately at right angles to each other, but there is nothing mandatory about the angle to be used and the punch work can cover a range as great as your imagination and skill will permit. Figure 24 shows the completed floorplate slightly undersize.

The 1917 Enfield floorplate is larger than either the Mauser or Springfield plate, so I have designed this plate with some larger scrolls along with several smaller ones. Human nature being what it is, the engraver must be prepared for any kind of design requirement. One customer may be completely averse to accepting large, bold scrolls as being artistic, while the next may think that fine delicate scroll work is too dainty and effeminate to grace a powerful rifle or shotgun. You must be prepared to cut both large scrolls and small scrolls so well that the shape and cutting is above reproach. So prepare yourself to handle the type of work that your occasional demanding customer is going to require. Most customers, perhaps even the majority, are open to the suggestions and recommendations that an engraver might offer. Then you can allow your experience and judgment to make designs that will be agreeable to the customer and a pleasure for you to work with. However, with this large Enfield plate, I have visualized a big man demanding some large, bold scrolls that will show up clear across the room when the rifle is standing in

a gun cabinet. Figure 25 is a plan for an Enfield floorplate. Here again you may want to develop your own design or some other plan that you particularly admire, so the plan is shown actual size for your convenience. Figure 26 is a layout made for tracing and transferring for the Enfield floorplate. After the plate was prepared and cut, it was photographed. The finished plate is shown at figure 27. The photographs of the completed Springfield, Mauser and Enfield floorplates are all pictured slightly undersize, while the drawings are shown actual size.

The hand graver is the one tool which seems to bring the most grief and difficulty to the beginning engraver. Let us go back to our example of the hammer and the nail. You know that you cannot take a nail and simply push it

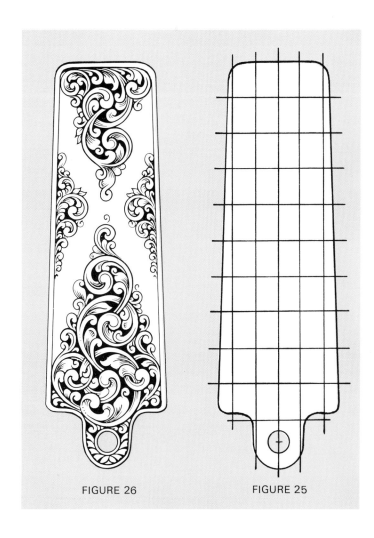

FIGURE 26   FIGURE 25

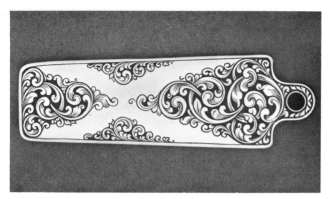

FIGURE 27

into the wood with your thumb. But, with a
few light taps of a hammer, you can start the
nail and then it can be easily driven into the
wood. The chasers hammer and chisel operates
on this principle, while the hand graver com-
pares more nearly to pushing the nail into the
wood with the thumb. The difference, of course,
is that instead of only the pressure of the thumb
against the small head of the nail, you have the
force exerted against the graver point distributed over the large handle of the graver pressing
against the heel of the hand. It is this steady
power expended through the hand to the tool
that must separate the metal to make the cut.
As you make a cut you must apply pressure not

only to force the tool forward, but you must use
varying amounts of pressure downward with
the forefinger of the tool hand and also against
one side or other of the tool as you move around
a curve.

The angles to which the tool is sharpened
and the degree of keeness to which the cutting
edges are finished both contribute to the per-
formance this tool will give as it cuts a line. In
determining the angle and the pressures at
which the tool functions best, you must get
what engravers refer to as the "feel" of the
tool. If the tool is carefully and properly sharpened and the work piece held securely, you

FIGURE 29

should soon become accustomed to the tool. Do
not attempt to remove a great deal of metal in
your initial efforts, but try for light, uniform
cuts and work to develop confidence in your
control of the hand graver. As your assurance
increases it will show in the quality of your
cuts, in the smoothness of your scrolls and
curves, and in the variety that you will get in
the width and depth of line.

Figure 28 shows the normal grasp of the
hand graver, seen from below. The thumb is

FIGURE 28

extended along the side of the blade, the index finger is on top of the graver while the remaining fingers hold the handle in position against the heel of the hand.

You will need to make some practice plates (perhaps many) to learn the technique as you did with the chasers hammer and chisel. You can take a practice plate, apply some Chinese White and draw some straight lines to be cut, or some parallel lines between which you can cut some curved lines as might be done for lettering or parts of scrolls. By working within these limitations, you will be developing a sense of control from the very start and not be working in a hit-or-miss fashion. Figure 29 shows a practice plate with straight lines and an assortment of short and long curves, scrolls and a small amount of lettering. (See the chapter on lettering if your interest lies in this direction.) Your main concern at the beginning will be to practice straight lines and curved lines. In doing the curves be sure to practice both clockwise and counter-clockwise curves until you can make a cut in either direction with equal ease.

FIGURE 31

FIGURE 30

Examine again those pictures that show the engravers using their hand tools. You will see the engraver is fairly well over his work and that the vise is quite close to the body (but not so close as to interfere with any free movement of the arms). Look at figure 30 and note the sturdy vise and the position of the body and the arms in relationship to the vise. Study especially the method that is being used for good positive control of the tool. The thumb of the hand with the graver is placed firmly on the surface of the work while the thumb of the left hand is positioned directly ahead of and against it. Pressure is applied to the graver while at the same time the muscles of the hand can add the exact amount of force necessary to force the tool through the metal. When the tool is controlled in this fashion, the thumbs remain stationary and solidly in contact with each other and with the work, while the tool slides past the thumb of the hand that is holding the tool. Figure 31 shows a cut being started on a practice plate. Notice that the thumb of the tool hand is extended so that the point of the graver is quite close to the end of the thumb as you begin the cut. As force is applied to the tool and the muscles of the hand thrust the tool

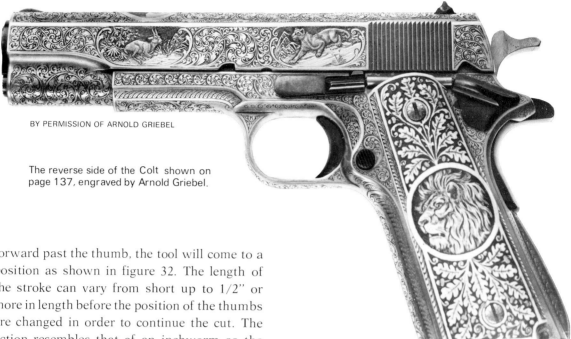

The reverse side of the Colt shown on page 137, engraved by Arnold Griebel.

forward past the thumb, the tool will come to a position as shown in figure 32. The length of the stroke can vary from short up to 1/2" or more in length before the position of the thumbs are changed in order to continue the cut. The action resembles that of an inchworm as the tool inches forward between pauses when the positions of the thumbs are changed. The movements and the actual cutting are much smoother than this description would indicate. In using the hand tool in this manner, some form of holding fixture is almost a necessity, otherwise the difficulty increases a great deal. One picture earlier in the chapter shows an engraver working on a plate attached to a block of wood, and the engraving being done on the top of the

bench. The engraver's ball is my personal first choice as a holding fixture for hand engraving, although preferences will differ. A swivel vise is perhaps the next choice and there are a number of vises that incorporate universal movements. Looking over illustrations of the different engravers, you will see that a number of styles of vises are being used. There should be no great difficulty in finding a suitable means of holding the work at a cost you want to invest.

While the method just described gives excellent control of the tool, much of your engraving by hand will be done as is shown in figure 33. Instead of the tool being forced through the metal while the work remains practically stationary, the tool stays more or less in one position while the work moves against the graver. The action is similar to that of a metal lathe which turns the work against the rigidly-held cutter bit. Engraving in this manner gives good freedom of movement in cutting scrolls. The advantages of a good ball vise are quite

FIGURE 32

evident for this style of work. The two reproductions of the Charles Daly trap gun show a
customary treatment of this type of scroll work,
and I have included two enlarged shots to give
a closer look at some of the detail in the engraving. Observe the treatment of the line
forming the back of the dog. This is not a hard,
solid line for the variation in the treatment of
the line gives a good suggestion of the forms,
and reveals the artistic handling of the cutting
by the engraver. You will also see some punch
work that was used on both the dog and bird
sections to give added texture, and note the
difference in the punches that were used in
these two parts to get the effect desired.

As you become accustomed to using the
hand graver and gain confidence with it, you
will find yourself loosening up and using a
combination of the techniques just described.
Sometimes you will find yourself using the tool
with the thumb of your graver hand in contact
with the surface of the work. You might even
use the graver with the index finger of the
graver hand contacting the work, and on occasion you might have both the thumb and forefinger in contact with the work. Experience
will give you confidence and you will use these
and some of your own methods with no conscious effort.

During the course of their visits many beginners have asked me about making simple
borders that they could do without too much
difficulty. One of the most troublesome borders
for the starting engraver is cutting a simple
straight line. The trouble lies not only in
having to maintain a uniform depth (and consequently width) of cut while at the same time
having to keep the graver on an absolutely

FIGURE 33

true course. The ability to cut a straight line is, of course, a fundamental necessity and most of your borders will eventually be based on it. However, while you are perfecting your straight line cuts, a wavy line such as is shown in figure 34a could be a good substitute. Small deviations in such a line are less obvious than they are in a straight line. In doing the first trial cuts of this wavy line, you can lay out three pencil lines as well as marks to space each complete curve evenly to help maintain uniformity. Refer again to figure 34a. The two outside lines are guides to control border width, while the spacing marks across the center line indicate the point at which the tool changes from cutting one curve to cutting the opposite curve. After you have become experienced, cutting such a line will be done without such elaborate guide lines. You will develop a sense of rhythm and timing that will enable you to cut this wavy line with a fine degree of uniformity. The simple addition of punch marks as shown at figure 34b changes the character of the line and makes it a delicate border.

All of the borders in the illustration are shown oversize. In your designs, you must fit

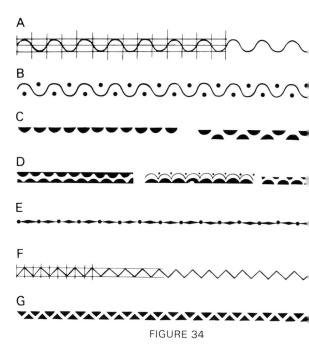

FIGURE 34

the width of the border to the area that you are enclosing, and you must also consider the "weight" of the border relative to the overall design. You may want a border that is heavy and decisive, or a border that is light and airy, or anything between these two extremes.

Figure 34c shows a straight line cut made with a flat graver. The scallops are done by raising one corner of the graver off the surface of the work slightly and driving the other corner into the work along a straight line; or if a curved border is needed, the graver would follow the curved line. As the tool enters the work, the hammer end of the tool is gradually raised until just before the maximum width of the scallop is reached. At this point, begin reversing the action of the hammer end of the tool by gradually lowering it as you cut the narrowing portion of the scallop until the tool leaves the work. You will find that if you use strokes of equal number and weight, you will come out with quite uniform cuts. As you practice cutting these scallops to develop your feel for the tool and your timing, try making both

An enlargement of the Chas. Daly on the preceding page. This detailed picture is included to show how the cutting was done.

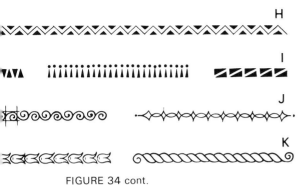

FIGURE 34 cont.

short and long scallops. You will also want to try cutting them as individual cuts with a little space between them, keeping both the cuts and the spaces uniform. The last half of line 34c shows two opposing rows of interrupted scallops.

The first segment at figure 34d shows an application of the scallop wherein each scallop is connected to the next to form a continuous wavy line one side of which remains a straight cut. A similar cut is made (moving the pattern forward one half of a scallop) opposite the first wavy line. This border is quite commonly used, and is very effective. When seen in the white, the scallops catch the light and shine like jewels on each side of the wavy, uncut center line. The last two segments of 34d show

variations in the use of the scallop. You can devise many more embellishments of this old motif which is one of the real fascinations of this art called engraving. You may find later on that a similar design has been used before, but that first thrill of making an original design will always be yours alone.

Figure 34e is made quite simply by spacing off dots, which can be punch marks. Between each punch mark two cuts are made with a square graver, each cut being made toward the center between two dots. It pays to be meticulous with your layout since it is deceptively simple looking. With the dots equally spaced, make all of the cuts with the square graver in one direction at the same time, to maintain a closer uniformity from cut to cut. When they are all completed in one direction, turn the work and finish the opposite cuts. The diamonds can be made wider or narrower depending upon the angle at which the square graver is driven into the work.

Figure 34f shows the numerous short cuts that make up this border and is self explanatory. It is quite simple to keep a short line straight. The only difficulty here is to keep your lines at the same angles and the lengths uniform with good connections.

Figure 34 g consists of cuts made with a square graver. The finished border will be

A fine example of Lynton McKenzie's artistry and craftsmanship.

the triangular cut. As mentioned previously, almost any shape triangle can be cut by changing the tool. Narrow, long triangles can be cut with the slender tool such as the point of onglette graver. The wider, shorter triangles can be made with the square tool. Still wider triangles can be made with a square tool stoned to an angle greater than its original 90 degrees. This tool will not only cut a wider angle, but the cut will also require less depth to obtain the greater width.

Both figures 34j and 34k are running borders that need no explanation. As a beginner cutting these borders, it would pay to make an accurate layout. By now you should have learned that a slipshod layout will only lead to an unsatisfactory finished job. As you continue to work and gain experience, your cutting will improve. Also you will continue to collect examples of borders and engraving that will serve as guides for your own future work.

I should like to give you one parting thought as we leave Chapter 6. Do not practice in an aimless, mindless manner or when you are very tired. By giving every cut your complete attention and effort your work will be sure to improve. This in itself is rewarding and you will soon find yourself making "just one more cut." When you have reached this point (the point where you don't want to lay the tool down) you are on your way to becoming an engraver.

only as good as your layout. Each individual triangle is cut by placing the square graver on the work and driving it into the work to cast up a burr. Then place your flat graver on the surface of the work at the base of the burr and shear it off cleanly. A light stoning of the surface removes any remaining trace of the burr and leaves the surface level. By not trying to remove the metal as you make the cut, you maintain a triangle that is sharp and clean in each corner with each side perfectly straight.

Figure 34h is a combination of the two previous border examples. After cutting the angular line as shown in 34f, the triangular cuts are made to give the border a little more weight.

Shown at figure 34i are three variations of

Chapter Seven
Advanced Engraving

ow that your basic experience is behind you, no doubt you are anxious to explore some of the more difficult—and rewarding—jobs that can be done; for example, gold and other precious metal inlays. An engraving job that incorporates such inlays always seems to be superior or more distinguished than those jobs that lack this extra effort in time and talent. I am assuming, of course, that the job is accomplished in a skillful manner, because if it is not the bright gold or silver only draws attention to the lack of craftsmanship. However, before becoming completely involved in this subject, there are some general remarks I should like to make, and some observations or comments that I want to repeat.

When you start to engrave an individual firearm, it will be disassembled and the parts engraved separately as a general rule. The exceptions are, of course, those parts such as the bottom plates of some double barrelled shotguns where the design will carry through from one part to the next, or other guns where the components to be engraved are connected in the final assembly. In disassembling these arms be sure that your capabilities are equal to the task. If you are a careful mechanic and have a good clear, complete set of instructions on the correct procedure for the disassembly of that particular arm, then you should have no difficulty. If there is any doubt in your mind, take the gun to a good gunsmith and have him take it down for you. When you are making your deal with him insist that you be permitted to observe the procedure and make notes. Don't just watch him, but observe carefully and make a step by step record of the procedure. A day or a week later when you wonder if he removed this part first or that other piece first, you can refer to your notes of the sequence of disassembly and be sure. After you have become familiar with the arm, you may feel capable of assembling the firearm yourself if you have good notes. Whether the gunsmith disassembles the gun or you do it yourself, you should have a stout container in which you can keep all the parts of this particular gun together. It is so easy to misplace or lose a small part, and many times they are difficult to replace. Not only should you have a good container (or two if necessary) but it should be clearly identified as to make, model and even the serial number of the gun. For disassembly instructions, you will find a number of magazines carrying diagrams and instructions covering a great many guns. Over the years **The American Rifleman** has carried many of these articles. **Gun Digest** has also many such reviews. Start now and collect these articles and file them so that they can be easily located; otherwise they will do you no good. Brownells, Incorporated have a huge book entitled **Encyclopedia of Modern Firearms Parts and Assembly** that will answer perhaps 95% of your questions.

With the gun completely disassembled,

148

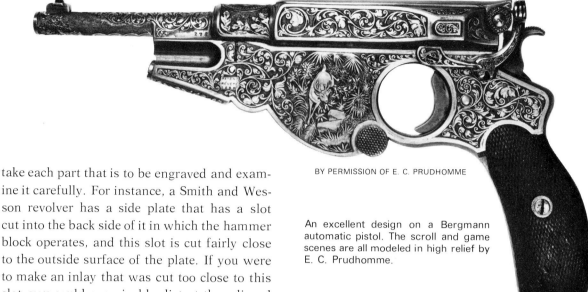

An excellent design on a Bergmann automatic pistol. The scroll and game scenes are all modeled in high relief by E. C. Prudhomme.

take each part that is to be engraved and examine it carefully. For instance, a Smith and Wesson revolver has a side plate that has a slot cut into the back side of it in which the hammer block operates, and this slot is cut fairly close to the outside surface of the plate. If you were to make an inlay that was cut too close to this slot, you could conceivably distort the relieved slot while setting the gold. By driving the bottom of the inlay down into this slot it could put a bind on the hammer block that would interfere with its functioning. Also, some portions of the bottom plate on the old Parker shotguns had some sections that were comparatively thin. By examining the gun critically before starting your drawings, you can arrange your design so that these thin areas will not require any heavy cuts or deep inlays. Most guns have ample areas that are suitable for your inlays and any heavier cuts that you may wish to incorporate.

If you find any thin sections on the parts to be engraved that you think require care, plot them carefully, and as nearly as you can indicate their location on the surface that you are going to engrave. By knowing exactly where they are, you can give them proper consideration as you work.

Many of these parts that have thin areas can be mounted on blocks with engraver's cement. By filling these grooves with cement and cementing the whole plate to a block, these thin sections can be supported from the back as they are worked on, and distortion of the underside of the thin sections is prevented. However, you must still use care and not cut into them with deep cuts or inlays.

The cement procedure works well when cutting on Springfield, Enfield, Model 70 and Weatherby floorplates since it supports the back of the plates where they have been milled out to take the magazine spring. Use a Butane torch to soften the cement and warm the metal part that is to be engraved. No more heat than is necessary should be used on the metal parts so that they can embed themselves in the softened cement. I am sure that the heat would be well under 200 degrees F. After the part has become embedded in the cement, extinguish the torch and allow the part to cool naturally. The part will now be supported and held firmly by the cement. After engraving, the part can be removed easily by warming it up again with the torch and lifting it out with a pointed stick or pliers. Any cement that adheres can be removed with a stick or knife while the plate is warm and any small amount remaining can be removed with alcohol. Engraver's cement is available from the jeweler's and engraver's suppliers listed in the back of the book. Any other precautions or tips that may save you some trouble with inlays will be given as the occasions arise. Now, let us get into the fascinating subject of inlays.

That John E. Warren is a master shows clearly in the sensitive scroll work, fine borders and detailed figures on this 1886 Winchester.

BY PERMISSION OF JOHN E. WARREN

Your inlays, because of their color, luster and contrast with the blued steel, are going to attract the eye and will be the first parts to catch the attention of the observer. For this reason, every bit of your skill and finesse should be applied to this part of your engraving. If your temperment is such that you do not have the patience to make such a project come out right, then you cannot expect to attain the quality of inlaying that is the mark of the true craftsman. This is an area in which one cannot just muddle through and expect everything to come out fine in the end. On the other hand, if you give careful attention to all of your cuts and especially to the undercutting and preparation steps, the actual inlaying is relatively easy and you should have no trouble in attaching the gold so that it is securely and permanently a part of the firearm. That is of course the first test of a good inlay, that it be firmly anchored in place!

Precious metals for inlays can be purchased in two forms; wires of different diameters and sheets of various thicknesses, and your inlays can be made using either form. Another method is to model the figures in wax or modeling material and make a casting which is then inlaid into the metal.

For practicing let us start by inlaying a short section of wire for a border. You will eventually want to inlay lines of different widths, like a double-line border around a barrel using one wide and one narrow line. Generally speaking, a gold border on a blued background should not be made wide and heavy because such a line is too conspicuous and can actually detract from your engraving by its overwhelming weight and attraction. For your first attempt at wire inlaying, cut a straight line approximately 3/4" long using the familiar onglette. Since we want to use a wire that is 25 or 26 gauge, which is approximately .015" in diameter, you should end up with a line that will be approximately 1/64" wide or slightly over.

For the benefit of the beginner, I will give specific recommendations so there will be a definite point from which to start. Engraving is a very personal experience and one in which individual preferences come to exert a great deal of influence. This is good, for it is because of this personal partiality and how an engraver chooses to do a particular job that makes for the individuality of each engraver. When specific instructions are given it is because they have been carefully considered and I think they will produce the result you are striving for in the particular situation. As an engraver you should always watch for new methods, new tools and different ways of improving and increasing the scope and range of your technique. So, when a specific set of instructions is given do not assume that this is the only way of accomplishing the job. If they do the job for you, that is fine; but you should still keep an open mind as to other ways of attaining equally good results.

To inlay our practice line, let us take the onglette and see how we can get the best results from it. All of the photographs shown here are taken of the tools that are of the sizes recommended in the text. These tools are the standard hand gravers that have been fitted with handles and were described earlier in the book. The number 5 size is recommended for the main cut that removes most of the metal. The undercuts are made with an 0 size onglette.

In shaping this onglette, keep in mind that it is being sharpened to cut only straight lines and should be used only to cut straight lines because of its entirely different shape. The onglette that was sharpened earlier for the normal cutting of curves was given clearance back of the cutting edge which permitted the tool to be manipulated in changing directions without interference from the heel of the tool. At figure 1a an onglette is shown as though it was making a curved cut. Imagine if you can that the tool has been stopped and that it has been sliced off even with the surface of the work. The main part of the tool has been raised up so that you can see the cross section of that part of the tool which is making the cut. You will notice that immediately back of the cutting edges the sides of the tool drop off rapidly so that there will be room to make the changes in direction that are needed (this is the clearance that was spoken of earlier and it is shown at the arrow).

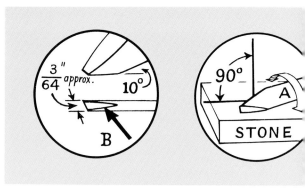

FIGURE 1c   FIGURE 1d

When it comes to cutting a straight line a new set of conditions prevail and several different characteristics are desirable. You can see that instead of a tool which can be guided through direction change easily, a tool that resists changes in direction and tends to maintain a direct course is preferred. Such a tool can be sharpened, and by following the explanation and examining figure 1b it will be easily understood. I have made no attempt to maintain the true proportion between the tool size and the cut, but have shown the cut large enough to convey the correct idea of the part that the clearance plays in the functioning of the tool. In figure 1a the heel of the tool is relatively short, and the smaller the curves and scrolls to be made the shorter this heel must be. At figure 1b, the heel is comparatively long and it is this longer heel plus the change in the clearance that makes this particular tool have less of a tendency to wander from a straight line.

To make a "straight-line" cutter, start with a number 5 onglette. Examine the point to see if the sides of the tool at the face have been rounded in grinding. If they are rounded, grind the tool back until the face of the tool and the sides are square with each other. While doing this, grind the face to an angle of approximately 50 degrees instead of the 45 degree angle to which they are usually ground.

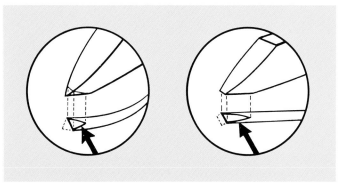

FIGURE 1a   FIGURE 1b

Next, stone the heel to give about a 10 degree lift to the handle of the tool, see figure 1c. While stoning the heel angle, the tool should be held so that the stoned angle is perfectly square across the thickness of the tool. Stone this down until you have a measurement of approximately 3/64" across the flat at the front edge of the tool. This will still give you quite a good

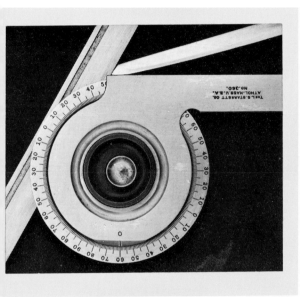

FIGURE 1h

clearance angle even with the longer heel as is shown at figure 1c at B. Figure 1h shows the tool that has been shaped with the protractor showing the 60 degree angle that is the sum of the face angle plus the 10 degree lift that was given the tool in stoning the bottom at the point of the tool.

In order to reduce the clearance and the width of the tool at the face, lay the onglette flat on the stone and by rotating the tool as shown in figure 1d at A, the angle of the tool face to the surface of the stone can be changed. It is obvious that if the tool were stoned at the 90

degree angle there would be no clearance. We do want a minimum amount of clearance so the main objective here is to see that the face angle of the tool to the surface of the stone is NOT LESS than 90 degrees. To put it another way, the angle of the tool face to the sides of the tool must not be over 90 degrees and only slightly less than the 90 degrees to get the result that we are striving for, see figure 1d. At figure 1e the finished tool is shown. The 3/32" portion shown should have practically no taper from the cutting edge to the trailing edge (which must not be wider than the cutting edge). You will note that while we were stoning the clearance angle we were also reducing the width of the cutting edge of the tool from approximately 3/64" to its final width of about 1/64". Your tool is now completed.

In sharpening the size 0 onglette for making undercuts, the first step will again be to stone the heel as you did the number 5 tool. Stone the heel back until you have a heel length of about 3/32" and a 10 degree lift, see figure 1f. In stoning the sides at the point you can follow the instructions given for the number 5 tool. The only difference is that the sides are stoned down almost to the center line on each side. This leaves only a small flat and the corners of this flat are stoned so that this bottom edge at the heel has a very small radius. This not only gives the point of the tool a little added strength but also gives more strength to the corners of the inlaid gold.

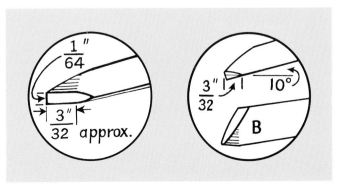

FIGURE 1e   FIGURE 1f

Figure 1g shows cross sections of the various steps to inlay gold wire. At A most of the metal has been removed with the number 5 onglette. At B the number 0 onglette is making the undercut. It is tipped over sharply, about as far as possible without contacting the opposite lip of the main cut. At C the wire is in position for punching into the cut. You can see that the .015" diameter wire lays into the cut about halfway which means that the first cut was about .008" deep. The depth of cut must not be so deep that the material in the wire is insufficient to completely fill it. You will soon learn to judge your depth of cut so that this will be no problem. At D the gold wire has been hammered into the cut and enough gold is left on top to insure that the line will be completely filled. The surplus gold is removed flush with the surface of the work with a flat graver of sufficient width, using care not to allow the graver to dig into the steel. It can then be polished with some 500 or 600 grit wet-or-dry automotive paper backed up with a flat piece of steel or hard wood to prevent polishing away the gold and leaving a rounded depression in the gold inlay. The surplus gold can also be removed with fine cut jeweler's files, stoned to remove any file marks and polished with the automotive paper.

FIGURE 1g

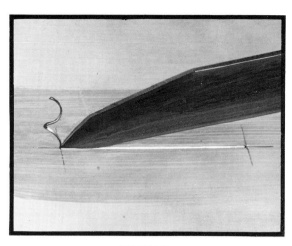

FIGURE 3

When sharpening the tools, remember that these drawings are exaggerated to show the details more clearly. The measurements given in the text are correct. On the drawings 1/64" looks big, whereas on the tool it will appear so small that you may think that it is incorrect.

The drawings that you have just seen may leave some unanswered questions in your mind on how to do a wire inlay. For the beginner the thought often occurs, "If I could only SEE someone do it". Since this isn't always possible, the next best alternative is a photograph of the various steps. In the photograph at figure 2, the steel plate was given a light coat of Chinese white and a straight line 3/4" long was drawn and the main cut made with a number 5 onglette. The photographs are shown slightly oversize. Figure 3 shows the undercutting of one side of the main cut. After both sides were undercut, the .015" diameter gold wire was laid and punched into the undercut groove, as in the photograph at figure 4. The punch I use is made of hard brass with the end squared on the lathe with just a very slight relief on the outer edge. This face is smooth but not polished. The punch is then given a fine texture by holding it about 1/16" above a piece of 220 grit automotive paper laid on a steel plate and tap-

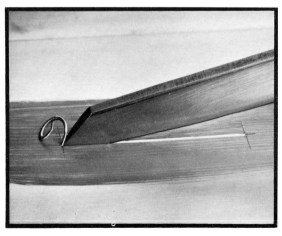

FIGURE 2

FIGURE 4

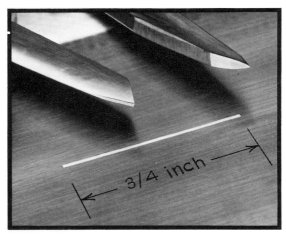

FIGURE 6

ping it lightly with the chasers hammer until the end of the punch shows a dull surface. This "textured" punch transmits more of the force from the hammer in setting the gold because the gold is held by the slightly roughened surface and is forced down into the cut instead of being squeezed out as well as down as it would be by a punch with a polished face. Figure 5 shows the surplus gold being removed with a number 42 flat graver. In stoning this flat graver on the bottom flat, the tang end of the graver is held about 15 degrees above the stone. As it is pushed forward, drop the tang end until it is between 5 or 10 degrees above the stone. This gives a slight radius on the heel portion just back of the cutting edge. By raising or lowering the hammer end of the tool this radius will raise or lower the cutting edge of the tool to remove just the right amount of excess gold. It is better to leave a little too much gold than to gouge cuts into the steel. Figure 6 shows the finished, inlaid gold along with the two tools that made the cuts.

You will find three photographs that you can study which are fine examples of the art of inlaying gold at figures 7a and 7b. The two pictures of the revolver cylinder are by A. A. White and are shown actual size (of the original photographs, not necessarily of the cylinders) in an effort to convey the excellence of the detail shown in the bird and the animal. Also shown is a fine old German shotgun (16 gauge) made by Emil Kerner. It has the typical fine stock carving and metal engraving, with a decorative carved horn fill-in piece back of the trigger guard but it was bought primarily because of the fine gold and silver scroll inlaying. The thin sections of these inlaid gold lines measure only .008" in width (only half the width of our demonstration line). The photo-

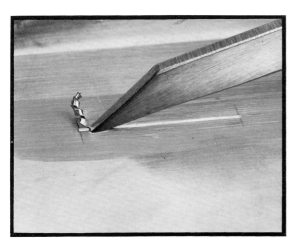

FIGURE 5

FIGURE 7a

The two sides of a gold inlaid and engraved single action Colt cylinder made on commission of Mr. R. P. Mellon, Courtesy of A. A. White Engravers, Inc.

FIGURE 7b

graph at figure 8 shows the gun at very close to actual size. Here again, a very important lesson can be learned. The engraved shotgun has many cuts that are quite heavy and bold, but it also contains elements in which a most delicate touch was required. In your own work you will want to develop your feel for the cut that is needed for a specific impression that you wish to express. As you experiment with smaller, more delicate scrolls and cuts, you will also want to learn to sharpen the tools needed to accomplish these finer cuts. To be specific again, I prefer a size 3 or 4 square or lozenge graver and an 0 or 00 onglette for fine work on steel. After sharpening the face angle, the heel

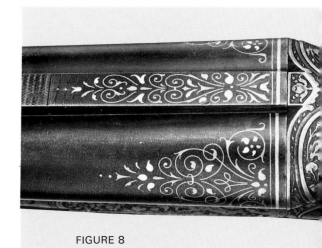

FIGURE 8

is given about a 15 degree lift by very light stoning so that the heel is no longer than 1/32". Glancing casually at the tool, the heel appears almost non-existent, but with your glass it shows up quite large, and with your glass you can see plainly whether or not your stoning is symmetrical, with the bottom edge continued in a straight line to the point of the tool.

Sharpening an onglette for cutting a straight line is shown because it is a definite help to the beginner who often experiences difficulty in keeping a regular tool from drifting from one side to the other. After you have become proficient in handling the tools, the coordination of your eye, the hammer and the tool will be such that you will be able to cut a straight line regardless of the tool being used.

Cutting and inlaying scrolls is no more difficult than cutting and inlaying a really straight line. It does, however, present several problems when it comes to undercutting the edges. (This is assuming of course that your scrolls are now well formed and smoothly cut.) The actual undercutting of the inside edge of a scroll is easily done since there is ample clearance and the tool can be manipulated freely. Undercutting of the outside edge is more difficult, especially when you are cutting smaller, finer scrolls for inlaying.

Lynton McKenzie was born in Australia. At sixteen, he was a well-established gunsmith to the Sydney trade. He left for Europe at an early age to improve his engraving and his work on antique arms. Studying in Italy, Austria, Germany, Belgium, and England, he worked in London for such famous gunmakers as Purdey, Holland and Holland, Rigby's, Wilk's, Westley Richards and Chaflin's. He now works in the United States for the New Orleans Arms Company.

FIGURE 9

The tools that were used for undercutting the two scrolls in figure 9, shown actual size, were a number 1 knife graver for the smaller scroll, and a double 00 onglette for the larger scroll. The knife gravers come in sizes from 1 to 3. The onglette is made in sizes 00, 0, 1 and numbers up to 6. It is not absolutely essential that you have the knife graver, but it does give some advantage in undercutting smaller scrolls.

When sharpening these tools for under-

cutting, they must be given quite a different treatment than was given the regular tools for these undercutting tools remove only a relatively small amount of steel. They also are required to make cuts with very small, sharp turns which calls for a very short heel to avoid any drag on the edge of the cut as the tool passes. Because the point has been stoned down to a size needed to make some of these small cuts, these tools will no longer have the rugged strength of regular gravers. As a consequence, you must use less force with the chasers hammer if you are going to preserve the points. You might use a heavy sledge to drive a wedge into a log while splitting it, but you wouldn't use the same force to drive a tack. Another

156

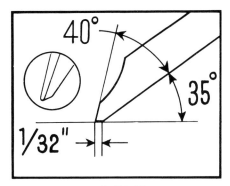

FIGURE 10

the face angle of the tool to a 40 degree angle with the bottom edge of the tool. Stone the heel to an angle of 30 to 35 degrees with the bottom edge so that the length of the heel is about 1/32" long (not over). This can be stoned perfectly flat at the angle given. After stoning the flat, the corners at the point are given a small radius as shown in the circle at figure 10.

Gravers are not the only way undercutting can be done. Punches are often used to displace the metal. Flat gravers can be given a chisel edge and used to form the undercut groove on straight lines and long curved lines. Round end punches can be made to form nice, round terminals on the inside end of scrolls to be inlaid.

Now that you have a firm grasp of wire inlaying and the importance of undercutting and the special tools this requires, let's look

very important point to remember is that the tool must be turned by the wrist to follow the curve as you cut around it, so that the point of the tool is always supported by the center of the heel. The farther the point wanders from the center line of the heel, the greater is the force acting to shear off the point.

Now back to figure 9. On this photo are drawn two gravers, a knife graver shown undercutting the smaller scroll, and an onglette undercutting the larger scroll. The difference between the two gravers shown is in the lift given each one. The graver at B is given the normal lift of 10 to 15 degrees while the graver at A is given approximately a 35 degree lift. The result can be seen at the arrows. You will notice that the flatter angle puts a greater length of tool back of the point down into the groove. In order to show the inlaid scrolls, the gravers were drawn undercutting the inside edge of the scroll which naturally gives clearance for the trailing edge of the tool. If this tool had been cutting the outside edge, the drag would have been much more pronounced. This drag not only roughens the edge of the cut, but a more serious result is that this contact prevents the heel of the tool from being turned far enough to maintain its maximum supporting position directly behind the point. To repeat, you may want to try sharpening an onglette or point graver as follows: first, grind

FIGURE 11

more closely at the basic methods of getting an inlay in place on the steel: hammering wire or sheet metal into place on the gun and later modeling it into figures, and either modeling or casting the figures off the gun and then setting them into place. First, let's discuss the process whereby wire is hammered into place in grooves cut side by side on the gun and the figure is modeled later.

FIGURE 12

.025" in diameter, with .039" wire being used on the remainder of the figures. I used the draw plate to draw the .039" wire down to .025", a distinct advantage of the wire inlay technique because wire can be drawn down to the size that will work best for the job. Figure 12 shows the two figures with the finer parts completely inlaid but with no detail as to modeling. Only the figure of the horse and hunter will be demonstrated here since it is the more complicated of the two.

These illustrations of the actual inlaying are shown twice over size for greater clarity. The drawback to showing them twice over size is that the novice may get a false impression of the size of the lines which in actuality are very small. Figure 13 illustrates the fact that while the inlay is shown two times the height of the original, it is in fact covering four times the area.

The actual inlaying of the body of the figure was begun at the left side of the figure which gave a fairly straight edge at which to start. It is also an advantage to run the lines in the direction that will give the greatest number of longer lines for it is faster to inlay a few longer wires than it is to inlay a greater number of shorter ones. About half of the wire required to complete the figure was inlaid using the same technique used to inlay single wire inlays—that is, cut a straight line, undercut both sides, set in the gold wire and punch it down—and an enlarged photograph was

On the use of the camera in Chapter Five I showed the preparation and transfer of a buffalo and mounted hunter scene onto a Model 94 Winchester, serial number 2040375, belonging to Mr. T. A. Bartels of New Jersey. Mr. Bartels has been most patient and considerate about the delivery date of the completed job which was left indefinite because of the work on this book. So it is with a great deal of anticipation that the job is to be finished as a demonstration of the inlaying of figures using the wire technique. This is to be done in high relief, using a .039" diameter wire to allow a generous amount of gold for a substantial undercut and to give an abundance of build-up for modeling a truly high relief figure.

After transferring the drawing, the background scene was cut. Sometimes this is done first, and at other times the figures are inlaid before finishing the supporting scene. This is a matter of preference and varying the procedure can add some variety and interest to the job. At figure 11 is shown the two figures that have had the outline cut and the outside edges undercut. These are shown actual size.

One advantage of using the gold wire is the ease with which the smaller details can be accomplished, such as the legs of the animals, the arm with the rifle and the reins. The reins are done with a gold wire that measured only

FIGURE 13   FIGURE 14

158

made, shown at figure 14. Here, the last wire that was inlaid is shown, with a punch being used to square up the edge of the inlaid gold. This punch has the same textured face as the punch described earlier, however, the face is ground to a slight angle to the body of the punch so as to leave a vertical face to the gold being upset. Also, the bottom side of the punch

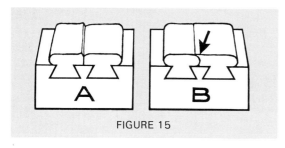

FIGURE 15

has a flat ground on it which contacts the steel. This gives broader coverage, see figure 14. The squaring-up is done so that the next piece of wire will have a square edge against which to form itself. At figure 15 are shown two diagrams illustrating this point. At figure 14 you will notice that the punch has upset the gold so that it is a little thicker than the level of the rest of the inlay. As the next wire is inlaid up against it, and the two wires are punched down together, they meet and form a solid joint from top to bottom. In looking at the drawing in figure 15 where the wire is not squared up, the wire that is being punched down must form itself over a rounded shape, as shown at the arrow. It can be seen that as the punch drives the gold down over this rounded shape, one side thins out to nothing when the two surfaces are level with each other. You will find that when you come to finishing and modeling these joints, the gold in these thinner areas will tend to flake off and there will be small pock marks

where the thin gold areas have been hammered into the gold beneath, but they have not attached to it. Quite often these imperfections seem to occur at critical areas of the modeling. By squaring each wire as it is inlaid, making sure that each joint meets squarely, the modeling can be carried to any depth that is required with the assurance that the gold will remain solid with no flaking. It is also important to keep any impurities from getting between the gold wires, so be sure to clean away all steel chips from cutting the dovetails, and to clean each dovetail and adjacent gold wire with a brush dipped in lacquer thinner before putting in the next wire. I find it also helpful to anneal the gold wire, and will describe the procedure later.

After squaring up the edge of the last inlaid wire, the next dovetail is cut, shown at figure 16. This cut can be made fairly close to the last inlaid wire. Naturally, the cut must not be made so close that the tool enters into the previous cut. If however, you find that the particular area that is being inlaid will require less thickness in modeling the figure, then the dovetail cut can be placed slightly farther apart. Nothing is gained by building up a thicker inlay than is needed.

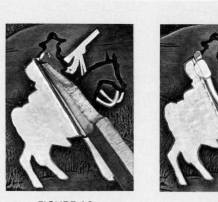

FIGURE 16   FIGURE 17

Figure 17 shows the gold wire laid in place and a single punch mark has set it. You will observe that the wire was set so that the end of the wire was slightly beyond the under-cut edge of the figure. After the wire is set into the dovetail cut, the end that overlaps can be upset the same as was done along the length of the wire. This will make sure that there is plenty of gold locked securely into the undercut along the outside edges of the figure. As each wire is laid in place, the excess gold that pro-jects beyond the figure is trimmed back to the original outline of the figure, making it easy to end up with your gold inlaid to the exact outline of your original figure. At figure 18 is shown the finished figure at approximately twice over size. The finished receiver, at figure

sired and it is usually available by the square inch. You might want to try some flat inlays on your first attempts. For this a thickness of .010" (30 gage) is plenty thick and in silver it is quite inexpensive. Another advantage of the silver is that on a flat inlay, the drawing of the detail can be engraved much as a pen drawing would be made. After the lines are cut, the silver can be treated with a liver of sulphur solution (buy the lumps at your local drug store and dissolve in water) to oxidize the sur-face. This of course oxidizes the incised lines as well. When the oxidized surface is polished, the lines being below the surface are protected and they show up as deep black lines on the bright silver.

For our demonstration here I shall inlay a gold figure on a Springfield floor plate. Once

FIGURE 18

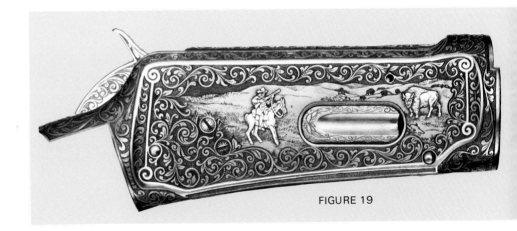

FIGURE 19

19, is shown approximately 75% of its actual size.

The use of precious metals in sheet form to make inlays is another common practice. The material can be inlaid so as to be flush with the surface or it can be inlaid to achieve a high relief figure. Gold, platinum and silver can be purchased in almost any thickness de-

again the exact details will be given for com-plete understanding. The inlay is made of 18k gold in sheet form, and is .031" thick. I pur-chase this material in 2 inch squares which makes for easy handling when sawing out the small figures. This piece is thicker than is needed, but with this thickness much of your modeling can be carried below the surface of

The reverse side of Mr. T. A. Bartel's 94 Winchester shown on the preceding page.

the steel into which the gold is placed, permitting a much greater latitude where you are after an impression of a really high relief figure. An example of this depth is evident in all of our coins which are modeled below the rim of the coin. If the area into which this inlay is placed has sufficient thickness, your gold can be sunk to a depth that doesn't leave a big blob of metal protruding above the surrounding surface. Naturally, you will want it to be a little above, but it should be a part of the surface and the design that surrounds it. It shouldn't look as though it was cut out and stuck on.

The drawing for the animal was completed and transferred to the plate, as has been described before. Next, the outline was cut and undercut, and you will notice at figure 20 that

the edges on the inside of the outline were bevelled with a flat graver. Normally I would not make this bevelled cut, but this is a good time to give a short resume of another approach to the inlaying of sheet gold.

In the February, 1950, issue of **The American Rifleman** there appeared an article on how Roy Vail inlaid a floor plate. It had a number of excellent photographs with descriptive material showing Mr. Vail actually doing the job. After the plate was prepared to accept the inlay, the gold figure was cut to fit using the technique of the repousse artisan. The gold was placed bottom side up on a lead block, and was beaten into shape from the back with punches to take on the general contours of the relief figure. After shaping, the gold was attached to a block of wood with engraver's cement and the details were completed from the front. With the figure cupped out, you can see the reason for the bevelling of the outline. This allows the back of the cupped figure to drop into the cutout with no interference from the metal on the inside of the outline. With this technique a very high, fully modeled figure is achieved with a minimum of material.

Returning to our project, figure 21 (three times over size) shows the outline cut and undercut. The metal is being removed with a square graver. After making all of the cuts with the square graver, a flat graver was used to flatten the bottom of the cutout which levels the bottom quite easily with the bulk of the metal removed. A word of caution is in order as you remove this metal. When you examine

FIGURE 20

FIGURE 21

line of the cutout in the steel going away from you, the scriber can be controlled quite accurately. Use a light touch with your scriber so that you cast up a burr that will not carry too much ivory black, and will consequently transfer a fine black line. The reason for scribing the line inside the edge of the cutout is that you can saw the inlay out right up to the line, but leave it intact. By leaving the line on, you can see exactly what you have, and leave a very minimum of filing and fitting. Ideally, the inlay should just drop into the cutout. You must make sure that the gold does not overlap the edge of the cutout. You might think that you can just drive it down into the cutout and make it fit. Even with 18k gold, forcing the figure down into the undercut will beat down the thin edge of the lip of the cutout and reduce its effectiveness. So be patient, and get a good fit between the gold and the undercut...which starts by getting an accurate outline for cutting out the gold. Another point: by using the clear plastic that forms to the curve of the plate, you are automatically compensating for the curved surface of the plate when you lay it flat on the sheet of gold.

the bottom side of the floor plate, observe the depth of the cutout and its relationship to the curved surface of the plate. As the curved surface approaches the side of the plate, it comes very close to the outside of the magazine spring cutout. The center of the floor plate is the thickest section, so your cutout can be made a little deeper in this area. Let the cutout become a little shallower as you come to the thinner sections. By being aware of how much metal you have to work with, you can judge your depth of cut accordingly. This should be one of your first concerns when making an inlay, being sure that you have enough metal to support your figure without distorting the underside while you are seating the figure into the cutout.

The cutout is now ready to receive the inlay. Take a piece of clear plastic sheeting and make a tracing as shown at figure 22 with the plastic taped securely to the floor plate. Be sure that the needle in the pinvise has a good sharp point. I try to scribe the line just a trifle inside the edge of the cutout, more a matter of feeling than measurement. If you have a micrometer, set it at .005" and see what it looks like. If you turn the work so that you can see the

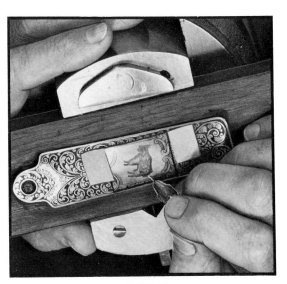

FIGURE 22

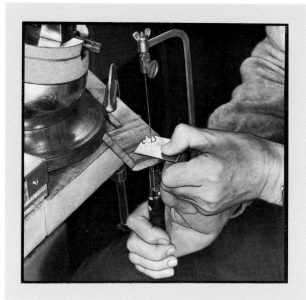

FIGURE 23

After you have transferred your tracing of the cutout to the gold and before sawing it out, give the transferred figure a light spray of a fixative used by artists to protect drawings and layouts. The tacky varnish has already picked up the ivory black, but it is susceptible to damage. The light spray coat of Blair Spray-Fix that I use protects the transfer and eliminates re-scribing it.

A good jeweler's saw is a necessity and will be found in some of the catalogs of companies supplying jewelers and engravers. Here are a few facts about the saws. As a reference point, one blade is designated size 0 or sometimes 1/0. This blade has a thickness of .011" and a width of .022". From 1/0, as the blades become finer, the number increases up to 8/0 which has a thickness of .0063" and a width of .0126". Going to the larger blades from 1/0, the sizes run from 1 to 14. Number 14 is .0236" thick and .069" in width. Naturally we need only the smaller sizes for sawing out sheet gold. The saw blade that was used to saw the figure illustrated was a number 4/0 and measures .008" thick and .0175" wide.

My set-up in figure 23 is simply a 5/16" hardwood board clamped to the bench. A narrow notch only slightly wider than the saw blade was sawed back into the board about 3/4". The saw blade is placed in the handle with the teeth pointing toward the handle. All of the cutting is done on the down stroke. The plate is turned (and the action of the saw is coordinated) as the saw progresses around the figure. Usually your figure can be laid out on the gold sheet so that all or most of the fine cuts can be made first. At figure 23, the small cuts around the legs were all made first. Then one cut was made down the front of the face and the horns, and the blade backed out. This left only the big main cut that is shown about one-half completed.

You now have the gold sawed out and flat. The gold must now be shaped to fit the contour of the plate, shown at figure 24. This was done with a round graver, jeweler's pliers and punches. The lead block is shown and just above it is a number 62 round graver. The rounded bottom of the graver was laid on the figure and

FIGURE 24

FIGURE 25

pad can be ground quite evenly on a grinding wheel. By holding the clamp at a slight angle, the wheel will spin the pad as it grinds, and it will reduce the size uniformly, as shown in the illustration. After grinding, all edges were stoned smooth. This clamp with the smaller pad is used to begin the setting. On this particular inlay the area along the back was clamped, and the setting of the belly line was started first. After punching the belly line into place, the clamp was shifted to this area to expose the section just above the shoulder and the back which was then set with the punch. With the back and the belly set into place (you will remember that this was the thickest section of the plate, and the cut was slightly deeper), the gold inlay is now held so that we can safely shift the clamps.

After the midsection is set, use the clamp with the larger pad and clamp this part of the figure securely. Now shift the clamp with the smaller pad to the head of the figure and continue setting the figure along the top of the neck, under the beard and along the front of

by tapping it lightly, the gold can be curled to assume the contour of the plate; however, any round piece of steel can be used to lay on the figure and shape it. By using the tools shown, the piece can be shaped to fit the contour of your plate and the cutout. From here on, it is a case of punch and try. You will soon find out how accurately your transfer and sawing have been. Do whatever filing and punching are necessary to fit the figure to the cutout. Be sure that the gold does not overlap the cutout at any point. The closer the fit all around the edge of the figure, the easier will be the job of setting the figure. This is one of those times when patience pays off.

If your fitting has been done accurately, setting the figure will be simple. Clamps are used to hold the figure in place while the punch is setting it. You saw what punches can do when you shaped the figure to fit the contour of the plate. At figure 25 are shown two clamps that were alike, except that the one clamping the figure in place has been altered so that the pad at the end of the screw which adjusts for uneven surfaces has been ground down. This

FIGURE 26

A typical example of Arnold Griebel's lively and detailed execution of two small game scenes. An excellent setting for the scenes is used, and the overall design concept should be studied by the student.

FIGURE 27

the shoulder. After these are secure, I would still use the small clamp on the lower part of the face, while the horns and forehead are set. After shifting the small clamp again to the horns and forehead, the face and beard are completed. By shifting your clamps so that the figure is held firmly in place while the punching is done, any stresses built up in the figure are controlled.

The clamps shown in figure 25 can be used to complete the job. However, in figure 26 are shown the two tool maker's parallel clamps that were actually used. These clamps come in various sizes. Looking at figure 26, it is most apparent that there is much more room to manipulate the punches and these clamps can be changed to secure the figure clear down to the last hoof. While the "C" clamps project above the figure, the parallel clamps require more room below the block holding the plate. In order to get this room, the block was set higher in the vise. You will also notice that the block is set in the vise so that the gold is be-

yond the vise jaws. In order to prevent the block from being driven down by the punching, a long wood screw was inserted into the bottom of the block and rested on the surface of the engraver's ball. Raising the block and putting the screw into the block gave the necessary room to adjust the clamps and hold the block steady. So, for a minimum of trouble, make good use of your clamps. The completed floor plate is shown at figure 27.

The processes that the engraver uses to inlay metals have been used since the beginning of the decorative arts. The next process that will be described is no exception. Using this process, the metalsmiths of India have fashioned many beautiful and intricate designs on metal items. The method has several advantages; completion can be accomplished more quickly, and complicated designs can be handled quite easily. As the process is explained, you will understand why this is so.

The subject chosen was a fine hunting dog belonging to Lloyd Thompson of Boone, Iowa. I had drawn this dog for use on his Parker bird gun, and inlaid the dog in gold with the quail in silver. The oversize drawing was made to his satisfaction from a snapshot of a pose that he liked. He also had some Polaroid color shots that were helpful in making up the drawing. The drawing was then reduced to the proper size, using the camera as was explained in

Chapter Five. Shown at figure 28 is the drawing and the reduced outline, transferred to the demonstration plate. The gold dog is 11/16" tall, so the reproduction of the outline should be close to actual size. The pencil drawing is shown about the size that it was drawn originally. In addition to the outline of the dog at figure 28, there are drawn three straight lines, 30 degrees apart.

The next step is shown at figure 29. A chisel is used to cut a series of grooves, similar to those of a file. The chisel I used is not sharpened like a cold chisel, but more like a wood chisel. The edge is more vulnerable than a cold chisel, but then you will not be beating on it as you would a cold chisel. The first series of grooves has been cut with the chisel tipped at an angle away from you. The flat side of the chisel is toward you with the bevelled edge away from you. You will find that as a groove is cut, the burr that is cast up will act as a guide for your next cut. The consensus seems to be that these cuts should run fifty to the inch, although a few more or less is immaterial. If your background is to be removed or stippled, the cuts can overlap the outline. If the

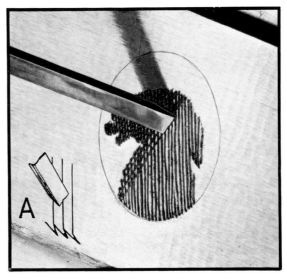

FIGURE 29

background is to remain smooth, you must stay within your outline. After you have cut all of the grooves in one direction, it is important that your next series of cuts are made cutting **into** the burr. This is shown in figure 29 at A. Turn the plate the same way when you make your third series of cuts (into the previous burrs). Naturally, on your first attempts you will be trying the angle of the chisel and the depth of the cuts. Also, you will need to actually apply your gold and test its adherence. For your own peace of mind you want to be sure that the gold will not come off without some real effort.

After the cuts are completed, a fine Arkansas stone is used to lightly stone any burrs that have been turned up higher than the rest. Figure 30 shows the cuts completed and stoned. A stainless steel fine wire brush is used with lacquer thinner to brush out any grease or oil and chips, so that the gold can make a good tight bond to the roughened steel. I pour out a little lacquer thinner into a small container and dip the brush into it before brushing. This is done about six times, absorbing the lacquer

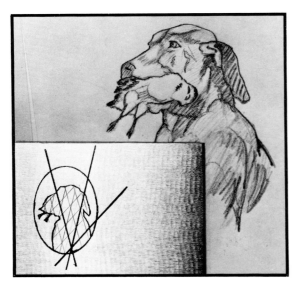

FIGURE 28

FIGURE 30

thinner between brushings with a clean cloth. Since the background was planned to be set back and roughened, the area between the bird's feet was disregarded and the cuts made to cover the whole area.

The outline made earlier on acetate is now carefully centered over the roughened area and securely taped into place. This is shown at figure 31. A strip of white paper has been inserted underneath the acetate to show the outline more clearly.

In this instance a sheet of .010" thick 24k gold was used. Although 24k sheet gold as thin as .005" up to as thick as .015" can be applied with this method, I have found that .010" is ample for an impressive high relief figure. All inlays of this type should be 24k gold (annealed) whatever the thickness used. At figure 32 an outline has been transferred to the gold plate and it is being cut out with a small flat chisel. The gold is placed on a piece of cold rolled steel, which allows the chisel to shear it cleanly with very little distortion. After the gold is cut, it must be annealed. I use a

common hardware store variety Butane torch and a jeweler's charcoal soldering block which can be purchased from jewelry supply houses. The charcoal blocks come in various sizes, and the one I am using is 4" x 7" x 1-1/4". If one is not available, a heavy asbestos pad works equally well. Light the torch and play it onto the block until a spot shows red. Then lay the gold cutout on this spot and play the torch on it. This torch does not have any tendency to overheat the gold, and in fact does not even bring it to a red heat. But, when the torch is turned off and the block and the gold are allowed to air cool, the gold is very soft and malleable.

After annealing, wash the gold cutout with lacquer thinner. From this point on be careful that no oil or grease contaminates the back surface. Pick it up with tweezers and place it underneath the acetate layout that we attached to the plate. After shifting the gold into place beneath the outline, it is staked lightly into place so that it will not be moved, as shown in figure 33.

The acetate outline that we taped into

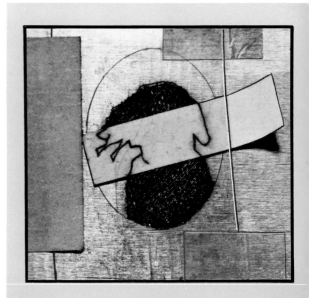

FIGURE 31

FIGURE 32

place is now folded back (do not remove it) so that the gold can be hammered into the roughened area that was prepared for it. Figure 34 shows the hammering process. A trip to the local sheet metal shop produced some small

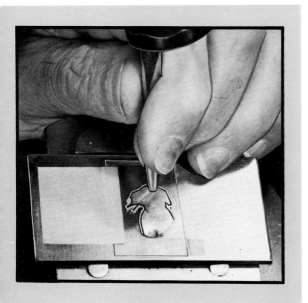

FIGURE 33

scraps of soft, sheet copper that are used as a buffer between the gold and the hammer. After you have hammered it down, you can see where the gold has been forced into the chiseled grooves. I now take the chasers hammer and planish the surface lightly. This levels and sets the gold. Do not worry about getting it perfectly flat and level as this is a waste of time and gold. The surface will be taken care of in the modeling.

FIGURE 34

With the gold set into place, the acetate is charged with the ivory black. Damar varnish is applied to the gold, and when it becomes tacky the outline is transferred to the gold. We now have our outline precisely over the prepared surface. In cutting out the gold, a chisel is first used to follow the outline and separate the gold. This cut need not go clear through to the metal. In using the chisel do not place the edge flat on the gold. Tilt the chisel to about 45 degrees and let the lower corner

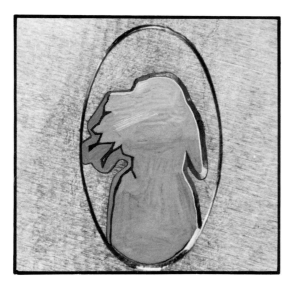

FIGURE 35

FIGURE 36 - Actual Size

enter the gold and follow the outline. This chisel cut is followed by an onglette (in one of the smaller sizes) sharpened to have a good lift (about 15 degrees) and the face ground until it is almost at a 90 degree angle with the surface of the gold. The chisel and this onglette produce a shearing cut that is always forcing the edge of the inlay downward. At figure 35 is shown the attached gold with the outline applied, and the bottom, top and right side of the inlay have been trimmed to the outline. On the left side of the inlay the outline shows on the untrimmed portion. After trimming, the figure is modeled and given its finishing touches. The finished figure and practice plate are shown at figure 36. By using this method, quite complicated subjects can be attached and trimmed.

One final comment on inlays before we move on; I'd like to pass along some remarks on casting gold and silver figures for use in inlaying. If you were working with modeling clay or plastic modeling material in preparation for a casting, you would have considerable leeway in which to change and experiment. The material lends itself to manipulation, adding to where needed, or being removed if not wanted. However, steel or gold is a much less flexible material, and your cuts should be made only when you know that they are right. A small amount of shifting and changing can be accomplished with punches, but it is generally faster to be precise and deliberate with you drawing and cutting.

However, casting figures for inlays is a practical and interesting method of achieving a precise and properly executed inlay, especially if a number of duplicates of the same figure are to be used. A wide range of textures is easily obtained, and is limited only by the ingenuity of the artist. Figure 36a shows some of the animals that have been modeled, cast and used as inlays. The photograph also shows some of the tools that are used in shaping and modeling the material. The initial investment for precious metal casting can be quite high. You would need a high temperature oven for the burning out of the flask and bringing it up to temperature; a casting machine, which could be either a centrifugal or vacuum casting machine, or a combination of the two; and the necessary equipment for melting the metal to be cast.

There are numerous books available on the subject of casting, and they go into the process in good detail. **Metal Techniques For Craftsmen** by Oppi Untracht, a book of some

471 pages, is very well illustrated and is available from Brownells, Incorporated. Another volume, **Creative Casting** by Sharr Choate, can be purchased from the Lapidary Journal Book Department. For those interested in casting, I am sure you will have no trouble in finding the necessary information and tools.

A design for a G33/40 Mauser trigger guard and floor plate. The design allows for the contours of the plate, and is very close to actual size.

FIGURE 36a

FIGURE 37

When the words "high relief" are used in referring to engraving, one immediately expects something special; and when the job is well done, it has a quality that really does make it mighty special from most of the engraving we see. I would like to discuss the high relief designs in which the forms of the scrolls, leaves, or decorative motifs are actually modeled, not merely shaded with incised lines. This extra shaping of the forms does require more time and attention to details. If you have an understanding of forms and can successfully represent them with shading cuts, then you should be able to model the forms without too much difficulty. Making a detailed drawing of your proposed design is recommended first. The drawing can be changed many times as improvements occur to you, and this is the best

place to make your changes. Once an ill-considered cut has been made in steel, it is most difficult to conceal.

For the demonstration of a high relief job, a Mauser 98 floor plate and trigger guard was chosen. The pencil drawing at figure 37 is a study for the design. As a change from the customary animal figures, I thought that it would be fun to do a conventionalized face of a girl. For the trigger guard, as a contrast to the pretty girl, I did a head in the manner of of the old grotesque masks. Many ancient artisans used this contrast of "beauty and the beast" in their decorations.

After the design is transferred, the next step is the same as in any relief engraving; the background is cut away first. At figure 38 this step is shown. On this particular plate, the bulk of the background was removed with an onglette. After this was completed I used a number 6 six-line graver to level the small ridges left by the onglette. This graver is a little over 1/64" wide (approximately .020"). A flat graver may be used but I like the line graver as it seems easier to control in attaining a flat surface. A number 6 two-line graver was used to get into tight places and corners in completing the levelling of the bottom. With the bottom levelled, a number 38 flat graver was used as a wiggle tool to give the bottom a texture. An advantage of using the lining tool to finish the bottoming cuts is that the wiggle tool takes hold easily and the background can be given a uniform texture in a very short time. At figure 38 on the left side above the head, the background has been cut away with the onglette. On the right side of the plate (same figure) the background has been levelled with the line graver. The bottom half of the plate has the background finished. There has also been some of the modeling started on the face.

Figure 39 shows the completed trigger guard and floor plate. Rather than go into detail on the entire job which contains a number of motifs such as leaves, flowers and figures, I shall take a single motif to execute in detail. This will give you all of the techniques used in executing a subject containing inside and outside concave surfaces as well as convex surfaces.

The professional wood carver has many,

FIGURE 38

FIGURE 39

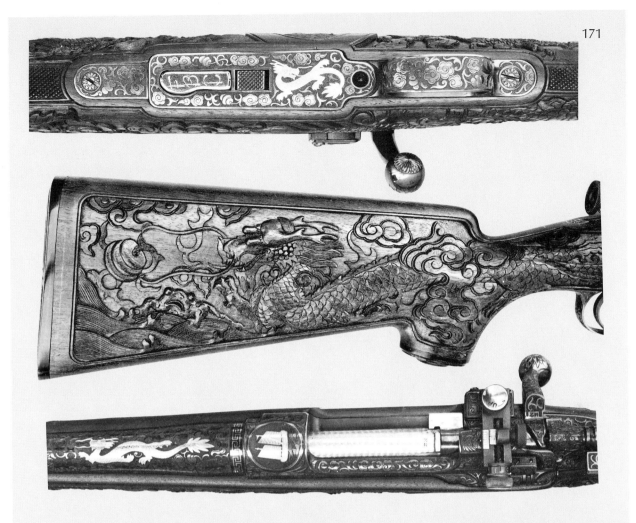

The following is from a letter Lt. Col. F. B. Conway, (Ret.), wrote about the above gun:

"The wood carving was done for a Marine Lieutenant in Mainland China in 1934, and the stock was inletted for a 1903 Springfield. I carried it around for some years with many ideas of what to do in the way of engraving for it, but did nothing until I was sent to Germany. I finally took it to Kurt Jaeger's engravers in Mainz.

"I told him I wanted the items on the stock represented in the metal with the junk and dragons in gold. The gun was there about five months. When I went to pick it up, I was told an 82 year old engraver had done

the work, and that it was his last job. He had gone into the hospital about two weeks later, where he had died.

"Now to the real point. About the second person that I showed the gun to when I brought it to the States was Lt. Col. Frank Palmer, Military Police Officer, who was in charge of security for the War Crimes Trials in the Far East following World War II. He looked at it and said, 'Very Nice! But how come you have happy dragons on the wood and unhappy dragons on the metal?'

"That floored me, so I said, 'How do you tell them apart?' He replied, 'A happy dragon has a toy to play with. If you look in front of the feelers of each dragon you will see a

ball-like object. That is his toy and to be correct, the metal work should have a gold toy to match the golden dragon. We found that particular design several places in the engraving but not related to the dragons.

"The point of the whole thing is that a craftsman, regardless of his technical skills, would have to study the customs and habits of an area in order to produce a correct piece of art work. How could we expect an old and skilled German engraver to know anything about Chinese mythology when my old Hawaiian friends of Chinese, Japanese and Phillipine descent don't know anything about it either?"

many chisels and gouges ranging from small half circle ones to large flat ones...and in all sizes. Thus, he has a big selection from which to choose the tool with which to cut the exact form that he wishes to make. The engraver's selection of tools need not be as extensive as a wood carver's collection of chisels. Glardon's die sinkers chisels are excellent tools for the engraver. Numbers 1, 2, 3, and 4 are flat chisels of varying widths. Chisels numbers 5, 6, 7 and 8 are round chisels that have progressively larger radii, and are also wider as they get larger. Numbers 9 and 10 are onglette gravers. Number 11 is a bevel graver and number 12 a knife graver. These are not absolutely necessary if you have a set of the round gravers (50 to 63) and a set of flat gravers (36 to 49). If you are beginning, and don't wish to invest any more than necessary, a very good job can be done with only a few of each kind. The regular gravers would, of course, have handles made for them, so that your chasers hammer could be used.

The beginner who is starting the study and practice of this fascinating phase of the engraver's art may have some doubts when it comes to getting started. As it was with our more simple engraving, a design or pattern is the first requirement. Do not slight this step in your impatience to start cutting. Try to draw a design that you feel quite sure you will be able to cut. For the plan or design there is a wealth of material that can serve as models from which to develop an idea. The fine silverware makers publish brochures with excellent reproductions of their various patterns. Furniture makers have developed decorative carved panels using new molded materials and plastics that defy detection from original wood carvings. The metalwork that the carpenter and cabinetmaker now use in the way of drawer pulls, escutcheons, hinges, et cetera, is the result of new methods of die casting and injection molding, and can be seen at the suppliers and in catalogs. The electrical industry also has a large selection of decorative outlet plates in high relief, molded in different metals and plastics, making them very attractive. From all of this material, along with the books and magazines on design and engraving that you will have collected, your high relief design requirements should be well taken care of. Eventually, one of your main satisfactions will be developing your own designs from all of this material that you have gathered. You may even want to go back to the original source of most of our designs, nature. Designs from animal life, plants, flowers and leaves can supply an endless source of ideas for designs.

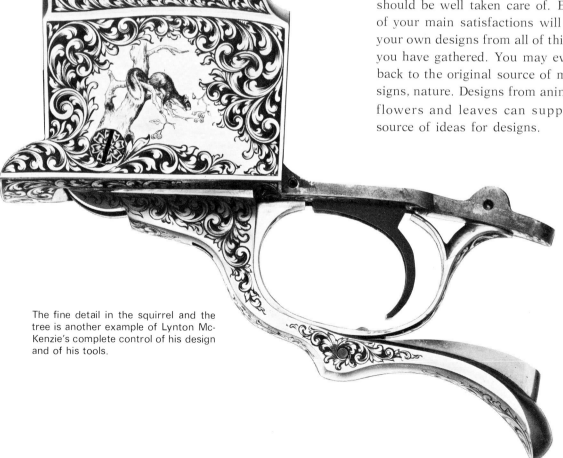

The fine detail in the squirrel and the tree is another example of Lynton McKenzie's complete control of his design and of his tools.

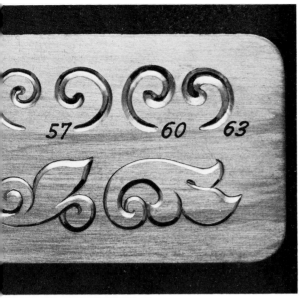

FIGURE 40

either on a polishing wheel or with some 500 or 600 grit wet or dry automotive paper.

In using these tools, if a single cut will produce the form desired, this is an ideal situation and you can be thankful. However, a single tool may not be capable of producing the variations that will be necessary in representing a natural form in high relief. In this case, a number of cuts may be needed. After roughing out the form with cuts that come as close as possible to the final shape, finishing can be accomplished easily and rapidly with scrapers (except for the final smoothing and polishing). The bottom row of cuts at figure 40 were all made with one flat graver, and are the basis for your convex forms. These convex forms may be made with one or more cuts as required, and are blended into the final shape with the scraper.

Prior to making a demonstration plate showing the progression and execution of high relief engraving, I want to cover some of the basic cuts and the tools used to make them. With round tools we shall be making concave cuts ranging from narrow to wide, and from shallow to deep. They may be straight, curved to the left or to the right, start shallow and become progressively deeper as they approach the end of the cut, or start from a greater depth and become shallower as they terminate. The top row of cuts at figure 40, shown twice over size, is made with round gravers number 54, 57, 60 and 63. The heavier, deeper cuts were made in two passes, no attempt being made to remove all of the metal in one cut. By sharpening the tools to a smooth, keen edge and giving the heels a high polish, a smooth bright cut can be made. The heels can be quite short, less than 1/32", and should be given a small radius instead of being flat as most of the heels have been heretofore. This small radius will give smoother entries and exits as you begin and end the cuts. Stone the heel to shape with a hard Arkansas stone and give it a high polish,

FIGURE 41

Our demonstration plate at figure 41 is shown actual size. The work done here is the same as you would do for any relief engraving. The background has been cut away first and given a texture. From now on, instead of shading the design with line cuts, each form will be modeled (cut to shape) to bring out the forms. This plate is designed specifically to show the execution of the different phases of high relief engraving, and has been made large and open to show the detail. It may appear somewhat

174

FIGURE 42

crude to the artistic sensibilities of the discriminating artist; however, if the beginner can get a clear picture of the correct process, the design will have served its purpose.

In most art forms, whether it be drawing, painting or carving, the artist starts with the big things first, such as action, proportion and character. This has been mentioned before, but it bears repeating. The details are not thought of until the last and they should fall into place without special attention. Since high relief engraving is actually a form of sculpture, let's discuss it from that point of view. If you had a block of wood or stone to carve, you would plan from each side the location of your figure. Having decided this, you would remove all of the excess material in order to start actually carving on your figure. You would not, at the beginning, start carving an ear or nose. This would be done only after you had established the action, the proportions and character so that you were sure that each part would fall into its proper position. Removing this excess material or planning your drawing or painting is sometimes referred to as "roughing out" the subject. After you have gained some experience in high relief engraving, you will find that much time can be saved in roughing out your design. By knowing your subject, the surplus material can be attacked vigorously. As you approach the finished surface, the time that you have saved can be used to better advantage in the accurate completion of the final form. This

technique applies not only to your engraving, but is also true for inletting and shaping gun stocks. Likewise, on machine tools and lathes, much material can be removed with heavy roughing cuts, approaching the final dimensions with care. At figure 42 the demonstration plate has been roughed out with no "touching up" of the cuts. The excess material was removed rapidly and the plate has been deliberately lighted and photographed to show these rough cuts.

The scrapers you use for refining the "roughing out" cuts can be made from drill rod. Figure 43 shows the tools that were used in cutting and finishing the demonstration plate. (You may not use all of the flat or round gravers, but the other tools were used at one place or another). There are some dental tools, donated by a cooperative dentist. The two scrapers with the wooden handles were made from drill rod. One was made for flat work and the other was given some compound curves that will accommodate different surfaces. They were filed to shape, hardened and drawn at about 350 degrees F. leaving them very hard, and then ground to final shape with a hand grinder. Great care must be exercised with the

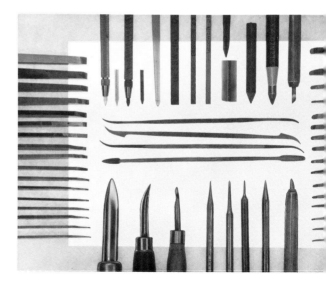

FIGURE 43

Edward C. Prudhomme, b. March 15, 1911. College background, especially in fine arts and liberal arts. American and European trained in engraving, having received the bulk of art training in France. Engraving instruction in England, Germany, Austria, Belgium, France and the U.S.A. Came under the influence of Kornbrath in 1935-36. Influenced by A. Griebel also. Started engraving on a hobby basis in 1932, and has become one of our finest and most versatile engravers.

much smoother chatter-free finish can be attained by holding the tool firmly at the desired angle with the right hand, while using the thumb of the left hand to propel the scraper forward with short strokes. This method gives fine control over the tool, and you can get into tight corners with no difficulty. If for any reason some roughness should develop, a few strokes along the length of any chatter marks will take them down level.

FIGURE 44

hand grinder as it is so easy to overheat the small tools. A light touch with the grinder and frequent cooling with a wet cloth are necessary. Finally, they were given a good, sharp scraping edge with a fine stone. The round gravers themselves make excellent scrapers. When they are used with the scraping edge at a right angle to the travel of the stroke, they reproduce the radius of the tool. By turning the edge to lesser angles, a variety of radii can be had from the same tool. Along with the cutting and scraping tools are shown the burnishers and stones that were used. Burnishing is an important step in preparing the metal for the final polish.

Figure 44 shows how to use these scrapers. When a scraper is used in one hand, it tends to develop a chatter that leaves a rough finish. A

The "roughed out" demonstration plate was refined with scrapers and files, and the result is shown at figure 45. Some needle files and die sinkers' riffler files were used after using the scrapers. The files do not remove any appreciable amount of metal, but they do carry the finishing process a little further along. The riffler files are 6" to 8" long with 1/2" to 1-1/4" on each end shaped and cut for filing. They are made in a variety of shapes so that the die maker can file about any form that is required.

176

FIGURE 45

FIGURE 46

FIGURE 47

The finer cuts, of course, leave a smoother finish so a cut no coarser than a number 4 is recommended. The cuts are usually numbered from 00, 1, 2, 3, 4, 5, 6; number 6 being the finest. You may occasionally encounter one numbered 8. In certain shapes, number 4 is as fine as they are cut. If you cannot locate such files in your local hardware or machinery supply stores, you can get them at Southwest Smelting and Refining Company, Incorporated or from Gesswein. Finer cuts also recommended on the needle files. You are not interested in removing any great amount of metal, but are more concerned with the finish they will leave.

After you have attained the modeling that you feel represents the subject, all that is left is the final finishing and polishing. This will do nothing to alter the form. If you feel that some changes are needed, make them with the gravers, scrapers and files. After the files, stones are used to remove the file and scraper marks. I prefer Scotch stones which are soft, slate-like material that breaks down easily and adapts itself to the contours. These stones are sometimes called "Water of Ayr" or "Tam O'Shanter" stones, and are usually available in sizes from 1/8" to 3/4" square and from 5" to 6" long. They are used moistened with water. Figure 46 shows a Scotch stone being used. Figure 47 shows the use of an engraver's chuck and point stone. Whenever I break a small tri-

Relief chiselled portrait of General George Armstrong Custer, by A. A. White. Courtesy of A. A. White Engravers, Inc.

angular oval or square stone on the bench, I keep the larger of the broken pieces to use in a corner, the point or a side to stone out unusual configurations. Stoning is continued until the file marks are all removed.

After stoning, burnishers are used. With a well-polished burnisher, the surface can be brought to a very smooth finish. If you are using a burnisher that is quite round, you will soon find out that it doesn't work too well on a flat surface for with a little too much pressure it tends to leave rounded impressions. So, in addition to the rounded burnishers needed for inside scrolls, you will need some that have an almost flat area on the bottom. This "almost flat" area should be led into with well polished radii, and can be shaped to get into corners or fit a variety of contours. I sometimes alternate stoning and burnishing, because a very small scratch may be eliminated quicker with the burnisher than with a stone.

FIGURE 48

There are still Springfield floor plates available, and they make fine plates on which to perfect your engraving skills. The Springfield plate shown here is done in high relief.

Burnishing should leave a bright, shiny finish. When you feel that the burnishers can no longer improve the finish, polishing can begin with 600 grit Crystolon abrasive flour. Shape the ends of small, round hardwood sticks to fit the areas to be polished. Apply a lubricant such as gun grease or oil to the shaped end you wish to use, dip it into the abrasive, and begin polishing. With most of the final finish put on by the burnishers, this final polishing is a minor endeavor, and can be accomplished quickly. Sometimes instead of using the oiled stick dipped in the abrasive, a small amount of abrasive is mixed with the oil or grease to make a paste which is spread on the engraved part to be polished, and the sticks used as before. After polishing with the sticks and abrasive, a clean soft cloth is used with a minute amount of abrasive to polish the engraving lightly. Crocus and rouge can also be used in the final polishing. However, this polishing will leave a very shiny surface which some may not like - myself included. This can be dulled slightly with a plain pencil eraser or given a still more satiny finish by rubbing with an abrasive pencil eraser, which has been mentioned before. The finished plate is shown at actual size at figure 48.

As you work on high relief engraving, you will undoubtedly develop some methods of your own that will suit your way of working. It is a good practice to be continually on the alert for better methods to improve your technique. I have tried polishing wheels for final polishing, hoping to cut the time, but they were difficult to control in many places. The method just described has worked well for me, and as a beginner I don't think you will find it too difficult.

As a fitting finish to the chapter, let us take a brief look at some English style engraving. The words "English style" immediately brings to mind many small scrolls cut with restraint. I presume that this is the result of hand engraving as opposed to the use of the

FIGURE 49

BY PERMISSION OF LYNTON McKENZIE

chasers hammer and chisel. Parkers, the better grades of Ithacas and L. C. Smiths show this same delicacy of touch.

Figure 49 shows a panel of scrolls in the English style at actual size. In corners 1 and 4 are shown small scrolls that are often used. In corner number 2 is shown a scroll seen frequently on Parkers, Ithacas and others. The process is quite simple, and a surface can be covered rapidly. Sometimes a liner is used in conjunction with this scroll to add a little more depth to the finished appearance. At figure 50 is a portion of the engraving of a single barrel

Charles Daly trap gun engraved with the English type scrolls showing the use of the liner on the scrolls. The number 3 corner in figure 49 shows a patch of small scrolls. It was a common practice to lay out a side plate with a number of panels, surrounded by borders of plain metal much like figure 49 is done.

It is difficult to find good reproductions of English engraving. When the fine scrolls are reduced for reproduction and the scrolls are broken up by the half-tone screen, much of the fine line work is completely lost. Stoeger used to carry many of the finer English shotguns, including W. W. Greener, Holland and Holland, James Purdey and Sons, Joseph Lang, Powell, Woodward and others. The reproductions in

FIGURE 50

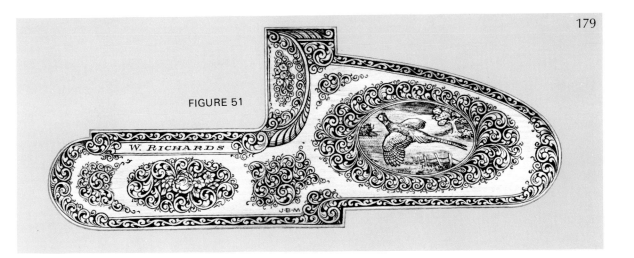

FIGURE 51

their early catalogs were good. Many of these have been reproduced in the **Shooter's Bible Treasury**. In the 1963 issue that I have, the reproductions are not too clear but they give a good resume of the number and quality of guns that were available. Of course, there were other fine English guns such as the Rigby and the current Webley and Scott. Over the years it has been possible to build up a fairly good collection of reproductions of fine English-style engraving from magazine covers and articles that have appeared.

Practicing the English-style scroll will definitely increase the range of your capabilities, for there are many places that large scrolls are unsuitable because they are so overpowering that any sense of richness of design is lost. The only comparison that occurs to me is that of a coarse, loud, over-dressed woman compared to a lady of quiet elegance. In each case the quality (or lack of it) is evident at a glance. You will do well to develop your small scroll and tool handling abilities so that you can execute those jobs well that require a finer treatment.

Figure 51 shows a simulated side lock cut to shape from a piece of cold rolled steel and engraved as an example. This piece is shown actual size. Notice particularly that working with smaller, finer designs calls for closer attention to details. This effort will not be lost when you return to cutting larger scrolls. In this style

of engraving, lettering, lining and scrolls are all cut to a lesser depth than the larger scrolls. Square or onglette gravers are used, and I use an onglette that has been stoned on each side, at the bottom, so that there is an included angle of from 90 degrees to 108 degrees. The onglette is preferred because of the narrow width of the face. The comparatively wide face of a square graver is somewhat distracting, unless the face is narrowed by grinding which is an extra effort and a little difficult to do

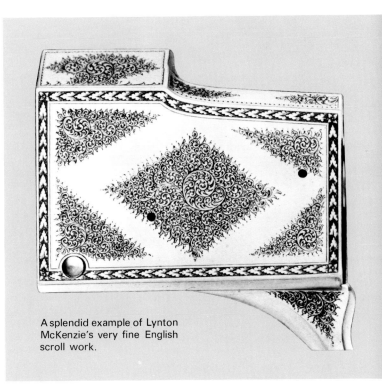

A splendid example of Lynton McKenzie's very fine English scroll work.

evenly. The heel of the onglette is kept quite short and is given about a 12 degree lift. By mounting the onglette in the sharpener (previously described), the angles can be set and stoned accurately with clean sharp edges. The time required is minimal because only a small amount of metal is removed. The graver sharpener is calibrated in 4 degree increments, so by mounting the onglette in the holder and setting it to 44 degrees, the heel can be set and stoned to the correct included angle in a few moments. By loosening the mount and turning it to 44 degrees the other side of zero, the opposite angle is stoned. Setting the holder at 36 degrees will give the more obtuse angle of 108 degrees. Of course, any angle in between that might be wanted can be stoned just as easily. By the same token, a tool with an included angle of less than 90 degrees can also be obtained.

By giving close attention to detail and making every cut to the best of your capabilities, you are bound to improve. If you find yourself cutting scrolls or designs in an aimless, hit-or-miss fashion, quit and do something else. Come back to it when you can concentrate and give it your best effort. In this way you will become a fine engraver. As an engraver you no doubt are of an artistic bent, so anything that will improve your artistic talents will benefit your engraving. I have found the magazine **The American Artist** a real help for it has articles each month on the works of practicing artists in various mediums, plus many advertisements for sources of supplies and materials. The printing and detail is excellent in both black and white as well as color.

Before going on to the last chapter, I would like to take a moment to especially thank the engravers who have so generously permitted me to show the many beautiful reproductions of their work in the pages of this book.

Chapter Eight
The Gravermeister

When one gets a lot of satisfaction or enjoyment from an experience, it adds to that appreciation if it can be shared. This is the reason for this short chapter on the Gravermeister which has given me both. I have been using my Gravermeister for a little over five years now, and it has given me thousands of hours of service. With reasonable care, simply following the manufacturer's maintenance instructions, there have been no repairs needed during that time.

John Rohner, partner in GRS Corporation which manufacturers and sells the Gravermeister, remarked during one of our many conversations that they have encountered some sales resistance to the machine. It seems to have come mostly from a few of the older craftsmen who have spent a lifetime mastering a hand craft, and are reluctant to throw it away to climb on the machine-age band wagon. There is that pride that comes from "doing it by hand" which they seem to feel they might lose. However, it is hard to imagine the extraordinarily gifted and inventive master-sculptor Michelangelo not using an air-powered chisel to speed up his work, if it had been available to him, for it would have saved him countless hours chipping away at those huge blocks of marble. After all, it is the master's hand guiding the tool - whether it be mechanically powered or hammer-powered - that controls the quality of the finished job, and in the end it is the finished job that will receive the critical appraisal,

regardless of how the job was accomplished.

I had been engraving by hand and with chasers hammer and chisel for thirty-two years when I had an opportunity to try a Gravermeister. It was a revelation. The speed and ease with which I could cut a scroll told me at once that this was a very practical and useful tool. This short chapter is not intended as a sales pitch. It is simply that I am using the Gravermeister; I like it, and feel that I can safely recommend it to anyone whose situation can justify such a machine. And, as far as I know, this is the only machine of its nature on the market today.

The Gravermeister was developed by John Rohner and his brother-in-law and good friend Don Glaser, a mechanical engineer and machine designer who holds over 100 US and foreign patents in the graphic arts industry with many related to pneumatic systems such as the one used in the Gravermeister. They primarily wanted to speed up their own engraving, but they also wanted to make it possible for a beginning engraver, who does not have a lifetime to devote to learning precise hammer control, to be able to learn the art of engraving faster. (By the way, both of these men's works have been shown in recent issues of **Gun Digest**). The machine is quite compact, measuring 16″ long, 9″ high and about 12″ wide, including the oil filter and muffler jars. Two flexible hoses lead from the machine body, one to the handpiece and one to the foot controlled throttle. These

182

are shown in the photograph at figure 1. Incidentally, this is a photograph of my own machine which has been in use for over five years.

The operation of the Gravermeister is amazingly simple, for what you have actually is a miniature pneumatic chisel that operates on the same principle as a jack hammer, but with the important addition of precise control of the power of the impact strokes by manipulation of the foot throttle. As the machine is being used, the weight or forward thrust of the stroke can be adjusted from light to heavy with the foot throttle. The number of strokes per minute can be controlled between 800 and

to your specific use from John Rohner, GRS Corporation, or from Brownells, Incorporated. I would like to cover a few of the main components here to give you some idea of their functions. The Gravermeister has four main parts: Pump, Handpiece, Throttle, and Speed Control. The Pump is the heart of the machine, and is a special rotary-vane type vacuum and pressure pump/motor combination that has been made especially for this purpose by one of the country's leading pump makers.

Two examples of John Rohner's use of his own Gravermeister.

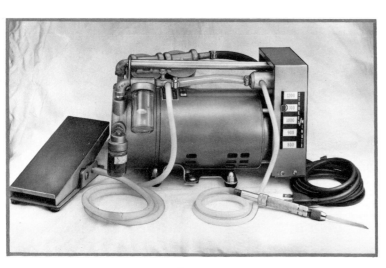

FIGURE 1

1200 by a control lever on the machine. The speed of the strokes per minute also affects the power of the stroke, for the slower the SPM, the more time the pressure has to overcome the rearward inertia of the piston, and consequently the more power that is delivered to the chisel.

I won't go into any great detail concerning the machine as you can get a complete, descriptive catalog, prices, and any special information about the Gravermeister's application

Another of John Rohner's examples showing the capability of his Gravermeister in cutting fine, delicate lines.

The Handpiece holds the engraving tools, and is essentially a custom-designed air-operated hammer. The universal chuck at one end accepts all tools up to 1/4" shank diameter and is permanently attached to a hollow tube. The other end is connected to the pressure-vacuum valving system of the pump by a flexible hose. The air pressure and vacuum coming into the piston chamber arrives in pulsed, alternating bursts instead of a constant push.

A vacuum pulse draws the piston back against a spring between the piston and the air hose connection at the rear end of the tube, and then an alternate pressure pulse drives the piston downward to an impact face at the forward end of the tube directly behind the chuck, creating the force that drives the tool. Control of the vacuum pulse varies the length of the stroke of the piston, and thus the magnitude of the impact stroke.

These controlled, alternating pulses coming into the piston chamber create the reciprocating action in the handpiece tube which, in turn, delivers the impact to the engraving tool being held in the chuck. It is a very ingenious and effective arrangement, and as you can see,

gives infinite variation to the amount of forward force exerted on the engraving tool.

The Foot Throttle is connected to the vacuum side of the pump by a flexible hose. The pedal is under spring tension, and as it is depressed, a bleed valve is progressively closed causing an increasing vacuum to be developed by the pump. The stronger vacuum pulse delivered to the handpiece increases the impact force delivered to the tool. This gives you a great deal of control over the weight of the stroke-from almost non-existant to very heavy-while both hands are free to manipulate the tool and guide the work.

The Speed Control is mounted securely to and is a part of the pump unit. The pump and speed control unit account for the bulk of the weight (45-lbs), which gives you some idea of the sturdiness of the construction of the unit. It is simply a lever connected to an adjustable pulley, and by changing the size of one of the pulleys, the speed of the pulses, and thus the stroke, is controlled. There is a change in the character of the stroke from the slower one to the faster.

As was mentioned before, the slower strokes are the more powerful and as the speed of the strokes increases, they become lighter. You will soon adapt to choosing the stroke that is best suited to the job that you are doing. With the wide choice of strokes offered through the foot throttle and the speed control, the Gravermeister responds quickly and easily to the operator's wishes. There is an additional control that has been added since I bought my machine.

(As a matter of fact, this "fine tune" control was added by the manufacturers at Mr. Meek's suggestion. Ed.) This is a small bleed valve on the vacuum side of the pump. It is adjusted by hand for even finer control, on the lighter strokes. For fine lettering, extremely fine scroll work or any intricate job, the force can be reduced from a light tap on down to the very lightest of taps. In fact, it can be reduced down to zero. Not only does the valve work on the finer, lighter strokes but you can use it for "fine tuning" the heavier strokes too. Used in conjunction with the foot pedal, you have a command of strokes that is as complete as any chasers hammer in the hands of an experienced engraver.

Having given a general description of the machine, describing its uses is more difficult. It was of course, developed for the purpose of engraving, but it can also be used for wood-working, bronze chasing, die cutting, stone cutting, print making, numerous jewelry oper-ations and even in the fields of speciman prep-aration in archaeology and paleontology. In engraving, any of the tools that the engraver customarily employs can be used, such as liners, knives and flat, round, point and bevel gravers. Used with an onglette or square graver, cutting scrolls, straight lines or removing back-grounds is no longer the time consuming job that it is with the graver and chasers hammer. For inlaying gold lines, it is almost unbeliev-able. The line can be cut and undercut, and the gold punched into place almost while you are thinking about it. Almost any punch can be used for background work. And, since you can use less power with longer sweeps to cut a line with the Gravermeister, the tips of the tools last much longer. Likewise, since the only pres-sure exerted by the engraver is the downward pressure necessary to hold the tool under the metal, there is not nearly the likelihood of side-slipping that so frequently happens with the chasers hammer and chisel. I have also used it with carving tools and it works beautifully. As Mr. Rohner plainly states in his literature, buying the machine will not instantly make you an engraver. But, with an artistic talent and a genuine desire to become an engraver, the Gravermeister will relieve you of the endless hours of practice and the many headaches and pitfalls encountered as you learn to master the hand graver along with the chasers ham-mer and chisel. Mr. Rohner has literature on the machine, showing engraving being done along with more detailed information, and he is also preparing a book that will give complete information on the many uses of the Graver-meister. For my own use, I'd much prefer giv-ing up the chasers hammer and chisel to ever surrendering my Gravermeister.

AFTERWORD

It is with feelings of relief and regret that I suddenly realize the end of the project is almost here. "Almost", because while the writing, drawing, engraving and photography are all completed, each page has yet to be arranged so that it is camera-ready for the printer. We learned early to be careful in talking about the book. My wife, Jeanette, casually mentioned something about the book to a friend whose seven year old son was one of the group. He was overheard to remark, "Oh, no! Not the book again." So, with only a few remarks about the book, and books in general, I shall get on to some thoughts in conclusion.

In planning the book, Bob Brownell and I decided that it should be written especially for the beginner. Questions may be asked as to why there was nothing on plating, antique firearms or whatever. An anecdote that occurred while I was attending the Chicago Art Institute will answer the question. The school decided that every student was to be required to have so many hours of Art History. In my case, the hours conflicted with a three hour drawing class that I had, five days a week. When I told the professor, his reaction was, "If you want to be an artist, draw and paint — paint and draw; you can get all of the art history you want on the outside." I drew and painted. So it is with the book. If the information presented will provide a good start for the beginner, it has served its purpose. The good engraver will go ahead on the "outside" and develop his capabilities in any facet of the craft that interests him.

There will be other books on the subject. The old idea that a process be kept secret may have had some justification in the minds of

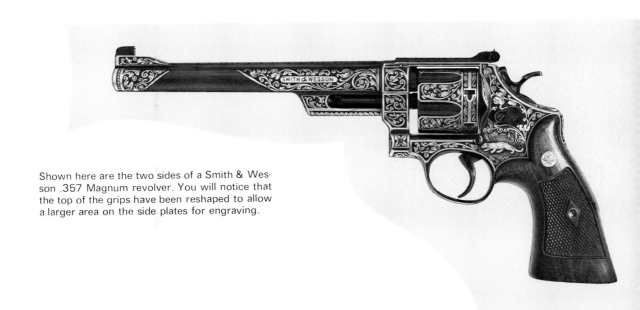

Shown here are the two sides of a Smith & Wesson .357 Magnum revolver. You will notice that the top of the grips have been reshaped to allow a larger area on the side plates for engraving.

those who practiced it. There is very little new today that has not been done sometime by the craftsmen of the past. Man is an ingenious character and it doesn't take long, generally, to unravel a secret. Then too, revealing a process does not mean that everyone who is aware of it is going to use it. Some are actually incapable, others are too lazy and many are simply not interested.

There have been countless numbers of painters, but there was only one Rembrandt, one Michelangelo, and One Leonardo da Vinci. If you get an intense enjoyment and satisfaction out of your engraving, what others do should not CONCERN you, only interest you. Who is to know, you may be the next Rembrandt of the engravers. It is striving for excel-

lence, and occasionally knowing that you have done something better than you had heretofore been capable of, that is in itself rewarding.

It is hoped that many of our fine engravers can be encouraged to write of their engraving because of their acknowledged excellence and years of experience. The old saying "You can lead a horse to water, but you cannot make him drink" and its paraphrase "You can stuff a man with knowledge, but you cannot make him think", is as true today as it ever was. In sharing processes and techniques, just remember that it is hard to beat a man at his own game.

So, to you the beginner, my "Best Wishes" for a long and pleasant affair with the art of engraving.

TOOLS, MATERIALS & SUPPLIES

Even though a tools, materials and supplies listing is included, it is more important that you be able to locate such materials and suppliers as you may need for yourself. We have all seen lists of suppliers in books that have become obsolete because some had changed their address while many others were no longer even operating. Below is the listing that I am currently using, plus a few pointers on how you can locate sources of materials and supplies.

Almost every craft, hobby or profession has at least one magazine that is published for its following. For example, **The Lapidary Journal** is one of the magazines published for the rock hounds. It is full of the advertising of suppliers of materials for creating polished rocks, gems and jewelry. Among these you can find sources of silver, gold, casting materials and even engraving tools. The magazine's book department has many manuals and texts on silversmithing, creative casting, stone setting and almost any subject related to gems and jewelry. Many of these books have lists of suppliers in the back.

If you have a friend who is in manufacturing or merchandising, he will quite likely have **Thomas Register of American Manufacturers** which is a complete listing of all U.S. manufacturers and their addresses. Among all of these 11 volumes of listings, you will find those who deal in whatever it is that you could ever want.

Catalogs are usually very informative and much can be learned from a careful study of them. Several catalogs supplying the jewelry trade are full of tables of weights and measures, conversion tables from decimal to metric measures, and the Brown and Sharp gage numbers with their various thicknesses shown in decimal and metric equivalents.

Machinery catalogs are another example. In one such catalog I found a description of a lathe bit that sounded as though it should make an ideal engraver's tool. I ordered two dozen bits, and I have found them to be extremely tough. The description read as follows: "1/8" square tool bits, Rex 95, SAE T8, approximately 2 1/2" long, high red hardness, superior abrasion resistance and good toughness. Contents, carbon .80%, tungsten 14.00%, chromium 4.00%, vanadium 2.00%, molybdenum .75%, cobalt 5.25%." These bits work very well in the Gravermeister and I have been using them for a number of years.

Many books on crafts such as Oppi Untracht's **Metal Techniques for Craftsmen** (Brownells, Inc.) have lists of suppliers of many materials from precious metals to rare woods. Check your library for such books that may help in locating materials you need. Don't hesitate to ask your dentist if he can help you locate a source of gold, or your jeweler to let you see his catalog or tell you where you can get saw blades, etc.

Following is a list of the books and magazines mentioned in the book, with the supplier listed in parenthesis.

American Artist (magazine)

An Atlas of Anatomy for Artists, by F. Schider (Dover or Dick Blick)

Animals In Motion, by Muybridge (Dover or Dick Blick)

An Atlas of Animal Anatomy for Artists, by Ellenberger, Baum and Dittrich (Dover or Dick Blick)

Animal Drawing, Anatomy and Action for Artists, by C.R. Knight (Dover or Dick Blick)

Animal Drawing and Painting, by W.J. Wilwerding (Dover)

Calligraphy, by Johann Georg Schwandner (Dover)

Constructive Anatomy, by Bridgman (Barnes & Noble, Inc. or Dick Blick)

Creative Casting, by Sharr Choate (**Lapidary Journal** Book Dept.)

Decorative Alphabets and Initials, by Alexander Nesbitt (Dover or Dick Blick)

English Furniture, Decoration, Woodwork and Allied Arts, by T.A. Strange (Publishers Central Bureau)

Encyclopedia of Modern Firearms, Parts and Assembly, by Bob Brownell (Brownells, Inc.)

French Interiors, Furniture, Decoration, Woodwork and Allied Arts, by T. A. Strange (Publishers Central Bureau)

Gun Engraving Review, by E.C. Prudhomme (E.C. Prudhomme)

Gun Digest, by John T. Amber (Digest Books, Inc.)

Handbook of Ornament, by F.S. Meyer (Dover or Dick Blick)

The Human Figure, by J. Vanderpoel (Dover)

The Human Figure In Motion, by Muybridge (Dover or Dick Blick)

A Practical Course in Jewelry Engraving, by Albert A. Winter (Swest, Inc.)

The Jewelry Engravers Manual, by John J. Bowman & R. Allen Hardy (Swest, Inc.)

Machinery's Handbook, by Erik Oberg and Franklin D. Jones (Brownells, Inc.)

Metal Techniques for Craftsmen, by Oppi Untracht (Brownells, Inc.)

L.D. Nimsche, Firearms Engraver, by R.L. Wilson (John Hintlian Books)

The Styles of Ornament, by Alexander Speltz (Dover or Dick Blick)

Techniques of Drawing and Painting Wildlife, by Fredric Sweney (Reinhold)

SUPPLIERS & PUBLISHERS

American Artist
2160 Patterson Street
Cincinnati, Ohio 45214

Barnes & Noble, Inc.
Harper & Row Publishers, Inc.
40 East 33rd Street
New York, N.Y. 10016

Dick Blick
P.O. Box 1267
Galesburg, Illinois 61401

Brownells, Inc.
Route 2 Box 1
Montezuma, Iowa 50171

Digest Books, Inc.
540 Frontage Rd.
Northfield, Illinois 60093

Dover Publications, Inc.
180 Varick Street
New York, N.Y. 10014

Paul H. Gesswein & Company, Inc.
235 Park Avenue South
New York, N.Y. 10003

GRS Corporation
Box 1157
Boulder, Colorado 80302

Hammel, Riglander & Co., Inc.
435 Hudson Street
New York, New York 10014

John Hintlian Books
273 Maple Hill Avenue
Newington, Connecticut 06111

Hoover & Strong, Inc.
119 W. Tupper Street
Buffalo, N.Y. 14201

The Industrial Press
93 Worth Street
New York, N.Y.

Lapidary Journal Book Department
P.O. Box 80937
San Diego, Calif. 92138

E. C. Prudhomme
302 Ward Building
Shreveport, La. 71101

Publishers Central Bureau
33-20 Hunters Point Avenue
Long Island City, N.Y. 11101

Reinhold Book Corporation
430 Park Avenue
New York, N.Y. 10022

Thomas Register
Thomas Publishing Company
461 Eighth Avenue
New York, N.Y. 10001

William Dixon Company
Carlstadt, New Jersey 07072

R. L. Wilson Books
P. O. Box 28
Manchester, Connecticut 06040

SWEST Inc.
(Southwest Smelting & Refining Co.)
10803 Composite Drive
Dallas, Texas 75222

INDEX